PEOPLE LIKE US

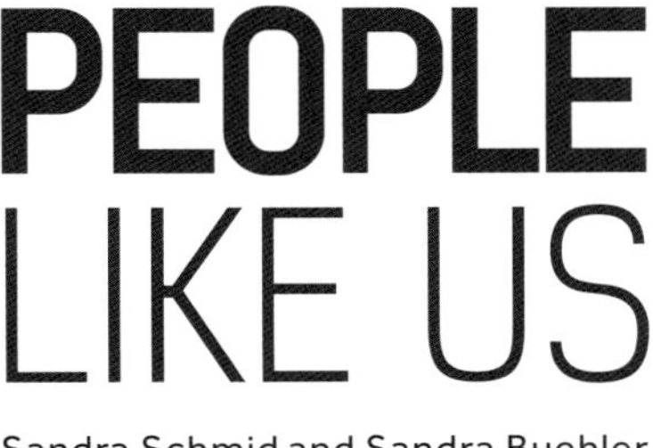

Sandra Schmid and Sandra Buehler

Unicorn Publishing Group

FOREWORD

Human beings are peculiar creatures – we fight and love, hate and forgive, condemn and make mistakes, yet essentially we are all the same. Yes, we might be white, brown, black, small, big, female, male or both, but we all need air and water to survive and we need love as to not wither away. We are all in possession of a heart that beats and when it ceases to do so we die. It's pretty banal actually; we are born to be on this earth only to leave it again, and no-one ever asked us where we want to live – we just appear somewhere on this planet surrounded by love or hate, wealth or poverty, good or bad luck. These circumstances influence the way we lead our lives, the way in which we discuss and then argue. Aren't we all capable of doing things we would never do under normal circumstances, things that have the power to drastically influence our lives? Wouldn't we all resort to murder if there was no other alternative?
A lot of people living in adverse conditions are ignored and condemned. It seems to be in our nature to render judgments within seconds, to form an opinion about someone's way of life or appearance without even knowing them. Everyone does it, and mostly without realising. Each judgment we make is a mirror reflecting something within ourselves – our own expectations, our beliefs, our self-created reality. Even if we seem to be completely different, we are all ultimately striving for the same things; we want to be content, experience joy and avoid pain, and we want to be treated with respect. Why don't we listen to one another before forming an opinion?
With this book, we want to honour and give voice to a few individuals and their uniqueness. Many readers may recognise themselves in one or the other story – no-one is alone, everyone has a story to tell. I have mine, you have yours. The sooner we begin to listen to one another, the sooner we will recognise how similar we really are while being completely individual. We might live in extremely different places, subject to different conditions, coming from Africa, America, Europe or Asia, but in the end, we are all People Like Us.

Sandra Schmid, Sandra Buehler
April 2018

STEVE, 48
DECEMBER 20TH, 2015, BOCAS DEL TORO, PANAMA

I was seventeen years old when I realised how fragile life is. My father died of cancer when he was 39. I began to live each moment to its fullest; I wanted to feel alive, I chased adventures and sought out rushes of adrenaline by skydiving.

I jumped out of planes more than a thousand times until the excitement wore off and I discovered BASE Jumping – a plunge from buildings or cliffs at much lower altitudes, thus increasing the risk. I was arrested after my first jump off an apartment building and was put on a surveillance list as it's illegal to jump off roofs, but I didn't care as I needed that kick.

Jumping off buildings at night was what gave me the ultimate rush. Skyscrapers in Los Angeles are perfect for it. I would sit at the edge of the roof and wait for all cops to disappear and the traffic lights to turn red. The moment right before jumping is the worst – the increased heart rate and overwhelming fear are feelings you just can't put into words, but it's also an addiction. It's about gaining control over oneself and being able to steer your fear. Sometimes you want to be the first to jump as the thought of being the last is terrifying. Sometimes you want to watch the others land uninjured first to feel safe before taking the plunge – either way, you just want it to be over. Some of my friends had to throw up before each jump.

It took days for my adrenaline level to decrease and normalise after each jump. BASE Jumping is an extreme sport, and just one tiny mistake can lead to death. A good friend of mine almost died when he broke his back jumping. That would have been the right moment for me to stop and I wanted to, but the addiction took hold of me. Six months after his accident, I jumped off a 200-metre high bridge and flew through a gorge. I grazed a tree and crashed, utterly twisting my leg and smashing my foot to bits. A helicopter had to transport me to the hospital, and I remained in a wheelchair for one whole year; afterward, I was only able to walk on crutches. The doctors tried to save my leg and reconstruct my foot with all means but to no avail. Pumped full of painkillers and constricted by the crutches, I decided to have my lower left leg amputated. The decision was a tough one to make, and it went against the doctors' advice, but I just wanted to be in control of my body again.

After the amputation, I continued jumping off cliffs, bridges, and buildings. My desire for adrenaline was stronger than the fact that my healthy leg wasn't going to tolerate many more jumps. At some point, I finally understood that I had to write a new chapter. I left Los Angeles and moved to Bocas del Toro, Panama – a place without skyscrapers.

These days I walk around like a pirate on one wooden leg. I kind of like this role. I bought a huge property with my wife, and we founded 'Flying Pirates'. We offer our customers tours on quads – adventures that come with a massive dose of adrenaline. My addiction to the rush has weakened, but it's still dormant in me somewhere. I still have my skydiving equipment, but will I ever use it again? I don't know. What I do know is that my life should be fun at every possible moment.

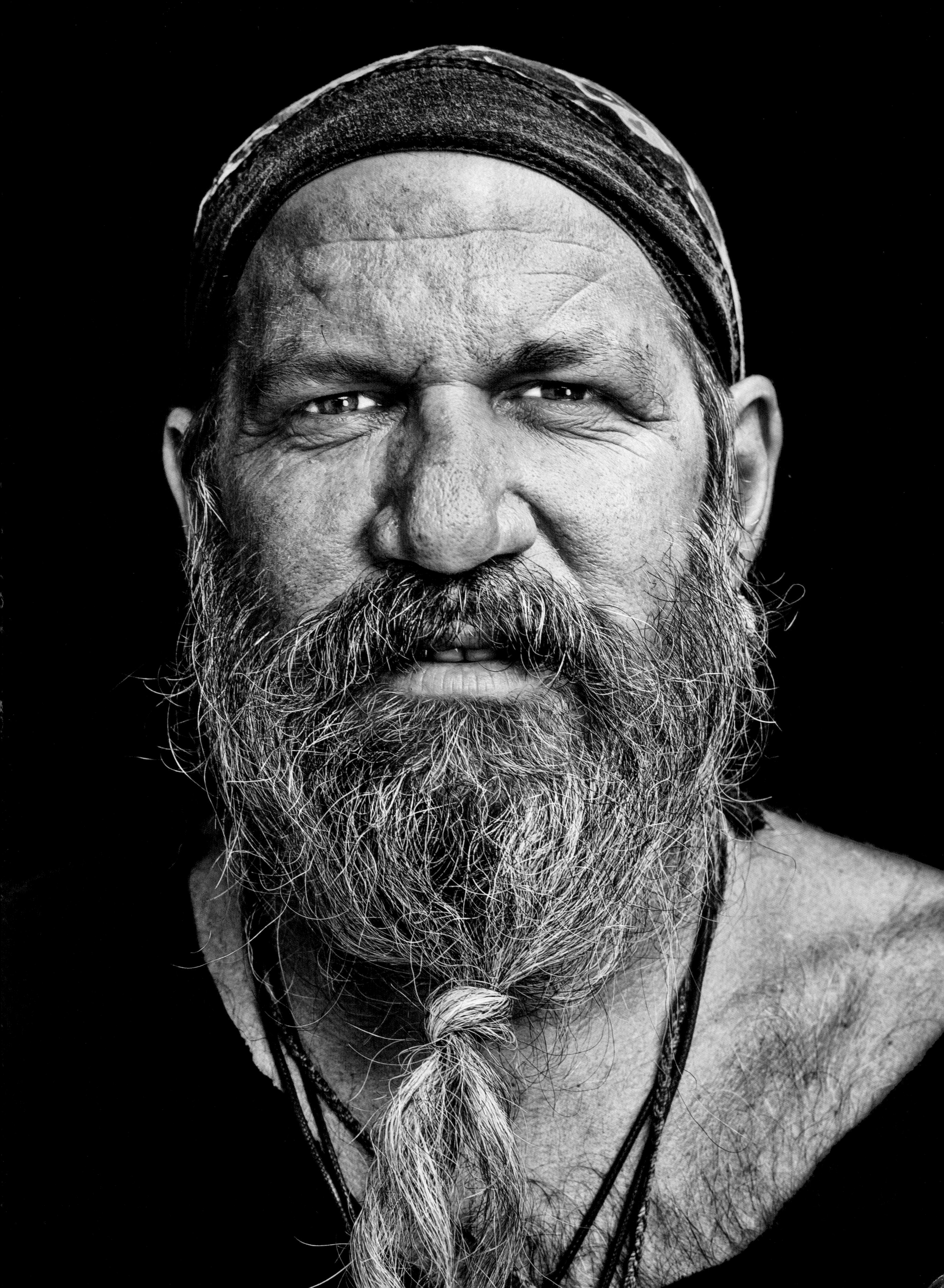

NATALIE, 27
NOVEMBER 2ND, 2016, BLIKKIESDORP, CAPE TOWN

I was out and about a lot when I was seventeen years old, including the night I was raped. I was scared to tell others let alone burden my parents. And the people around me would have probably said it was my fault, so I remained silent.

I was unbelievably angry; I felt dirty and was suffering from inner turmoil. I began to take crystal meth – that drug is like sweets, available at every street corner. The drug made me aggressive, unpredictable, and disrespectful. I destroyed things and was insufferable towards my parents. I lied to them and sold their belongings so I could afford my drug habit. My secret was eating me up from inside.

I got ill, and after several tests and examinations, I discovered that I was HIV-positive. My tormentor had infected me. Thousands of thoughts rushed through me; I was scared to death and felt utterly lost. Would anyone ever come close to me again let alone touch me?

My destructive drug addiction made it easy for the HIV to attack my immune system. I was so weak that I was unable to move. I could only lie there without being able to perceive what was going on, then I lost the strength to speak and was hardly able to breathe. I was skin and bones, and each day it was uncertain if I would live or die.

One day I was visited by Viola from the aid organisation 'HOPE Cape Town'. She made it clear to me that my parents would be childless if I were to die, and that they would mourn terribly for me. I knew how painful this kind of loss could be, as my brother was shot and killed on the street ten years prior. The thought of my parents suffering horrified me. At the end of our conversation, Viola wished to see me on my feet the next time she came to the hospital.

My stay in the hospital was my only chance of survival. My family and other members of the aid organisation visited me, hugged and kissed me. They were all there for me giving me the encouragement and support to find my way back into life. 'Life is not there to tread the path on one's own, Natalie!' I was bound to a wheelchair for the following months, and often tried to put my feet on the ground so that I could feel the ground beneath me and maybe even walk to the toilet on my own, but there was no chance. My mother motivated me to train so that I could walk again. I was to be an inspiration for people of Blikkiesdorp; I was to prove that you can battle this virus.

It was a Wednesday evening after the nurses had already left that a massive wave of power suddenly rushed through me – I took one step, then a second. I was able to walk again! My body began responding to the medication, and it became clear that the treatment had been worth it. I was overjoyed.

One year has passed until Viola revisited me again. When she saw that I could walk on my own two legs, I was able to fulfil her wish.

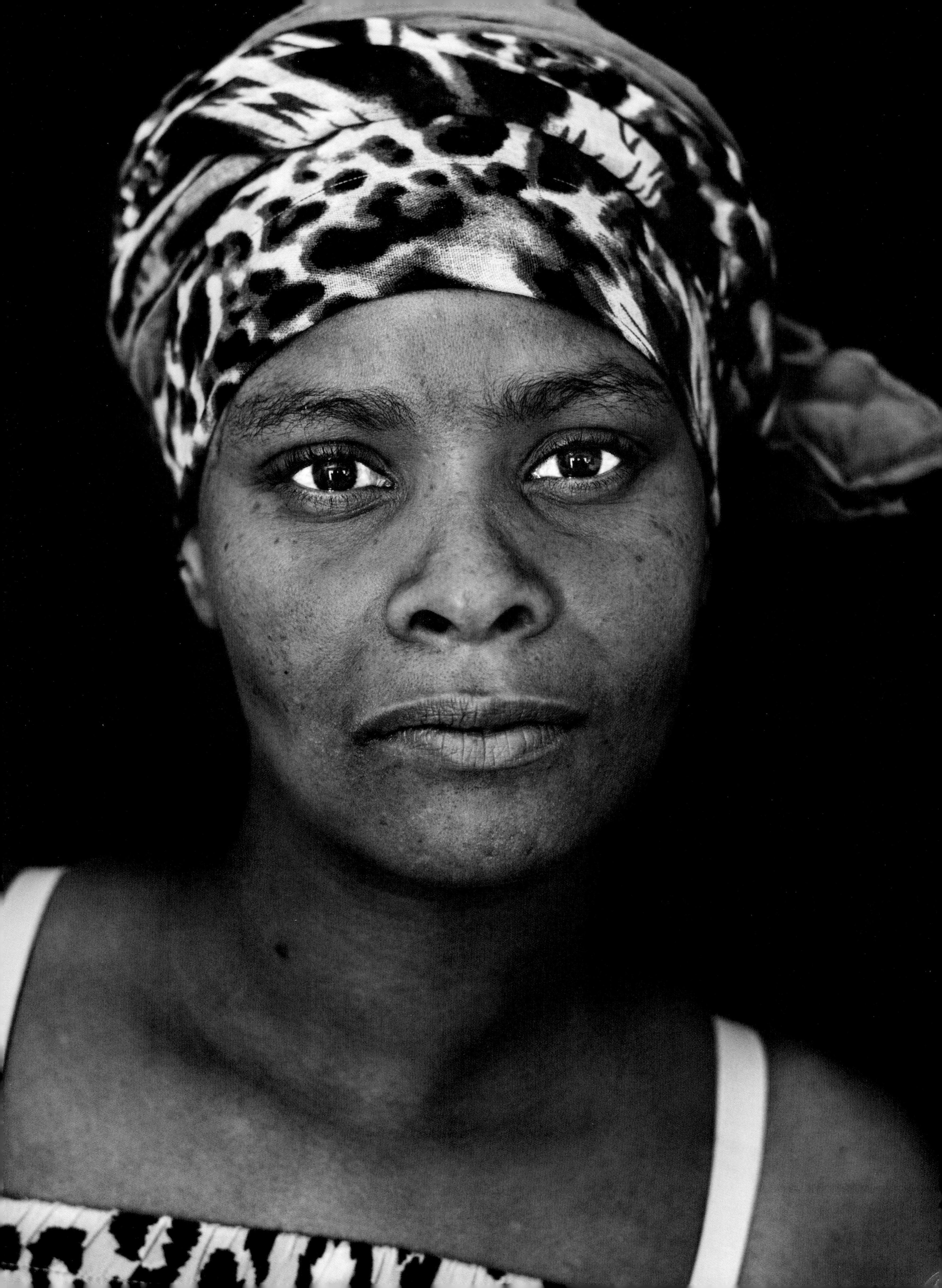

FELICIA, 45
NOVEMBER 14TH, 2015, POTOSÍ, BOLIVIA

I was sixteen years old when I married my brother-in-law's brother. My sister, at the time 25 years old, forged my passport so that I'd be old enough on paper to get married. It was just the two of us, so she was in charge and there was no opposing her. I was too young to stand up for myself, so I left home for a man I didn't want and travelled from La Paz to Potosí. I never saw my sister again.

After some time, I came to terms with my prearranged life and the first few years were alright. After a year had passed, I gave birth to our son. Six more children followed. Then my husband began to change: he started insulting me, and soon after he started to kick and hit me again and again. He was an alcoholic and was already wasted and uncontrollably aggressive in the early mornings. I wanted to flee, but I was dependent on him as I had no money or support system of my own. I saw no possibility of providing for our seven children on my own. With every year he became worse – constantly drunk and too lazy to work. He spent the last of our money on booze and his need to attack became stronger and stronger: 'I am first going to kill you and then the kids!'

When he beat up our eldest son, I reached my limit, and reported it to the police who then forced him to sign our divorce papers. The following months were the worst. It's brutal to survive here as a single mother. I didn't have any money to buy water or bread. I would walk several kilometres to collect rainwater. The water there was dirty, but thankfully our stomachs were resistant. In the evenings I would sit at the side of the road begging for money or bread. I felt dirty, worthless and degraded but I had no choice – I needed food for the children and myself.

After one year my eldest son found a job at the mines of Potosí. It's a tough job with low wages. Shortly after the mines employed me as a guard, my son and I were slowly able to fight our way back into existence.

Nowadays my whole family lives next to the mines in a small house. I have even begun to receive water from the union. I still struggle with money problems, but with each month our condition improves. It's been eight years since the divorce. My ex-husband and I rarely cross paths these days but when we do, I'm no longer scared – he seems old and frail, whereas I feel strong.

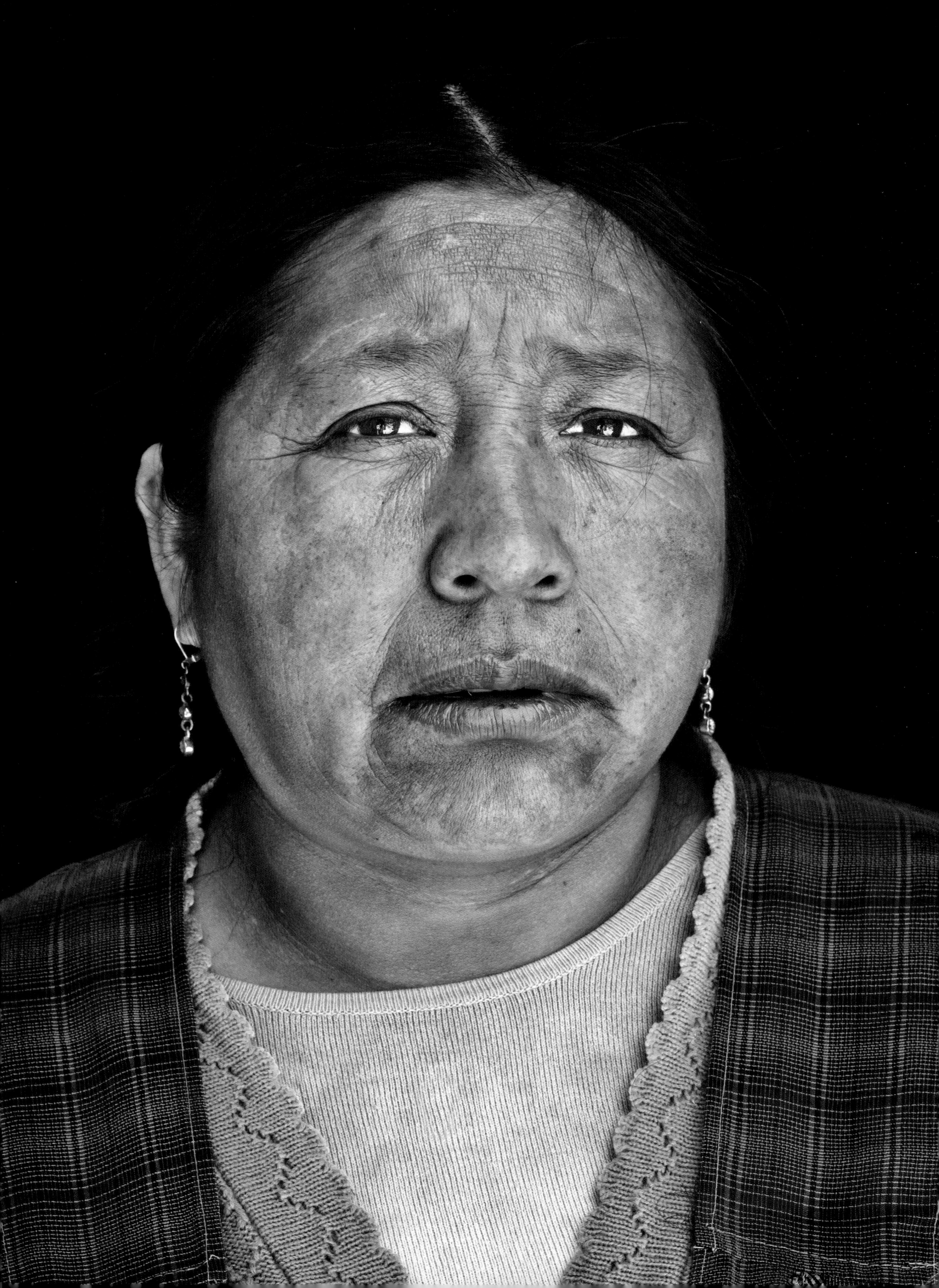

DAVID, 43
JUNE 8TH, 2017, MANHATTAN, NEW YORK

My life revolved around money. I was an investment banker at May Davis Group, and I was greedy, egotistical, cold and impatient. I worked sixteen hours a day and still wanted more money.

It was Tuesday, the 11th of September 2001. I left my house that morning without saying goodbye to my then-girlfriend as we were arguing. I was sitting at my desk on the 87th floor of the World Trade Center's North Tower, looking out the window towards the Statue of Liberty when there was a huge bang. The building swung to the side, with such ferocity that I thought it would fall over and whip back up. I clamped to my desk as if I were on a rollercoaster ride. It was unreal and horrifying – then, suddenly everything went silent.

We were fourteen people in the office. No one knew what had happened. We had no phone network, and no alarms were going off, so we stayed put until, about fifteen minutes later, smoke began to infiltrate our office. We went to the staircase and joined a massive queue of people heading to the ground floor. The atmosphere was almost tranquil – there was no notion of panic. At some point, we crossed paths with firefighters who were on their way up, and they told us about an airplane hitting the tower, and that it was a terrorist attack. They also said that the South Tower was hit. It took us about an hour to reach the lobby, which had become a setting for unthinkable chaos: firefighters continuously ran past us, and big bangs continued to echo throughout the building. When I looked outside I saw those people, who so hopelessly tried to escape the fire from the top floor, plunge onto the street. There was blood everywhere, body parts and corpses. I saw a bisected body in an illuminating yellow dress. That yellow dress still won't leave my mind's eye.

My first step outside was the exact moment the building began to collapse. It felt like a rattling train that was coming closer and closer at incredible speed, with no time to flee. The South Tower collapsed. A dense cloud of dust engulfed me. The sirens, the screams, the panic – they were all suddenly silenced. It was dark and I was unable to see or breathe. For a moment, I thought I was dead. The people around me were coughing, shouting, crying. I ran around aimlessly and then the North Tower also collapsed. I began looking for a colleague of mine but Harry, our friend and father of two, was the only one from our office who didn't make it out alive. He had decided to stay behind and help an injured person on the staircase. I asked myself again and again why I didn't convince Harry to leave the building with us. I also asked myself why I hadn't been the one to stay behind.

9/11 – I knew that after this day, my life would never be the same again. I felt a plethora of emotions coexist within me: shock, fear, anger, and guilt. I wasn't able to board a plane for a long time, and it was incredily nerve-wracking to take the subway. I had panic attacks whenever I wasn't in control. The images still haunt me and the sound of human bodies hitting the pavement rob me of my sleep. The guilt of being one of the survivors still tortures me as I ask myself why so many heroes, firefighters, police officers, and paramedics, lost their lives trying to save others. Perhaps I could have saved someone too.

The airplane hit the tower six stories above my office – merely eighteen metres separated us from a sure demise. Up until that point, I believed I knew how life worked and now? I have to cry every time I visit Ground Zero. I sit on a bench, inhale deeply and realise how precious life is. Money became secondary. I still work a lot but less than before. I care more about the people around me, talk about my feelings and try to help others as best as I can.

Now, when I leave my house to go to work, I give my wife a kiss knowing that each day can be the last.

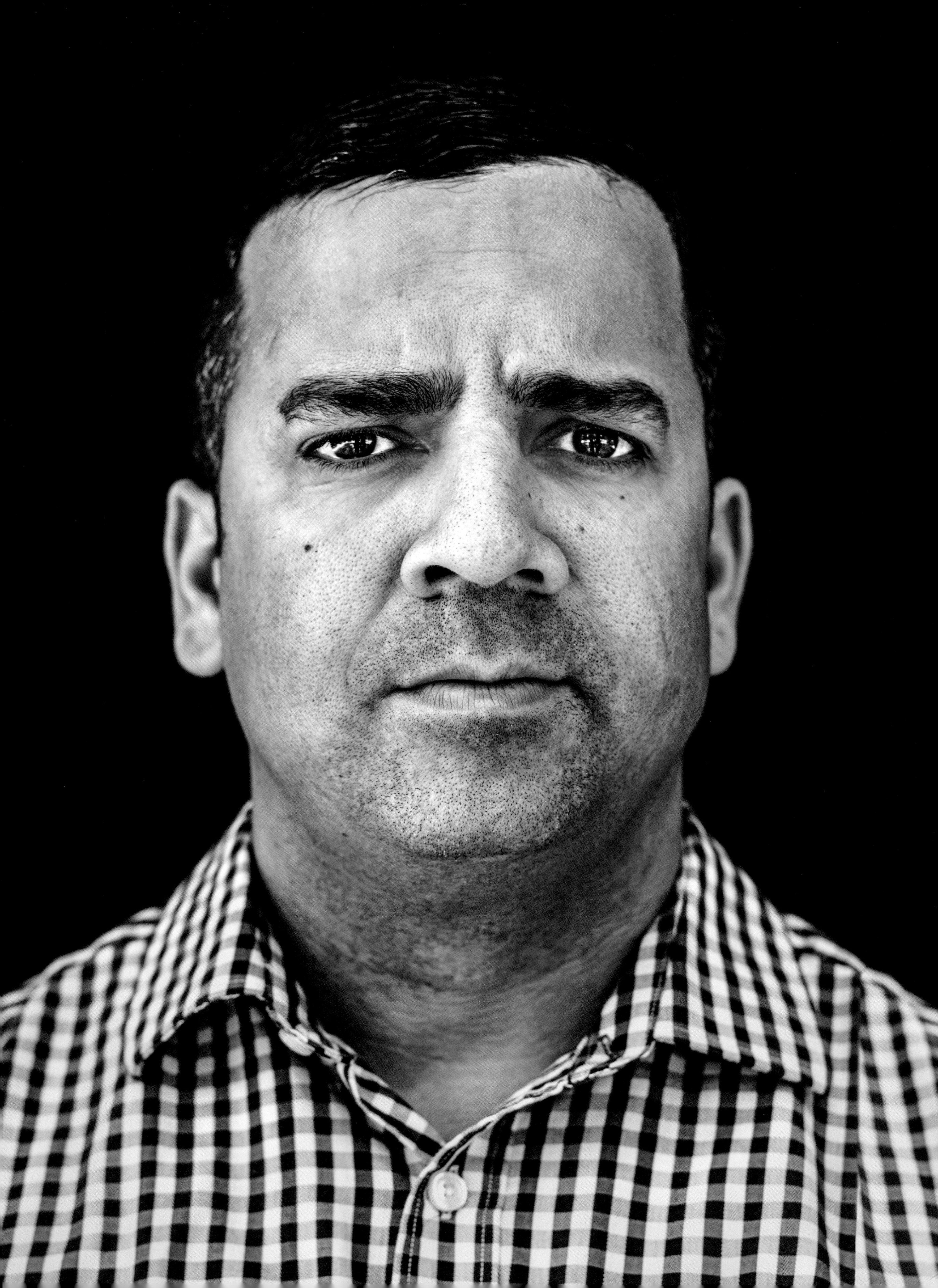

DIONNE, 30
JANUARY 17TH, 2015, ZURICH, SWITZERLAND

My parents fought all the time when I was young. My father, the total opposite of my mother, was an adventurer and jack of all trades, and one day he left without coming back. I only got to know him properly when I was fifteen. We had great discussions and had things in common. I liked him a lot, but then, just two years after reconnecting, his heart failed. I was unbelievably angry at him for leaving me again, and this time for good.

When I was 19 years old, I only cared about one thing: partying and disappearing into another world where I could be unburdened and detached. My boyfriend at the time was a drug dealer and took cocaine. I wanted to feel how he felt and wanted to understand why he took drugs. I let the substance into my body, and I liked it.

My Jamaican mother, a bank employee, had raised me strictly, so the fact that my life took a negative turn did not evade her. I left home and didn't come back. My boyfriend was unemployed with a lot of problems that crept more and more into our relationship: he was violent and treated me terribly, yet I loved him.

Then I accidentally became pregnant before turning twenty. First I thought of getting an abortion because I was so hopeless, but then I decided to keep the baby and take on this huge responsibility. Within a year I matured a great deal while my friends continued to party. I was forced to change my life around completely and leave my first big love which broke my heart, but I had to put my child first. His lifestyle, characterised by drugs and violent crimes, sent him to prison for eight years. My son Davin became the centre of my world, and he gave me a reason to feel an unbelievable sense of pride. He gave me strength and joy. Former desires and feelings became invalid. When Davin was half a year old, I took him to prison to visit his father, which was extremely hard for me to do but, knowing what it is like growing up without a father, I wanted to give my son the chance to meet his father. I wanted him to decide for himself how he wants his relationship to his father to be.

I always had the romantic notion of living in a house with my family, but for a long time that wish seemed unrealistic – until I met my husband, Sam. Davin calls him Dad, while he calls his biological father by his name. I have a good relationship with his Dad today – I don't want Davin growing up with fights. We're a patchwork family that works very well.

Life is full of tests. Obstacles you'd rather avoid come your way, but it's precisely these things that allow us to grow and turn out to be the most beautiful gifts. A lot of people judged me when I became pregnant, yet having Davin was the best thing that could have happened to me. He forced me to wake up and gave my life purpose again.

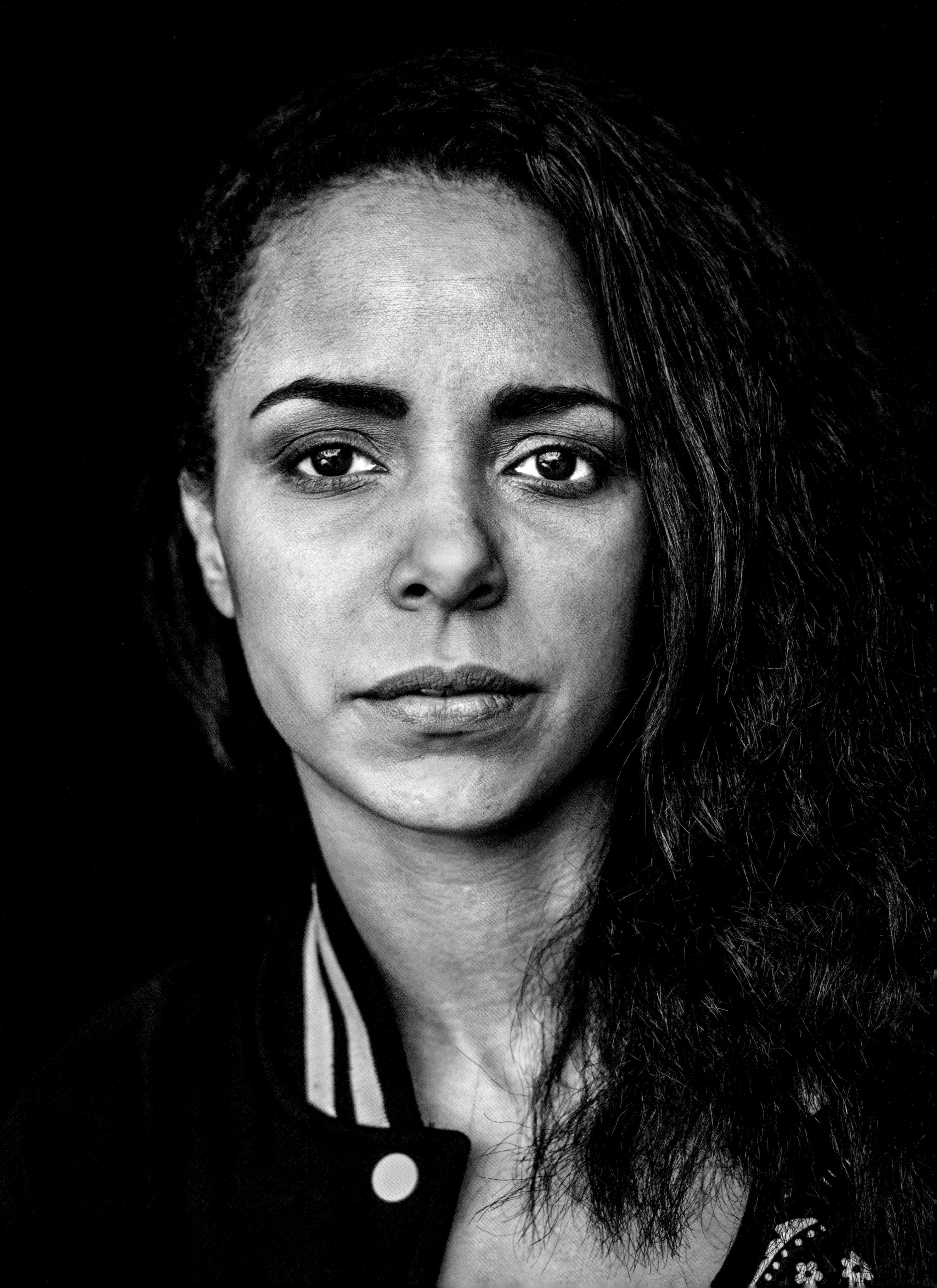

THOMAS, 48

OCTOBER 20TH, 2015, HOLLYWOOD, LOS ANGELES

Every child is creative, and you shouldn't put obstacles in the way of creatives. You have to feel free as an artist, you have to be able to fly.

I spent a lot of time in nature as a young child, where I would collect leaves in all forms and colours, I would study their structure and memorise it. At home I spent hours zooming in on my atlas, exploring all the fine lines, the lakes, streets, and mountain ranges. I realised that life isn't linear – it's full of many paths one can take, and I wanted to explore them all. My curiosity was insatiable. I wanted everything and preferably all put together. Some said I was too dreamy and that I would amount to nothing.

I left Germany, came to Los Angeles and founded my own art studio, and became very successful with my work. A lot of people ask me how my ideas come about: I'm in tune with nature. Mother earth creates the most beautiful structures and tells the most exciting stories. I look into the sky and discover creatures, I break up known structures and create new ones, I look into the ocean and come up with stories, I see beyond the horizon and start to dream. Sometimes I spend hours just roaming in nature, and then I jot down my ideas.

I believe that humans forget to dream. They are afraid to let go and be free. They lose childlike characteristics that allow them to experience colours, invent stories, frolic through fields and dream. It doesn't matter how old you are; life is pure love. When you stop dreaming, you stop growing.

One of my best ideas came to me as I was lying in a field of grass in Central Park and hundreds of dragonflies fluttered by me. This became the look of 'Tao' an award-winning restaurant in Las Vegas, which I designed. I was allowed to work on many such inspiring, exciting, out-of-the-ordinary and challenging projects. I was able to fully unfold myself in my work, yet I was lonely. As an artist, I lived a very introverted life, and dreamers are belittled. My image to the outside world was one of being strong, able to accomplish anything, always healthy and happy. I was convinced that if I were to allow my weaknesses to show, I would lose all my strength, so I never spoke about my feelings. It was a mere two years ago that I learned that this is wrong.

A slipped disc brought me to a complete standstill. I was in an insane amount of pain, but an operation would have put me at risk of becoming paralysed. For the first time ever, I told the people in my life that I wasn't well. My friends came from all over to support me, and this was an incredible feeling. Everyone was there. I realised that showing fragility is a strength and not a weakness. Decade-long friendships became more intense and my life more honest. Another side effect was that people also started to open themselves up to me, and I realised that they have precisely the same fears as I do.

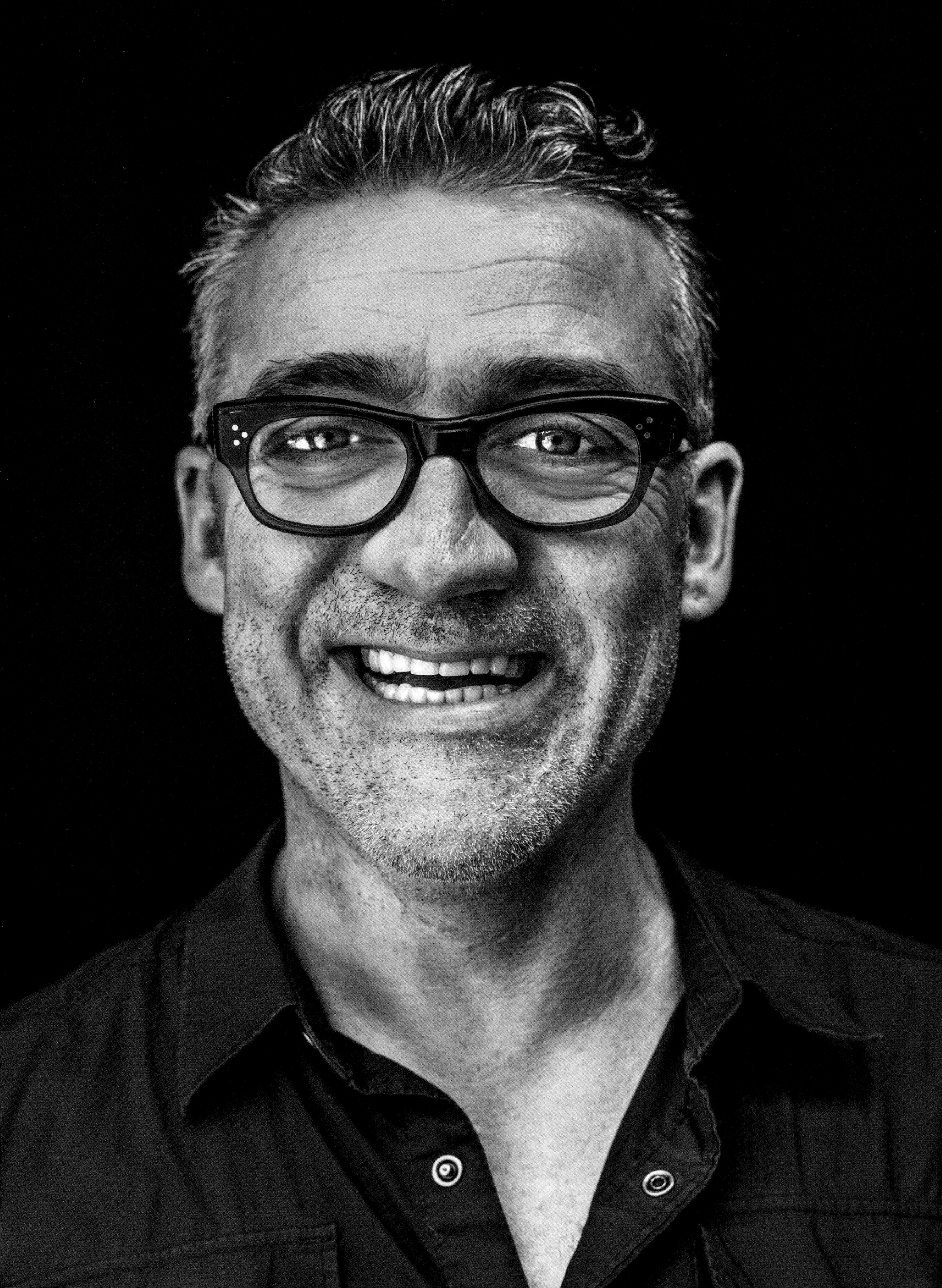

ANITA, 51

JANUARY 31ST, 2015, NIDWALDEN, SWITZERLAND

The water came towards us like a brown wall, thirteen metres tall. What happened next, I can't remember. The moments after have been erased from my memory.

December 26th 2004, Khao Lak, Thailand. My husband Remo and I were on vacation eating our breakfast on the beach when suddenly the water drastically receded. You could see the water rear up beneath the horizon, and the build-up of foam – a tremendous spectacle of nature. I wanted to get closer to see it, but my husband grabbed my hand and screamed at me to run for my life. We managed to run about thirty metres when the monster of a wave seized us and ripped away the ground beneath our feet. It catapulted me through the rubble, with no up or down distinguishable. I lost consciousness, and when I regained it, I was drifting towards the inland on some debris.

The impact of the wave had ripped the clothes off my body, now covered in wounds. I used the last of my strength to climb onto a roof and was able to endure the second and third wave. Then deadly silence, as if the world had stopped moving. There was no one anywhere. It was apocalyptic and sinister. I felt completely alone. I continuously yelled out my husband's name but to no avail. I saw corpses as the water receded again, on the palm trees on the streets, simply everywhere. I became desperate. Where is my husband? Then the first survivors began to assemble, but Remo wasn't there. Where was he? Was Remo alive? Hours later, supported by a local and heavily injured, he dragged himself through the destruction towards me. Through a miracle, we both managed to survive.

December 27th 2004, Khao Lak, Thailand. The day after. The sun was rising, the light rays were spreading themselves all around. In this moment I realised that the world kept going around as if nothing had happened.

Today, over ten years after the tsunami, there are still moments in which I burst out in tears. Why did so many people right next to me have to die, and why were my husband and I allowed to live? I realised that we are only guests on this planet, and that we should use the time we have here with a purpose, and should carefully consider what our values are. I live way more consciously today. Time is relative, that's why I no longer wear a watch. I try to see the beautiful moments in every day, and even small things can be significant – when you give them meaning. You write a new chapter with each passing day, and you are mainly in control of what that could be.

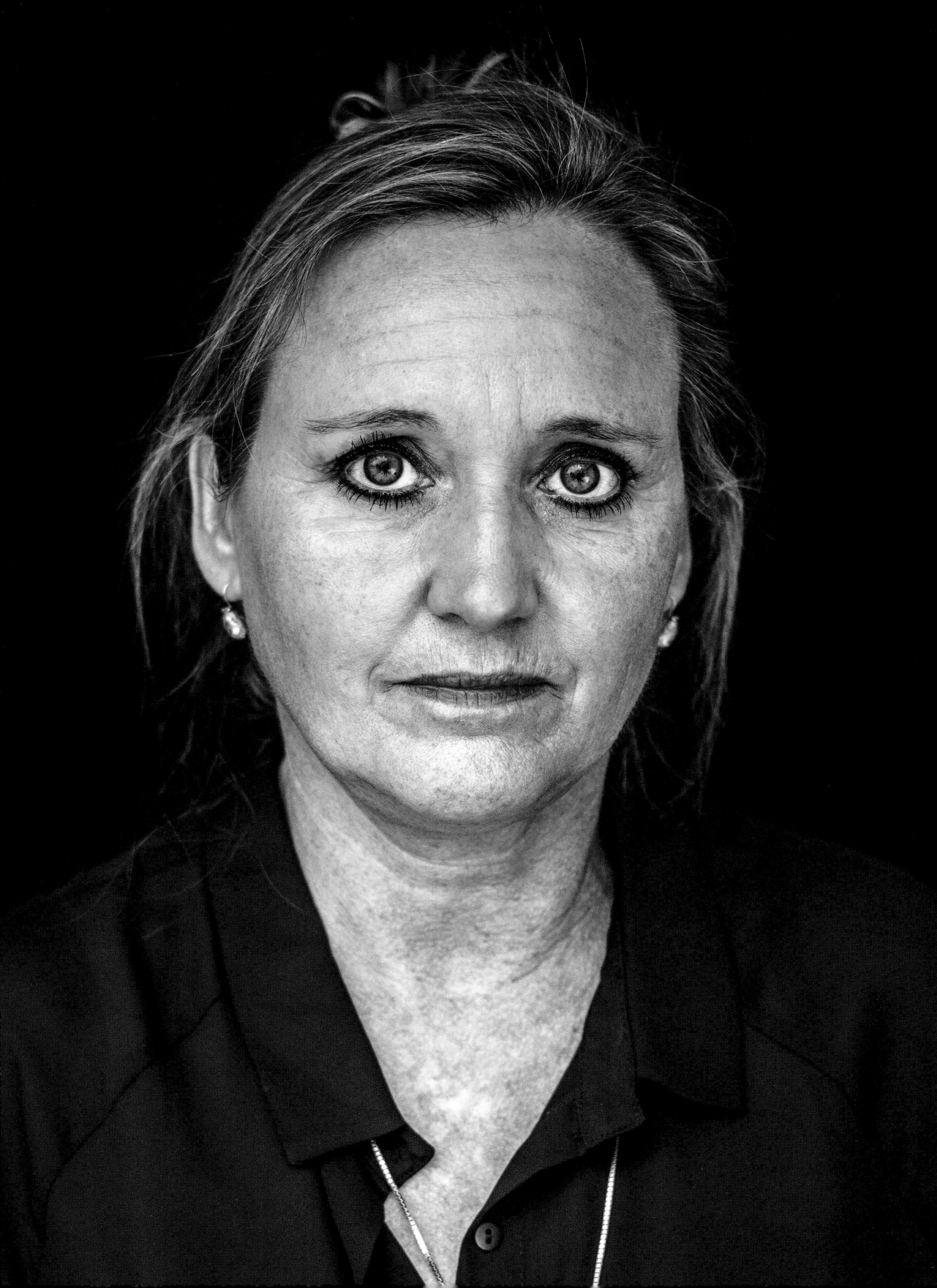

Hollywood turns men into fighters, machines, robots or superheroes; but that's not who we are, and it's not who we have to become to be happy.

In the past, everything just revolved around me. Being an artist, actor and musician enabled me to earn my money with the things I loved. I was successful with Sens Unik, the band I founded, and travelled often. I met many interesting people and discovered many new places when I began my acting career. I was goal oriented, motivated and focused. I wanted to be better and more important, and each step and decision was made to bring me closer to my goal. I began to judge people that were average. We only have this one life.

My childhood home was simple. My parents were immigrants from Spain, and they worked hard to live in Switzerland, but I was striving for more. I went to Hollywood and managed to snag a role in a James Bond movie. My life was excellent, and everything was beautiful, yet I began to lose myself in the severe and permanent pressure of having to be better and stronger. If you're too weak, you fall behind. Hollywood is a place that lets people shine, and so I presented myself to others as being superior, strong and smart but was just lying to myself. I owned a lot but had nothing.

My attitude towards life changed through the birth of my son, as suddenly there was a tiny creature in my life taking centre-stage which was more important to me than I was. Children are unburdened – they play, laugh, and the simplest of things entertain them. They live in the now without concerning themselves about what will be. I realised how superficial and ephemeral my job was, and how egotistical and arrogant I was. It was my son who made me realise that there are people without careers who achieve happiness, and it's precisely those people who have what I was missing from my life for a long time: contentment.

We're all just people. I couldn't control and influence my son's development in the same way I could control mine. I was no longer able to hide my fears and doubts beneath the mask I was wearing, and so I became gentle and fragile. If you allow yourself to be delicate, you'll gain strength; this is especially important for men, as our society often expects men to be tough regardless of the situation. I believe people who are aware of their weaknesses and accept them are the strong ones!

Today I lead a different kind of life. I am less focused on my career but more focused on my skills, and I no longer care about red carpets or winning an Oscar but care about doing the best possible job in a movie that can change the world. I dared to take a step back and readjust my priorities. I want to wake up in the mornings and be happy; I want to be a terrific father, and I hope that one day my son will tell me that he is happy and content with the life he has.

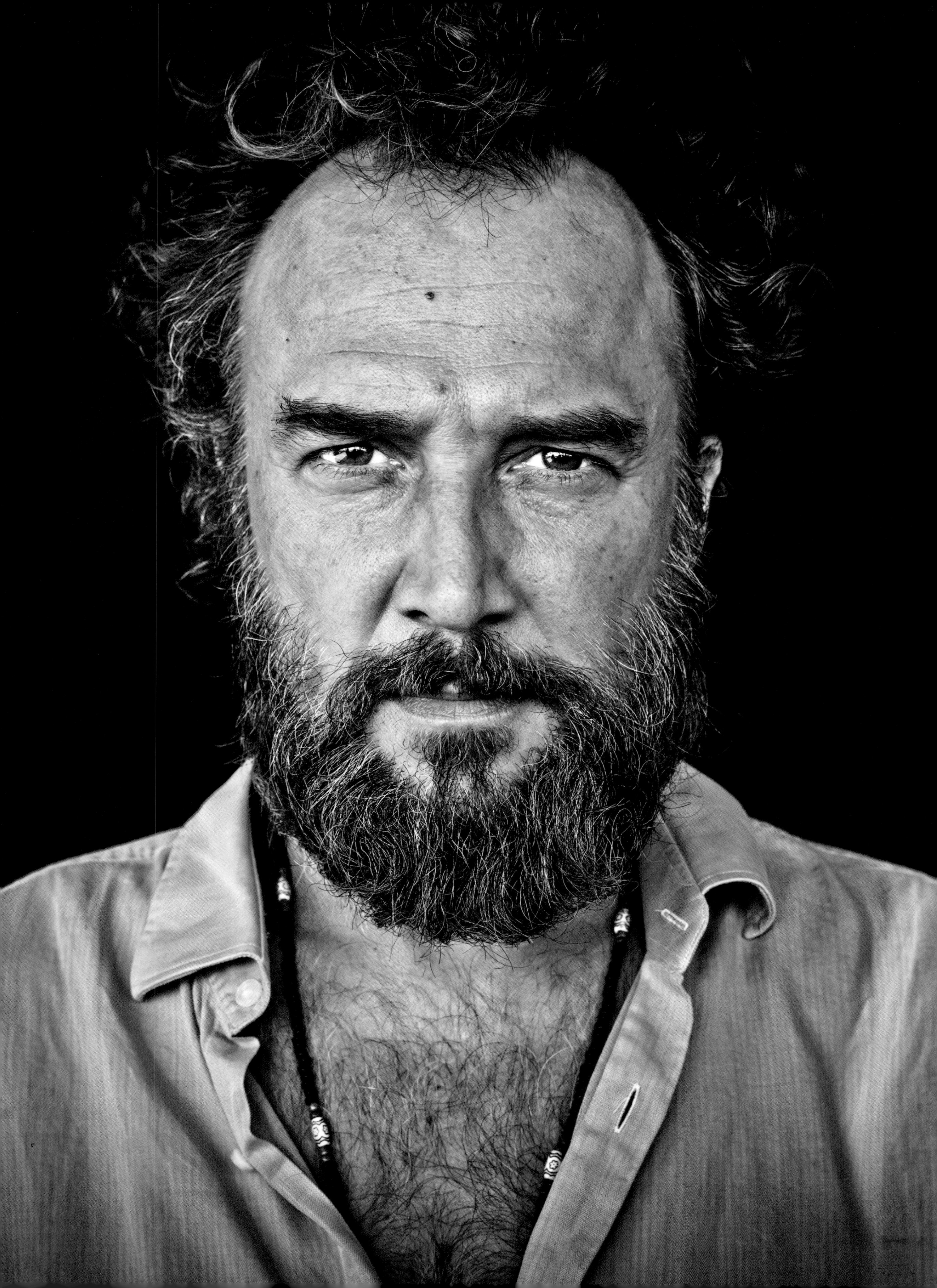

EMANUEL, 53
NOVEMBER 1ST, 2016, WATERFRONT, CAPE TOWN

Kaffir, bushman, and scum – I was the black lad, number five of thirteen children. I spent my childhood on the streets and in numerous farms owned by the whites, but my family stuck together.

My father laboured in the fields and my mother in the household. We were strictly forbidden to enter the house of the whites. Their property was always kilometres away from the rest of civilisation. We slept in the fields and watched as snakes violently snatched chickens and made small bonfires in the evenings to cook pap. It's out of habit that I still eat this white mash of corn today.

My two older brothers worked on the farm. Therefore, the master of the estate allowed me to go to school. I had to leave at 5:30 am every morning to arrive on time at 8:30. I had no shoes to walk the 50 kilometres it took to get there and back. I would meet other black children along the way, and as we walked together, the school buses filled with white children overtook us slowly so that they could pelt us with their rubbish.

The school for blacks was on the other side of the river so that, to cross and not get ripped away by the current, we had to build a human chain. We received beatings if we arrived late for school. I had to work on the fields on the weekends, and when I was able to read and write I had to start working during the week too – we weren't granted education that went further than these basics, and the farmers never compensated our work.

A lot of the owners were barbarians: one of the owners forced me to accompany her to their winter house for two weeks. It was freezing, and I only had on a thin pair of pants and a T-shirt while sitting on the cargo bed of her pick-up truck for the entire duration of the long drive. I wasn't able to walk upright once we arrived and so she beat me using a broom handle. Then she forced me to clean the pick-up truck using bitterly cold water. She would have kicked me out and left me on the streets if I had refused. I was twelve years old.

We had no rights during Apartheid. We had to treat white people with respect, bow down to them and serve them. If we were no longer of use to them, they chased us off their property and onto the streets where we were in much greater danger. Whenever we heard an approaching car, we ran away. Once I witnessed my parents get beaten up by young cops, I was unbelievably furious but was unable to do anything. My father explained to me that everyone has to fight their own battles. When I asked him why they are allowed to beat us, he said: 'Because they are white'. At some point, one just accepts that these living conditions are part of being black. One begins to think it's normal.

I was circumcised when I was fifteen-years-old. I had to go to a mountain for this and met many people living in townships who told me that there was a massive political movement in the making. I wanted to find out more, so I would eavesdrop the radio announcements through the open kitchen window back on the farm. This way I heard about Nelson Mandela and black power, but back then I had no idea what it all meant. I began to read newspapers and so my understanding of the country and how it worked increased. Previously there was only 'the law', and I understood that our government was behind these laws. I learned to see the bigger picture and not to despise the whites as such. Sure, some enjoyed torturing us and played with their power, but I also met good white people like a couple who once said to me, 'Emanuel, you should be allowed to play with our kids and decide who you want to hang out with, but our laws don't allow it.' It was 1979, and their farm wasn't far away from the city. I was allowed to work in the city and earned six Rand (in 1979, this was worth around 3.5 British Pound) per month. Three years later, when I was nineteen-years-old, I had saved enough to get my family off the farm. We fled into the townships and were finally free.

Today I am repeatedly asked whether I feel hatred towards white people, but why should I? I don't want to blame specific people – it was the government who failed us.

I make my own decisions at home now. My children shouldn't know any difference in colour. They should accept people for who they are. It does not matter what I've been through because I am alive and I always knew that as long as I'm alive, I'll be happy one day.

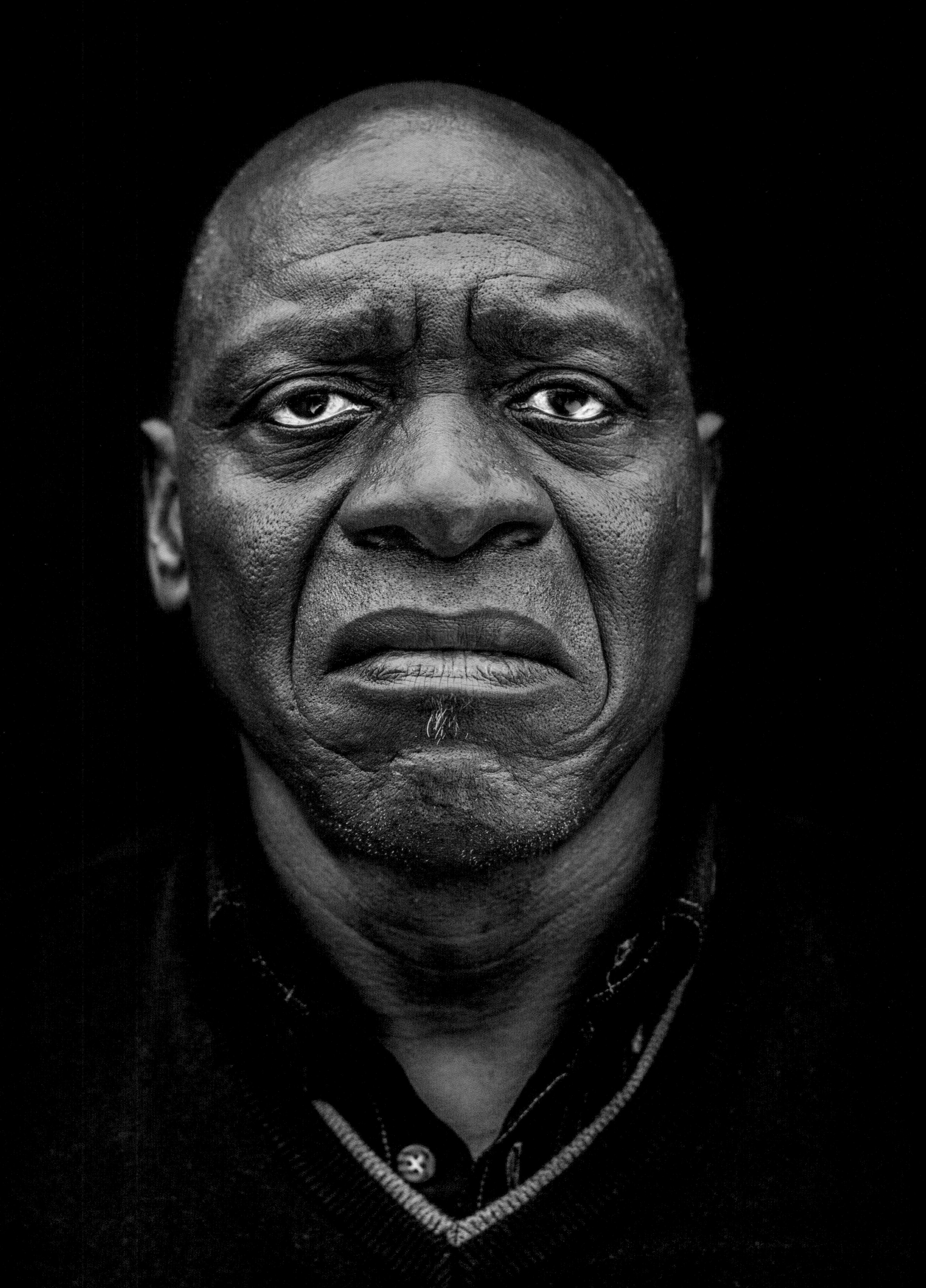

KATE, 26

OCTOBER 28TH, 2015, VENICE BEACH, LOS ANGELES

I was eight years old when my father's friend first abused me; I was thirteen when I finally defended myself. For a long time, five years, I was unable to understand what he was doing to me. I was too young, weak and powerless to stop his abuse.

As a child and a teenager I was always on the run, hoping to escape my memories. When I was finally old enough to go to college, I immediately left home, but I never settled down. I dropped out of school and moved restlessly from place to place, wanting to be free and independent; but I just ended up feeling lonely and empty.

At some point, I was offered a job as a model, though at that time I wasn't thinking of a career. I just accepted the offer because I didn't know what else to do. They put me up in a model apartment in New York, rent-free for three months, while I was meant to go to castings. I didn't go though, so I was kicked out; but I just moved into the next model apartment for free, only to get kicked out again. This cycle continued for a while until I met Nora, a model from Germany, who gave me a self-help book and taught me to be in control of my own thoughts. As a nineteen-year-old, this was a huge turning point in my life, as I began to realise that a bunch of things had gone terribly wrong in my life. I had moved six times in two years, was unable to settle down, lived in my own abstract world and was a stranger to myself. Hoping for some change, I went back home to North Carolina. One evening, drunk at a friend's house, I bought a one-way flight to Los Angeles. I was twenty-years-old and determined to finally get my life in order. Two days later I was off.

Los Angeles is strange and overwhelming, whilst being cool and fascinating. I spent the first few months alone. Any person I met was just a fleeting contact. Days went by without hearing myself speak. The loneliness ate me up from inside, and I found it hard to be with myself, but that's how I learned to bear my own company and to give my emotions space. I was able to connect to myself this way and focus on the future.

I still live here, and these days I'm going to castings on a regular basis, I'm getting a lot of jobs and can decide which ones I want to take. As a model I feel like I did when I was a child: I pretend to be someone else for others, yet the good thing is that this forces me to extract the childlike aspects from within myself again and again. That's how I lost my fear and gained the ability to feel carefree. My old fears are forgotten now.

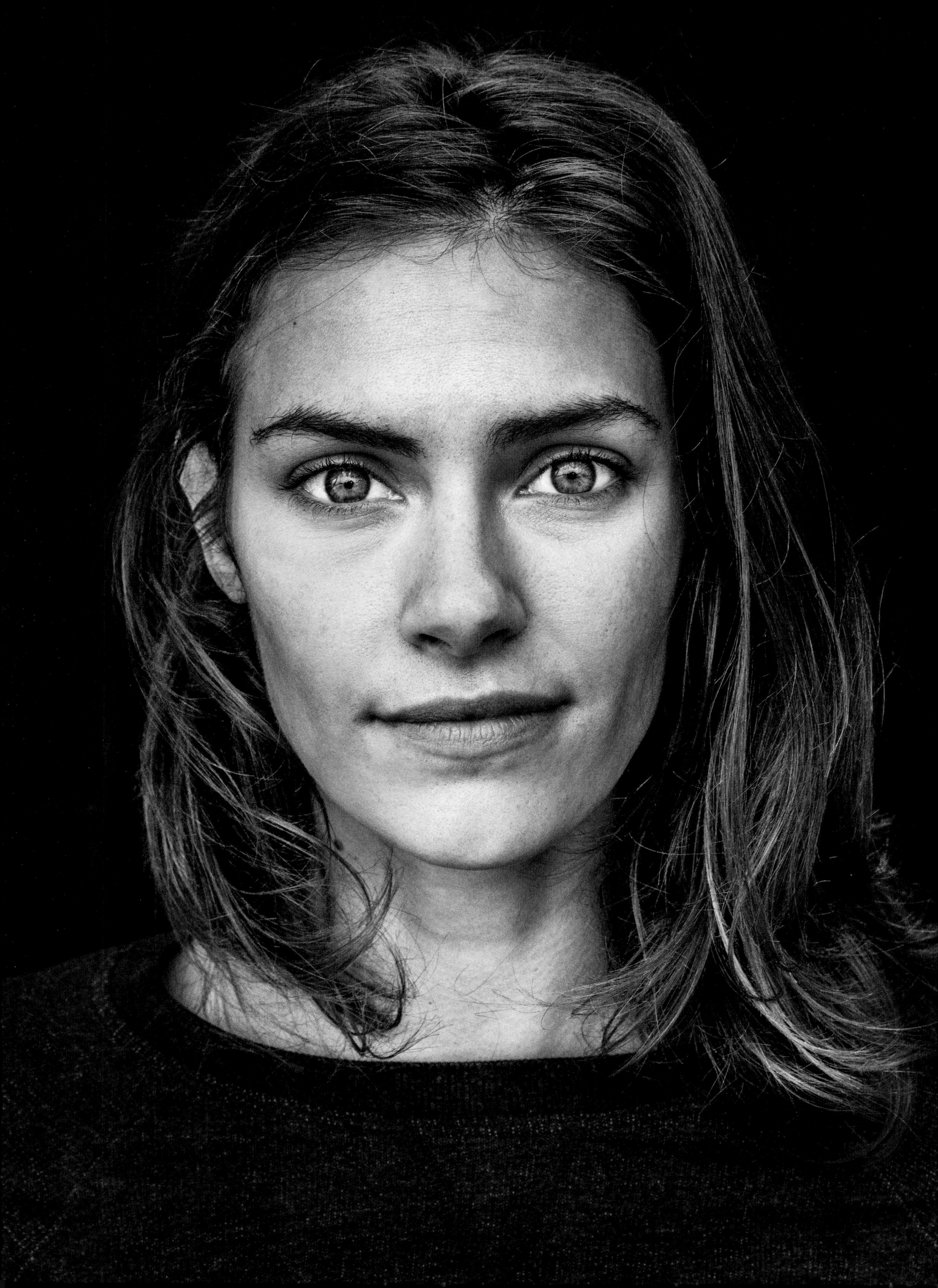

I was quiet and insecure as a child. I kept my thoughts to myself out of fear that I would say something wrong. It was my wild afro hair that would make me feel that I wasn't enough. If my mother could have had her way my hair would have been shorter and straighter – you shouldn't draw attention to yourself as a person of colour.

I was seventeen years old when my life suddenly and drastically changed. It was August 1985, and Apartheid was nearing its end. Back then schools were still divided by race. I was in my final year of the Catholic school Marist Brothers when we rebelled against the Apartheid regime with a school boycott. Our parents and teachers called an assembly into order in which they tried to force us to end our resistance and return to school. It was there that a massive wave of anger suddenly rushed through me and without thinking I jumped up and yelled: 'If we believe in God like we say we do, we would no longer tolerate the injustice in this country! It's our biblical duty to protest and boycott the Apartheid regime!' It was the first time I ever voiced my opinion, and hundreds of people were sitting around me. It was the moment I realised that I too have a voice and that I should stand up for my rights.

One month later, I gathered outside of the school with other students. Our hands were balled into fists as we took to the streets to demonstrate for freedom and equality while screaming 'Power to the people!' We demanded our right to vote, the right to a democratically-elected government, and the release of political prisoners. More and more people joined our march until it turned into a mass demonstration attended by over 600 people. Suddenly the police and military intervened by following us in all directions, and then they began to shoot at us. We were unarmed and defenceless and had no means to protect ourselves from the violence directed towards us. There was a mix of tear gas and smoke in the air while the streets were full of burning tires and tear-gas canisters. It was war. I ran for my life as fast as I could, but I ended up running into the direction of the military. As I jumped down from the top of the fence, a rubber bullet burst through the vibracrete fence I was hiding behind. I ran through the streets and jumped over fences until eventually a woman pulled me inside a house and locked the door behind me. On the floor was another teenage girl who yanked me down. My heart was pounding like crazy. We remained in this hideout for several hours until the situation outside calmed down.

I suppressed this day for many years, until one day a group of students asked me if I wanted to share my story from this event. It was difficult for me to precisely rehash this incident as I was still traumatised, so to process what I had experienced I turned my feelings into a hip-hop track called 'Butterflies Fly By'. I put the song on YouTube, making a video out of original film recordings from the demonstration. Hundreds of thousands of people saw the video, and many people thanked me and wrote to say that the song helped them to process those times.

Thirteen years after the mass demonstration I founded the project 'Heal the Hood', through which I want to give teenagers the chance to express themselves using music and dance to provide them with a sense of self-worth. I want them to gain self-confidence and self-esteem and stand up for their opinion.

Together we write songs, produce music and partake in international competitions with our dance crew. 'Heal the Hood' means the world to me, and every day it becomes more clear what we can reach collectively. So far over 130'000 teenagers from different parts of Western Cape have participated in this project. Within the project, they learn that it doesn't matter where we come from and how we grow up, because if we believe in ourselves anything is possible.

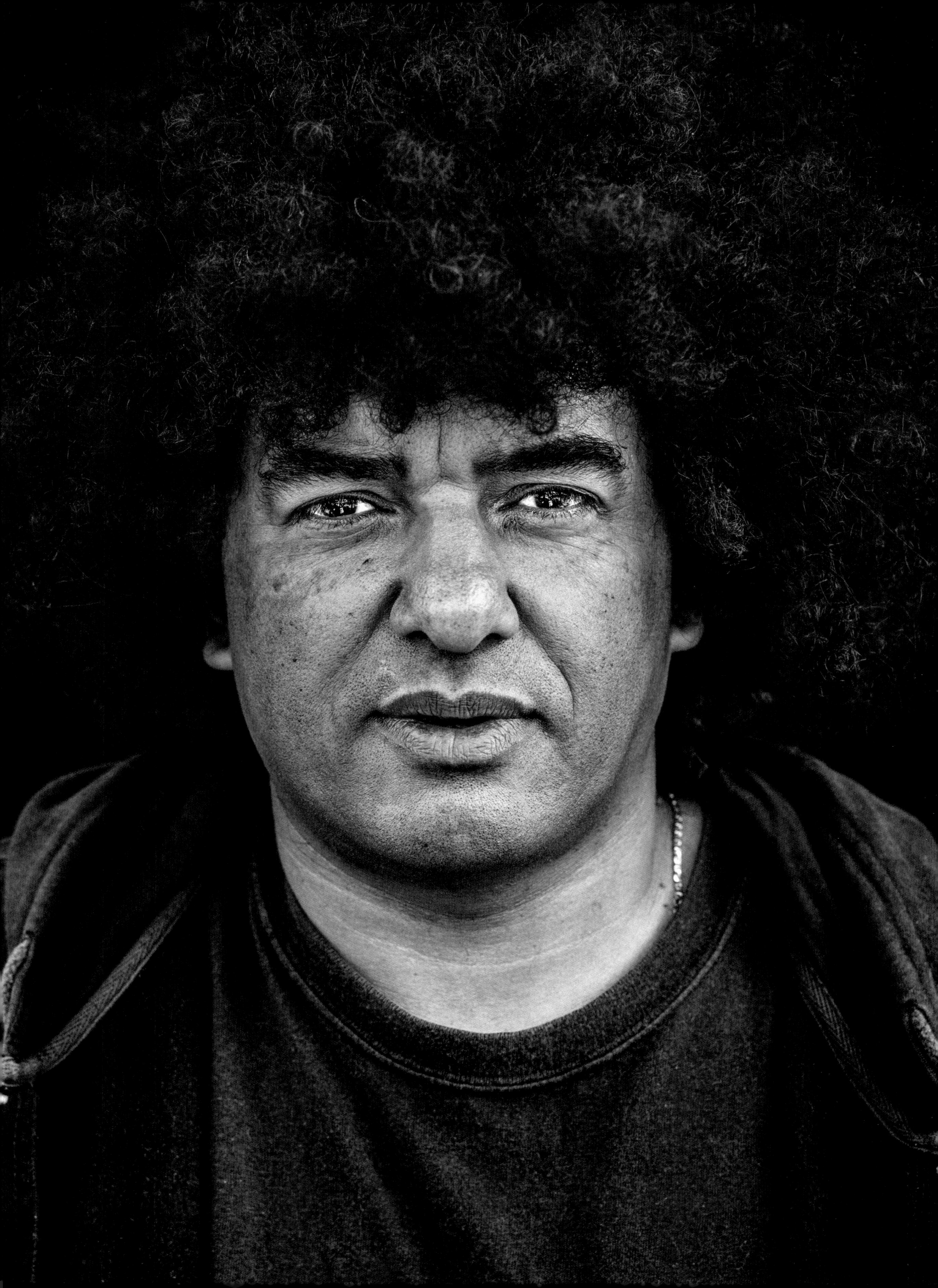

SONJA, 40

FEBRUARY 6TH, 2018, ZURICH, SWITZERLAND

I had to carry a burden as a child that was too heavy to handle, as my parents were full of traumas and psychological problems through the aftermath of the war. My father, an alcoholic, froze to death on a bench under the influence when I was eight years old. My mother didn't give me any sense of protection or support. She was full of abandonment fears, always scared that I would leave her and that she would die alone. I felt responsible for her from a young age, even later when she had a cheating partner. Life at home was a disaster. We always moved around, and things happened to me no child would be able to process, and my mother and I seemed to continually attract bad things. I was completely overwhelmed with life.

I went crazy when I turned thirteen and started going to parties, dancing all night long and using drugs; first weed then chemical drugs, to numb my mind. Partying with other lost teenagers gave me an identity and a sense of family, things I lacked at home. When I was fifteen years old, a guy gave me an overdose of ecstasy. When I regained consciousness, I was lying on his bed. He had raped me and then, as if nothing had happened, he gave me a lift home. It felt as if he thought the whole thing was a fair deal: he had given me drugs, and in return, he got access to my body. This event destroyed the very last trace of trust I still had in me, and it was the beginning of a five year long downward spiral.

I quit school, disappeared and drifted around without any orientation, just looking for any sort of distraction. I lived on the streets and had nothing in my pockets, so that at one point I even sold my birth control as drugs.

To be sought-after and cared for as a woman is something I had never seen at home or elsewhere, so I began to confuse sex for love; bit by bit, men went on to shatter my dignity, until I had none left at seventeen. I started to sell my body to buy cocaine. An older man wanted me as his playmate, paying me daily so that I would always be on call for him. I agreed. I would often ask myself what my purpose in life is. I didn't

understand how it had been possible for me to stoop so low and I desperately wanted to quit prostituting myself and managed to do so. But then I had no money, and I landed at a private escort service, where I had to give 60 % of my earnings to the pimps. The money that was left over I wasted on drugs. I took everything I got my hands on, just to experience a little high. I tried to suppress my thoughts during sex, but they always caught up with me. I felt worthless, restless and unbearable; my soul was bleeding. I was at rock bottom and needed more drugs to numb my body and mind. I was in a situation and place I didn't want to be in, but I kept taking more appointments for the escort service – I was in an unstoppable downward spiral.

Often I'll hear that prostitution is something one chooses to do, but what exactly does that mean? Mostly it's girls and women who are affected and who have completely lost themselves. Some girls I knew on the streets ended up committing suicide. Looking back, I know that Jesus was my life saviour. Getting in touch with him gave me the strength to find my way back into a healthy existence.

I managed to get out when I was nineteen and made a drug withdrawal. I was in a filthy apartment for several days with no money for food or anything. I packed my things and went back to my mom's place. Shortly after that, I found out that I was pregnant with my last relationship. That was my new beginning.

Through my son, I finally experienced love, while love through a partner still seemed impossible. For a long time I felt an intense hatred towards men but the more space I gave Jesus, the better I felt. Today I feel as if I've been reborn and can proudly say that I lead a beautiful life. I have an excellent partner and four sons – five men that I love more than anything. And I have my faith which fulfils me, and which enables me to pass on hope to others; something I didn't possess for a long time. A wise man once said to me, 'The tears of your past are pearls for those you meet tomorrow'.

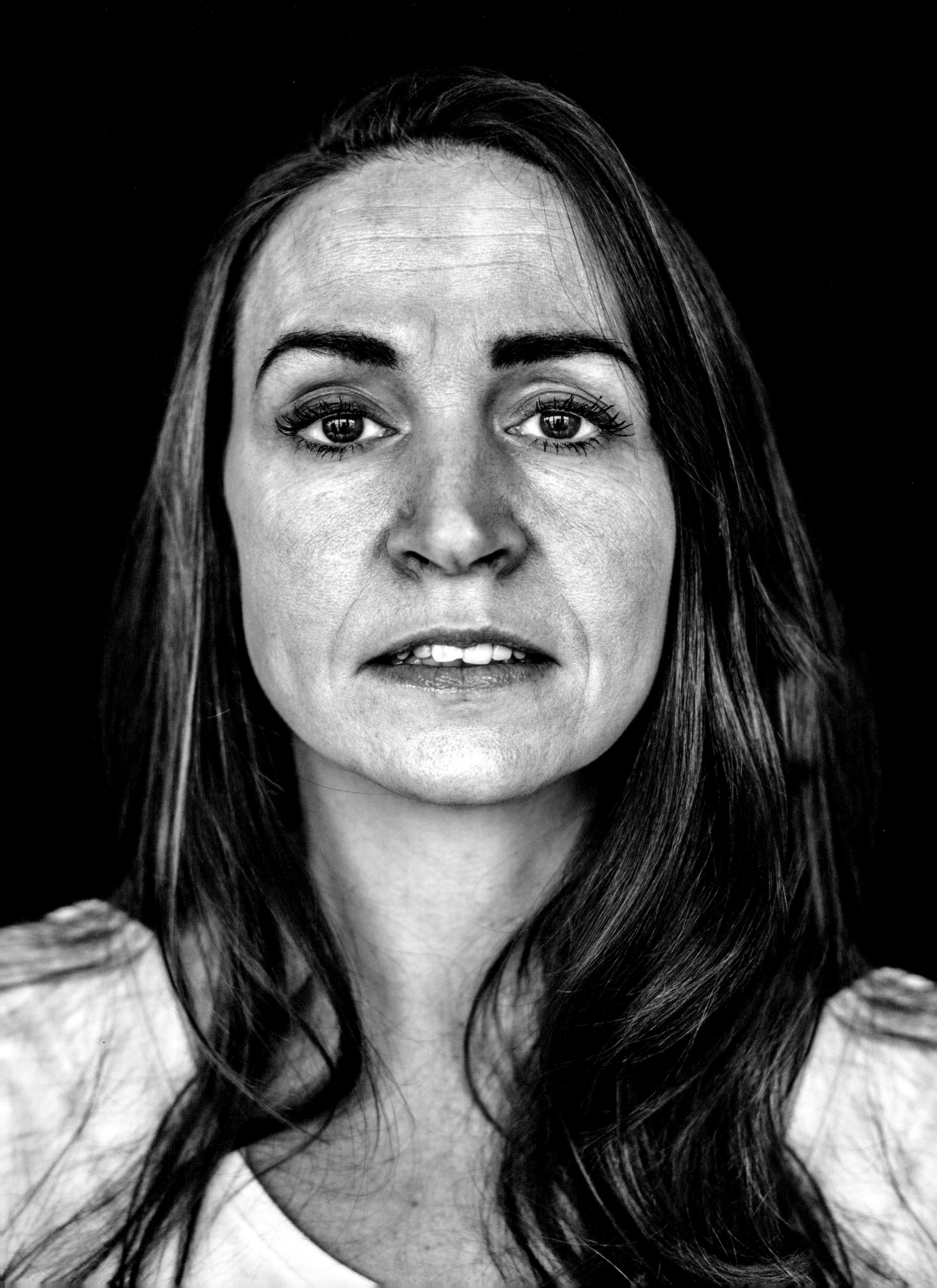

ANDREW, 51

APRIL 18TH, 2014, MANHATTAN, NEW YORK

What had the most significant impact on me? My family, especially my mother who was a single mother of seven, working sixteen hours a day to provide a good but minimal living for us.

My mother would be on her way to work before I was up and got home after I went to bed. When I was small, it was mostly my eldest brother tucking me in. He was the best storyteller and would make up tales about us being able to fly and taking over the world. We spent a lot of time together, and he was always able to make me laugh or teach me something – all the things a father would have done. I knew that with him by my side nothing could happen to me; together we were unstoppable.

I didn't see my mother very often, but when I did see her, she embraced me with warmth and always let me feel her love for me. She would often repeat: 'We have a home, and warm clothes and aren't hungering. We have everything we need to be happy'.

Sure, there were days where it was painful to see the wealth of my friends, days in which I felt we weren't privileged. It wasn't always easy to endure the injustice of my mother having to work herself to the ground while others hoarded their wealth, but mostly I was able to deal with it. It would have been wrong to feel jealousy towards those who were more successful and wealthy because, after all, we had each other and so nothing was really missing.

My relationship with my mother and siblings didn't change after I met my wife and started my own family. We knew that we could always count on each other. This was put to the test when my eldest brother was diagnosed with incurable cancer. He was only forty and a father of three. As a family we tried to fight for his life, we prayed to God, but he saw his sickness as God's will, as his fate.

Contrary to our advice, he decided against chemotherapy as he didn't want to leave us in a broken state. He wanted to remain in our memories as we knew him: as a proud husband, father, uncle, son, and brother. That was his last wish, and so cancer kept spreading through his body, and shortly after that, he passed away.

My brother's death left a massive hole in my heart. I never understood his decision to go without putting up a fight, but I had to accept it. He was my big brother, my protector, my companion. I'm grateful for every experience he shared with me and thankful for every realisation I had through him. He made me into the person I am today.

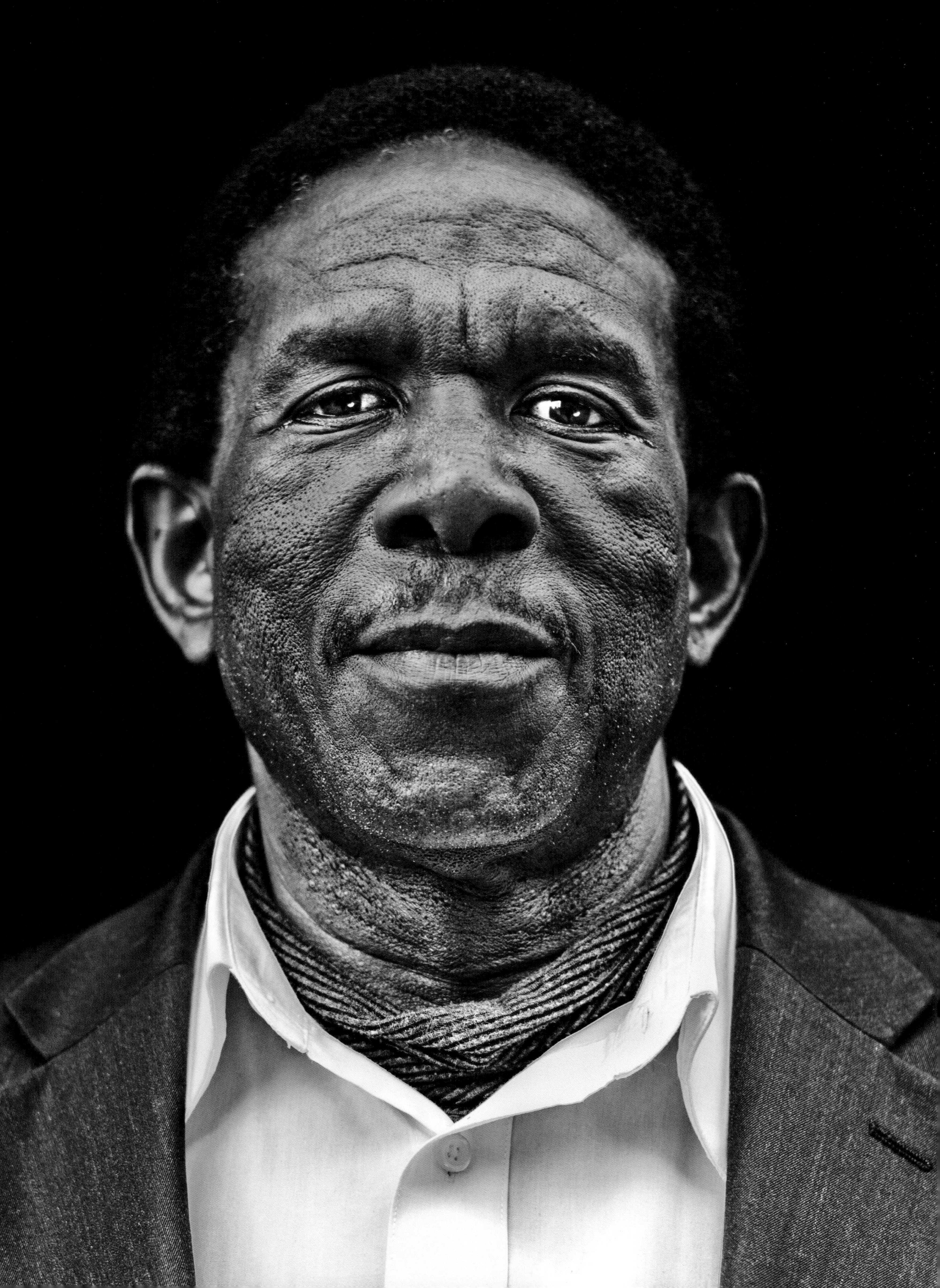

DINA, 40
DECEMBER 1ST, 2017, BALI, INDONESIA

In Indonesia, old traditions still in use say that women should submit themselves to their husbands. Women should keep whatever goes on inside their minds to themselves. They accept what men expect or demand of them.

I met my husband when I was 20, and one year later we were married. I was totally in love and did everything to be a good wife. I even began to visit my mother less often, because that's what he wanted. All my attention was to go towards his family, as is the custom in Indonesia – their problems become your problems. On top of that, we lived with his mother. What was unconventional in our marriage was that I was the breadwinner as my husband had lost his job.

I worked in the advertisement industry and earned quite well, so I was able to travel. I loved travelling and gaining an insight into other cultures. I dreamt of exploring the whole world, but then my husband ordered me to stay at home and not to go on holidays any longer. I wasn't to frivolously spend money, but save it for buying a house. When I had saved enough money to buy a house, he suddenly had no interest any longer. He stalled the purchase until we no longer had any money. My entire savings were spent, and it was only then, far too late, that I noticed my husband's drug addiction. He had continuously used my credit card to buy cocaine. He began to blame me for everything that went wrong in his life: his unemployment, his discontent, and his drug addiction. He also accused me of being responsible for our bank-

ruptcy. He was unable ever to take responsibility for his mistakes. I did everything he asked of me, I even apologised to him and began to believe that I was at fault. Then after five years of marriage came the final blow: my husband told me that he had never been happy with me and with those words he left me. He began to spread rumours about me and degraded me until I broke down. I felt deceived, unloved, useless and empty. My life was no longer meaningful, and for a short while, I even thought of ending it.

Five years went by until the divorce papers arrived and until that point, I remained responsible for his debts as his wife. When I finally wasn't able to be held accountable, I just wanted to leave. I took on different jobs in different Asian countries and travelled from place to place in search of myself. I desperately tried to flee from my past to find happiness again. It took me years to understand that my joy isn't dependent on other people, and that my husband's mistreatment hadn't been my fault.

To start anew, I decided to leave Jakarta for Bali. I don't have much money, but I can pay my rent and bills. I have food, a spoon, a fork and two plates. I live on my own. As a divorcee, I often get strange looks, and other women are afraid that I am in search of a married man, but I don't need another man to be happy. I don't need anyone telling me what to do. I have my own life now, and I'm satisfied with it.

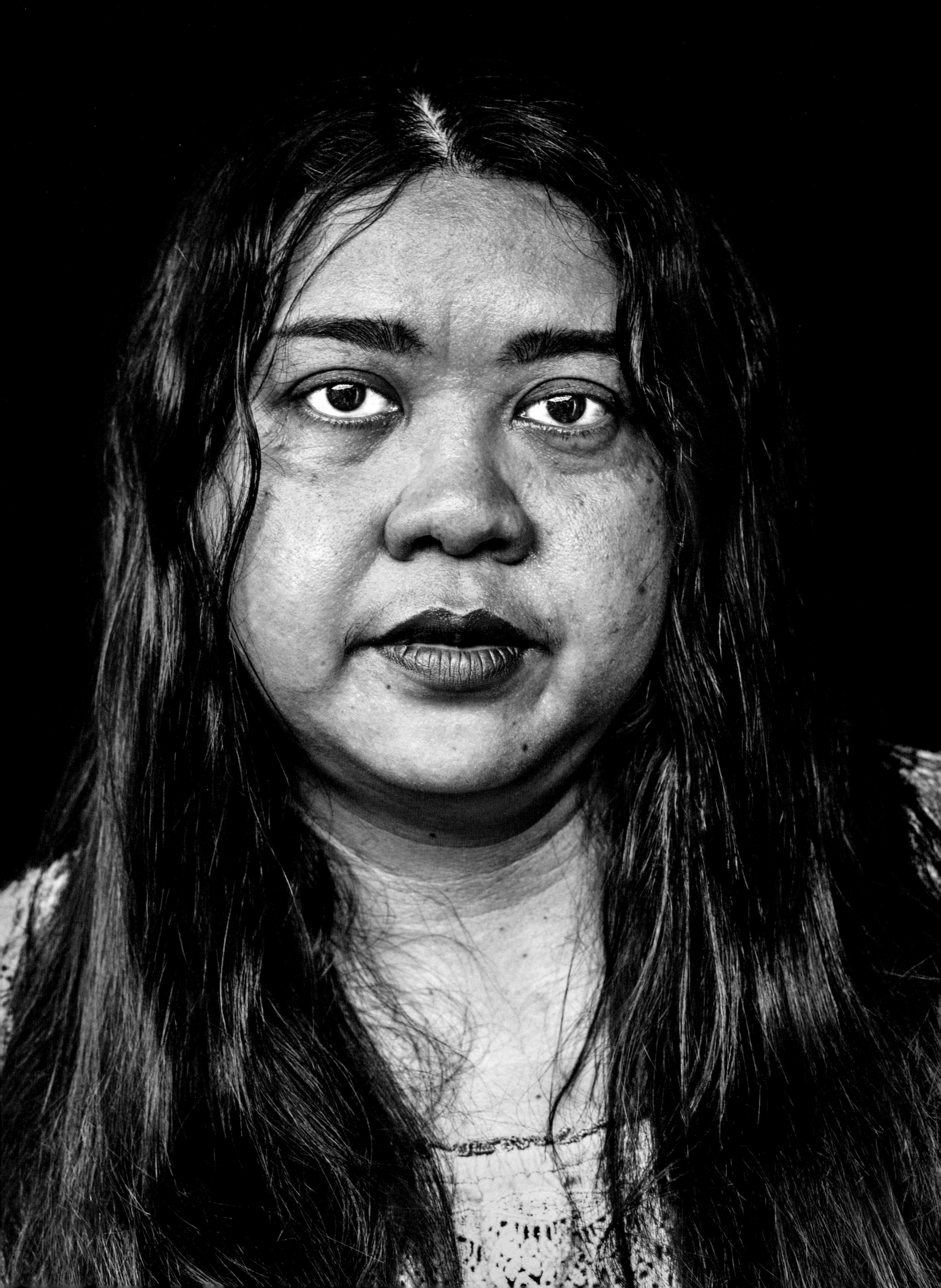

CARLOS, 43

NOVEMBER 3RD, 2015, AGUAS CALIENTES, PERU

My parents passed away when I was young. I can hardly remember my mother, whereas my father is still quite present in my memory. Both died from an illness and left behind a vast empty space.

As an orphan, I grew up with nuns. They were good to me, yet I missed love and comfort. They weren't able to fill up my empty heart, and so I yearned to be close to my mother and father my whole life. I left the orphanage when I was eleven and travelled to Aguas Calientes, my parents' place of birth, to find my roots. From that moment on I was dependent on myself, and I've been living here ever since.

Living among these mountains, I am surrounded by something magical. I miss my parents to this day, but I notice how my connection to them has increased here. It's at the peak of the mountaintop that I am closest to them, I feel connected to them, to God, the moon and the stars. I feel my inner peace at this height.

I worship nature just like the Incas did before me, and like them, I believe in the power of offerings. Every single morning I hike up to the top of the mountain to bring the gods corn or coca leaves. These offerings are meant to help keep the balance between nature and humans in check, since many treat mother nature without any respect – dumping their trash everywhere, polluting the waters, poisoning the air and destroying the forests. It's our own home we are killing. On the mountaintop, I pray for the reflection, responsibility, and stability of my fellow humans. During my ritual, I feel the unruly energy of the mountain deep within me. I have learned to reach an altered state of consciousness, to reach a level of trance that allows me to speak to my mother and get advice from her. This state of mind releases a power within me able to assist others in the healing of old wounds and blockages. I pass this power on through my hands, and that's how I try to help others heal their hearts.

I reclaimed my own heart in these mountains and healed it through my spirituality. Today I know that I carry my parents within me.

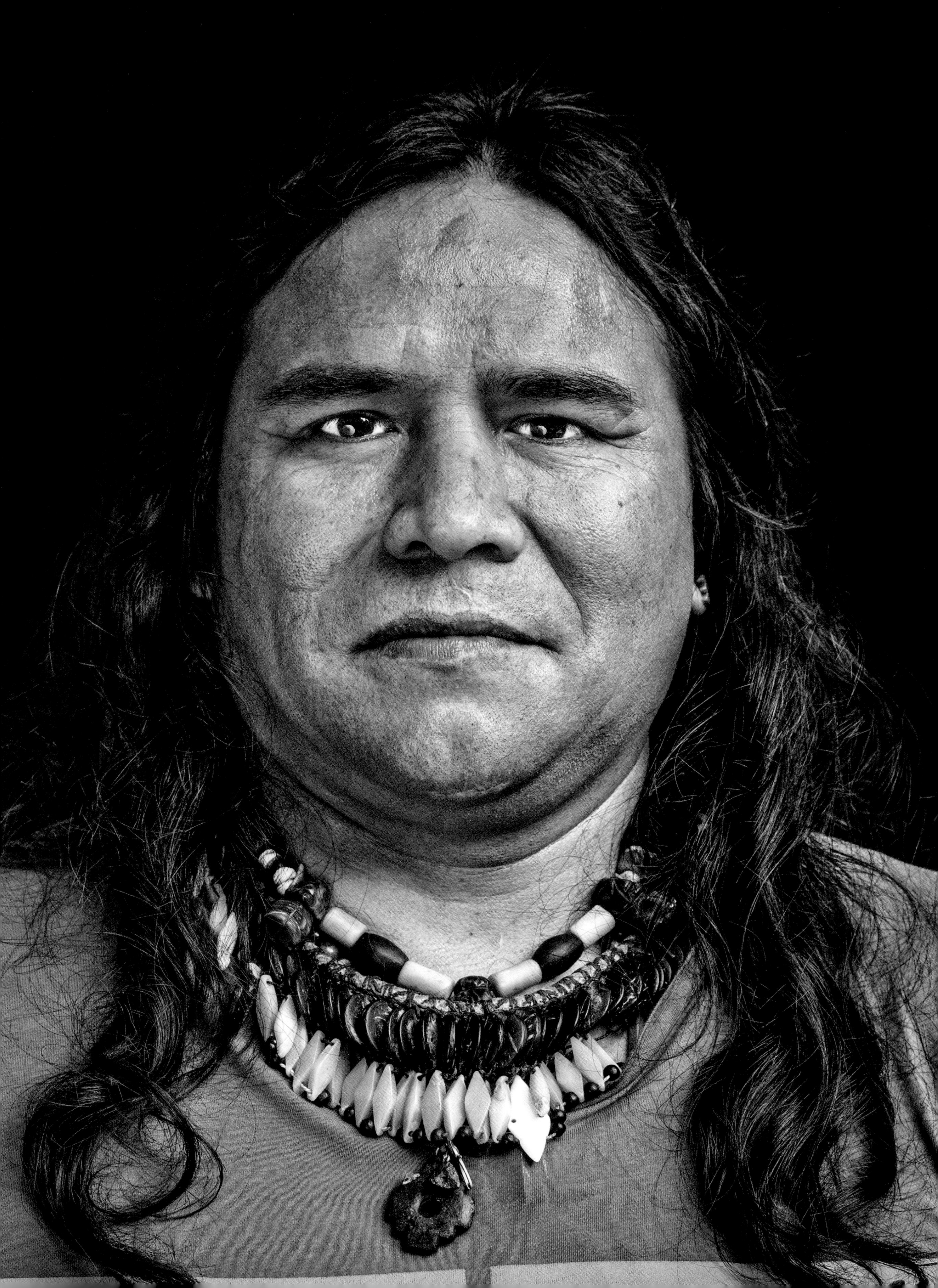

MARKUS, 30
JUNE 20TH, 2015, ZURICH, SWITZERLAND

At a certain point, I'm no longer Markus, and you'll have to start calling me Barbara. With every brush stroke, Markus disappears more and more.

I'm shy, down to earth, stubborn, Gemini and extremely fickle. Without Barbara, I would have never approached my current boyfriend. As a drag queen, I was able to create a second personality. I love beautiful and opulent dresses and started making my own as a young child, first for Barbies and then for people who appreciated my clothes. I sewed a robe for my friend when we were fourteen years old, and after putting it on she said she would ask me to make her bride's dress and really, over ten years later, she sent me a photo of her engagement ring with the message 'Markus, hereby I'm ordering my bride's dress'. It was unbelievable. I sewed her a dress that looked like it could belong to Sissi, the Empress of Austria.

I wanted to study fashion design, but all the state schools told me that my style is too set in stone and there was nothing left to teach me. They suggested I try to make it without enrolling in school like Karl Lagerfeld had done. My parents wanted to send me to the best fashion university, but they couldn't afford to.

These days I work in a hotel and design clothes as a hobby without any pressure, which I'm glad about. If I were forced to make several collections a year, I'd probably be burnt out by now.

My clothes are unique and extravagant and inspired by the '50s and '60s. I look at old photographs and get inspiration from films, 'Sissi' being one of them. I come up with designs in my head in such detail that I'm able to see the pattern before me and then I just pick out the fitting fabric. Or I'm in a store, discover some excellent materials and come up with a design that matches.

I keep my clothes in a big chest, but I also want to present them the way artists show their paintings in galleries. I take my clothes out of the chest and put them on as Barbara. With her, I've created a platform that allows me to show my creativity to the world. Most of all Barbara is there to generate attention and to generate some controversy.

I entertain people and make jokes as a drag queen. Barbara is less shy, and she says things that Markus would never dare utter. Like Barbara, I could theoretically say 'You're an asshole', but in such a sweet way and with a smile on my face that no one would feel insulted. I'm much more approachable when I wear dresses, and it's something unusual and exciting. People engage with me and want to take photos with me. Barbara has many facets that enrich my life.

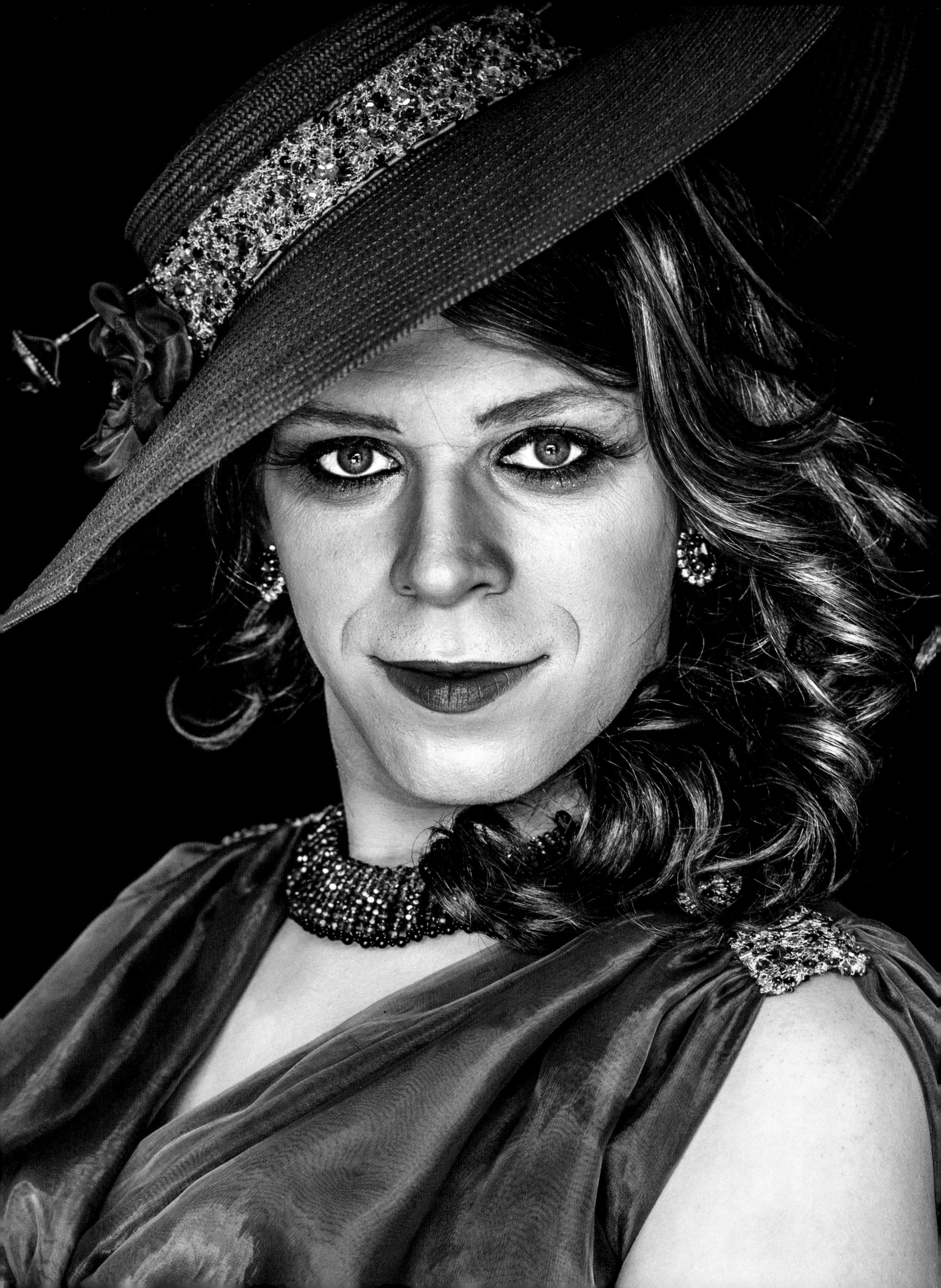

Specific fates are predetermined to form our character and to turn us into the person we are meant to be.

I've been living on the streets of New York for several years. Sometimes it's a severe struggle to survive, especially in the winter when the bitter cold creeps its way through your skin, and your airways begin to tighten up – that's when life can get damn hard, but at some point, you get used to it as much as you possibly can.

There are thousands of homeless in New York, many of whom have already given themselves up. You can either accept or decline your fate, and everyone has a different way of dealing with it. I live my life after the credo 'bend but don't break', and try to make the best out of my situation.

One year ago a stranger gave me the book 'Love Signs' by Linda Goodman, a famous astrologer who wrote this book to show how our hearts are influenced by the constellation system. She studied 78 sun sign combinations and thus decoded the mysteries of love. Her fascination with this topic captivated me.

I learned how astrology interacts with humans, how we are consciously and unconsciously influenced by it, why certain people are good matches and why others should just remain friends. Suddenly a lot of things from my past began to make sense, and my fate gained a meaning.

This book gave me the courage to wake up and engage myself again. I came up with an idea for a dating website based on astrology; every star sign is a sign for love, and every sign has its own way of being perceived. The site is meant to help women and men find one another via the perfect star sign constellation. My idea is still just a draft, but it's given me an aim in life.

Living on the streets has taught me that there is no obstacle I can't overcome, and this I truly believe in. No matter what situation I find myself in, I'll realise my dream, and it's just a matter of time – and time is something no one can take from me, after all.

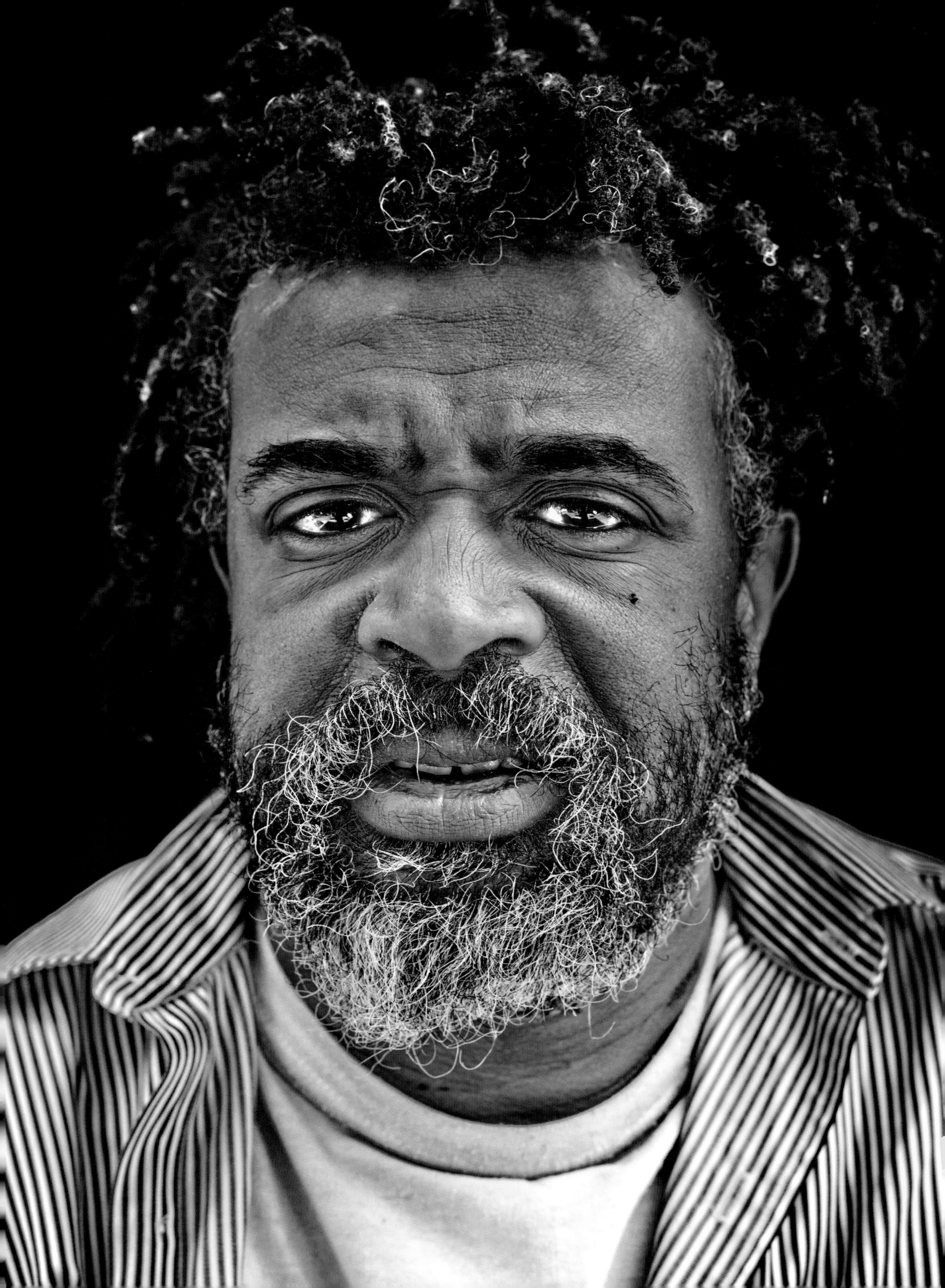

MARK, 27
OCTOBER 26TH, 2015, HOLLYWOOD, LOS ANGELES

When I was four years old, my Dad took me to a marine's airshow. I was fascinated by the fast airplanes and their earsplitting noise, the way the elite soldiers moved, their uniforms, the national anthem and the cheering masses. At this moment I knew that I wanted to become a marine! I could have never imagined that this dream would one day destroy me.

Throughout my whole childhood, I proudly watched the President give speeches about our country's role as the protector, and I watched countless movies about the marines, convinced that we were the 'good guys'.

When I was nineteen years old, I enrolled in the US Marine Corps to receive training so that I could join the best troop in the world – finally, I was one of them. The first four months were incredible and exactly how I envisioned life as a Marine to be. I was part of one entity, and I was healthy and happy. Suddenly we were informed that we had to go to Iraq. It only took a few weeks before I found myself travelling in a convoy on a mission. There was a sudden explosion that catapulted me out of the vehicle. I could only hear an incessant beeping in my ears; I felt stupefied and had no idea what had just happened. I couldn't even comprehend if I was still alive.

Our group was hit twice by an explosive device. I remained unharmed, but I realised that I would not survive the war. An emptiness that worsened with each passing day crept over me, as I fluctuated between patriotism and despair. My dream began to disintegrate as I realised that the war was pointless. The whole thing was a pile of shit and a never-ending downward spiral. The next few years I spent giving orders, while all I wanted was to leave that hell and just survive. It took four years until I was able to leave the Marines.

We had risked our lives for our country, but no one cheered for us when we returned – the state didn't even take care of its veterans. We were let down by our nation. It was impossible to continue civilian life where I left off; I had reoccurring nightmares, suffered from panic attacks, and was profoundly traumatised. It felt as if my thoughts, emotions, simply everything, had collided and exploded like a bomb. Fear followed me everywhere. Many of my colleagues had committed suicide, and I often thought of doing that too.

Sounds and smells triggered my war trauma – just a whiff of petrol or the sound of a slamming door was enough to bring me back to the desert of Iraq. I was trained to pay attention to everything that was able to explode, and I was incapable of letting this controlling mechanism go. Frightful anger joined this compulsive disorder. I persistently screamed at my parents and commanded everyone around me. I didn't notice that I was unbearable for everyone around me, as I thought those around me were just weak. It took time for me to see that the war had changed me.

I fought hard to find a way back to myself and learned how to listen to myself and to take my emotions seriously. I regained my self-belief through mediation, but there are still situations that overwhelm or panic me, yet my inner voice is more positive than ever. I can see the progress within me, and that helps me to know that I have the strength to lift myself out of moments of despair.

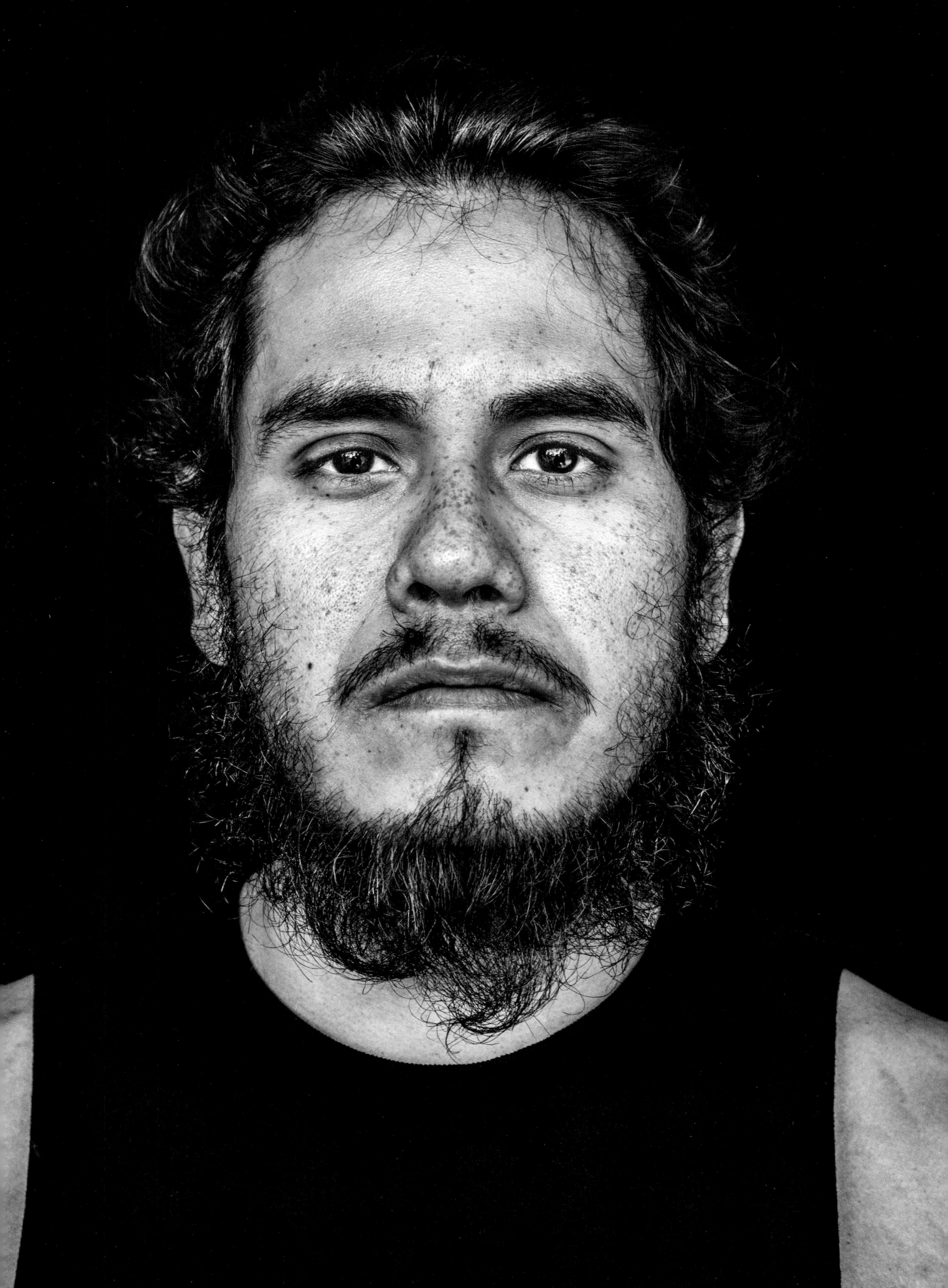

SANDY, 29
JANUARY 28TH, 2018, ZURICH, SWITZERLAND

You don't become a freak, you are born one and either you take your own path, or adapt to society's expectations.

My personality has always been both a blessing and a curse. I think I was born an anarchist. Whatever my parents wanted for me, I wanted the exact opposite and was able to vehemently stand my ground. Even as a young child, I was drawn to people with unique characteristics – burns, scars, pigment disorders. What others considered to be flawed, I liked.

As an only child, I was alone a lot as I didn't really have a connection with other kids. My mother is Swiss, my father is Italian. Italians like to doll up girls in dresses, tights, and patent leather shoes for festivities, and I just hated it! I shaved my hair off when I was five years old, thereby getting rid of the cute blonde girl. From then on people thought I was a sweet boy, but I could live with that.

I learned early on that my decisions aren't always right and especially not always easy but knowing that I could go my own way, no matter how hard this may be, fulfilled me. My strong sense of self-will continued throughout my youth. I got my nose pierced when I was twelve, and a belly button piercing soon followed. At some point, I knew that I wanted to become a piercer. My parents thought that it was just a passing fad, but when the topic of me finding an apprenticeship came up, I refused. My parents said I would have to choose between finding an apprenticeship or moving out, and so I took their empty threat to heart and moved into my boyfriend's place when I was sixteen. I was excited about starting my own life, but I knew the door to my parents would always remain open.

I worked hard during my teenage years, sometimes having three jobs at once while still being broke. I yearned for freedom, but I had a goal in mind and fought hard until I attained it, and that's how I became a piercer with my own studio at the age of nineteen. I fulfilled my own dream.

Body cult is my passion, but people dismiss me on account of how I look. How I feel, think and perceive things makes me believe that I don't belong into this world. I'm sensitive and delicate, and it hurts me to see how bitter, intolerant and narrow-minded our society is.

One day I saw a car crash into the side of a house. An old man having an epileptic seizure was behind the wheel. I was the only one who tried to help him. He clawed onto me desperately until a police officer pulled him from me. He told his colleague to check if the old man still had his wallet on him. Then they sent me away. I wanted to leave behind my business card so that the old man could contact me once he was better. I wanted to know if he was going to be okay, but they threw my card away. Those moments make me think that not belonging is actually the right way to be, as I never want to be as degrading and hurtful as that.

Already kids are indoctrinated to think what is right and wrong, how they should behave and think. Girls are meant to wear pink and boys blue, but why not the other way around? Perhaps the little boy wants to wear a pink dress? If we would allow certain things to be acceptable, then many wouldn't have to wait until they are grown up to realise that they aren't living a free life.

I've heard several kids say to their parents that they want to be like me when they pass me by on the street. The parents' reactions were intense, some even crossed to the other side of the road. But really, what's wrong with looking like me? I'm not a convicted felon, nor am I a junkie. I don't drink alcohol, and I avoid going to parties. I spend most of my time at home or in nature with my husband and my two dogs. I like the quiet and am probably more square than most others.

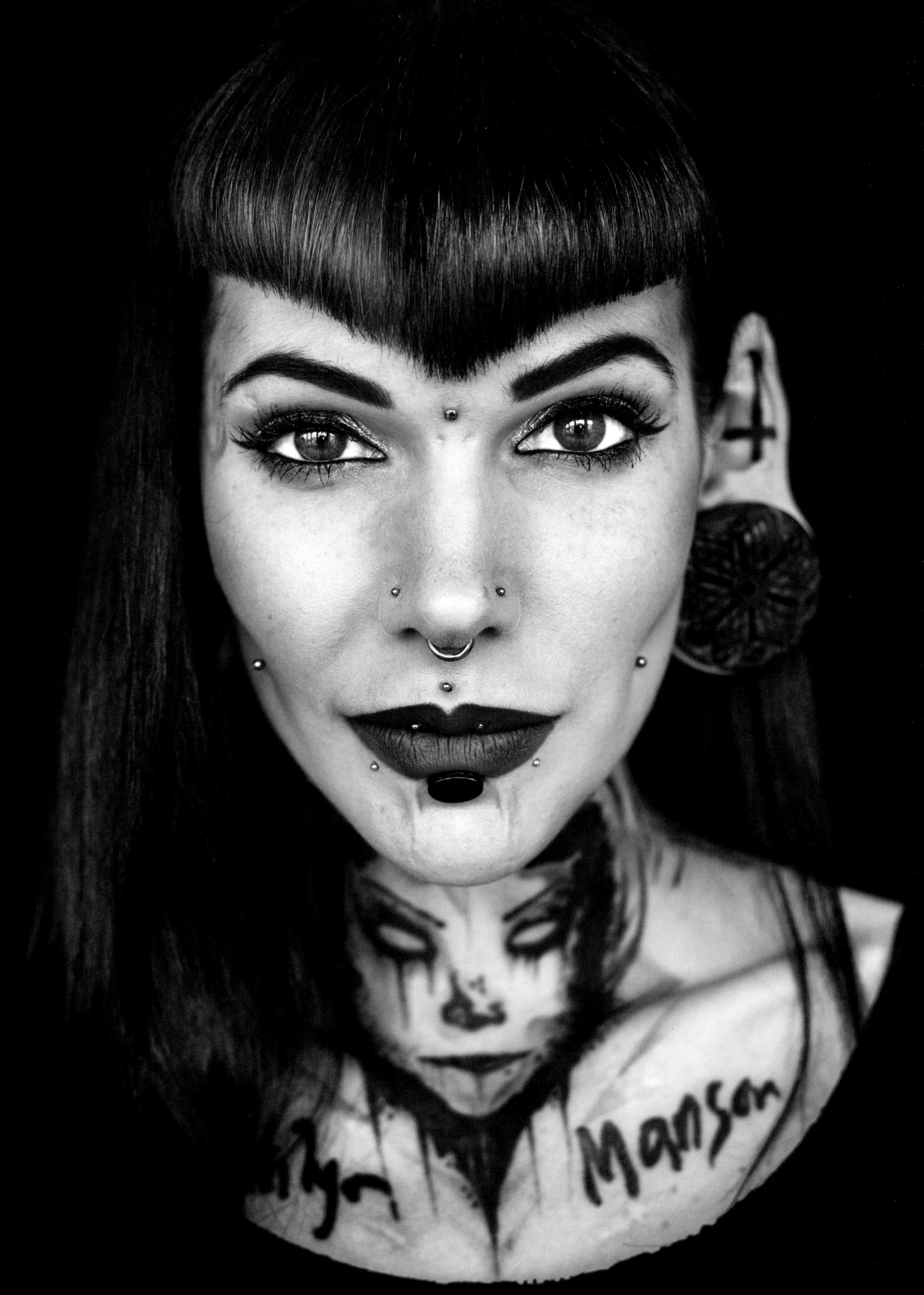

Manson

ALAN, 57
APRIL 19TH, 2014, BROOKLYN, NEW YORK

The headlines exclaimed: 'Gay plague! Gay plague!' An epidemic plagued New York in the 1980s that was quickly blamed on the homosexual community. The trigger for the death this disease was causing was unknown, yet many said that it was 'a well-deserved punishment for faggots'. Us gays were despised, and not just out of hatred but out of fear of the unknown.

Illness had always played a significant role in my life, as I was diagnosed with leukaemia when I was fourteen years old. I was able to battle it successfully and went on to work for a large bank where I made a lot of money and discovered the world. My life was incredible until I lost the love of my life to AIDS when I was 30. This loss changed absolutely everything. I had also lost friends to this deadly disease, and my anger was immense.

AIDS always leads to a terrible and painful death, and it came with extreme stigmatisation: health authorities demanded that no more homosexuals should be let into hospitals or emergency rooms, and in some cases homosexuals were even thrown out of their hospital beds. Funeral homes refused to bury the victims of AIDS, as no one knew how the virus was spreading.

To commemorate the many victims, a procession throughout the city was organised. We walked through the streets of New York holding candles to raise awareness for this deadly virus and its prevention. I began working as an activist and became part of 'ACTUPNY' – Act Up New York. I wanted to support those affected, and I wanted to help bring the hidden to the surface. It gave me hope and strength to be engaged in this group fighting the virus and the discrimination against gays that came with it.

I've been part of this group for 27 years now. We meet with politicians and health officials to demand money for research and free access to medication. I felt a huge glimmer of hope when my friend discovered that he is missing the CCR5 gene, which makes one immune to HIV – a defect applying to about 3% of all humans. He donated his blood to research institutes to help them find a cure, but then he took his own life, and I lost hope again. Two more partners of mine died from AIDS in 1989 and 1992.

No medicine can cure the disease to this day. There's a medicine that stops the virus from breaking out, but they are sold at such a price that most people can't afford to buy it. My biggest wish is to conquer this epidemic during my lifetime. I'll keep fighting for this until it happens, or until I die.

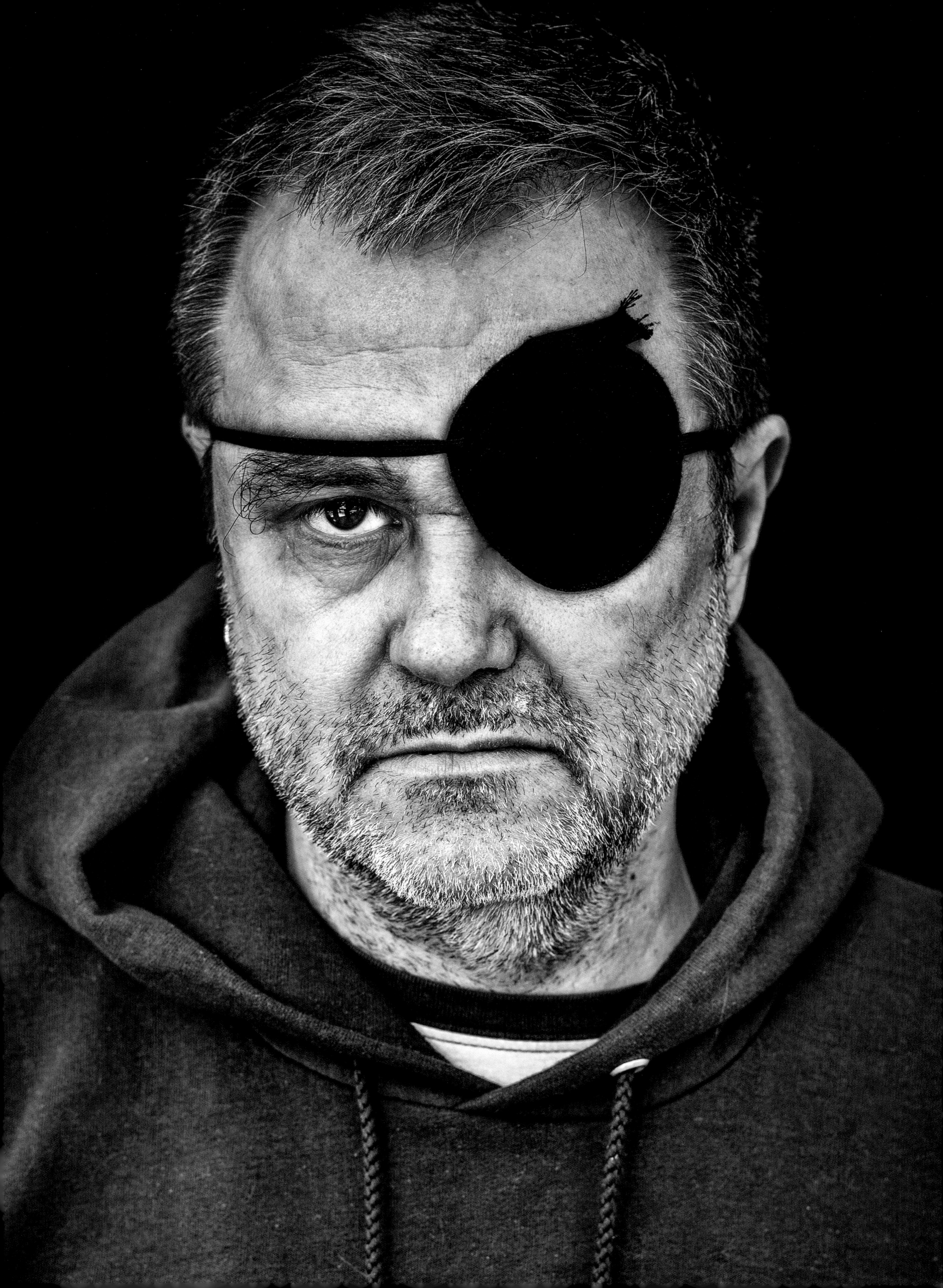

SIMONE, 35
NOVEMBER 1ST, 2016, CLAREMONT, CAPE TOWN

I've already had a few turning points in my life. The first one occurred at the age of eight when my mother died in a car accident, but the most severe turning point was still to come. Three years ago Murray was born, our miracle child as doctors had told me I was infertile due to my cancer treatment. A few months after his birth I became pregnant with Bella – she was unbelievably beautiful and perfect. Our family life was just as we had wanted it to be, until I received a call that abruptly changed everything: I was at work when our nanny called with the news that Bella was lying there motionless. She had choked on her own vomit in her cot. She was only seven months old.

It destroyed my world, and I fell into a deep hole. My husband cried solidly for the first 3 months, but I was in a state of shock. I didn't want to accept that Bella was no longer with us and that I could never hold her in my arms again. I didn't want to give in to her death.

Only Murray gave me a reason to get up and function in the mornings. He had already lost his sister and I didn't want him to be impacted by my grief. Work was a place of comfort for me and I tried, at least for seconds, to have other thoughts. To this day, Murray still asks me about Bella. When he does so, I take him into the garden and tell him that Bella is in heaven now. When he senses that I am sad, he says: 'Mommy, my sister's doing well in heaven'.

Then I became pregnant again and hoped that the birth of our son would bring some peace into our lives, but Thomas was born prematurely and died within several hours of being born. At this moment, I felt as if I had sunk to the bottom of the ocean. I had reached my lowest point and thousands of thoughts were going through my head in an endless loop: Bella, whom I would never see standing at the altar; Thomas, whom I could never congratulate on reaching milestones in his life. My pain was almost unbearable. During these times, I felt the real value of family and friends who were all there to carry us when we were unable to carry ourselves. My husband and I grew even closer to one another. He began to write openly about his feelings on a blog. At first, I was shocked, but then I also experienced how good it felt to write. We were able to express ourselves without speaking and give the people around us a chance to comprehend our pain. Many people thanked us for being so open, including other parents who had lost their children. Until this day the blog helps us to keep the memories of our children alive, and by giving others hope and by assisting them to navigate their grief, the death of our children gains some meaning.

My story still seems surreal to me. Some days I am so weak and just want to crawl into bed and often I think 'What if …?' The question has the power to swallow me up as I take apart every detail and begin to question everything, but then I come back down to earth and accept that I can't change what has happened. If you don't leave the past behind, it can eat you whole.

I was robbed of two children, but I still have my son Murray. To be a witness to his developments is incredible. He is very active and wants to test out all boundaries. In the mornings, I would love to wrap him in bubble wrap out of fear of losing him too, but I have to hold myself back from always wanting to protect him. He should have the chance to explore life, the chance that his brother and sister were robbed of.

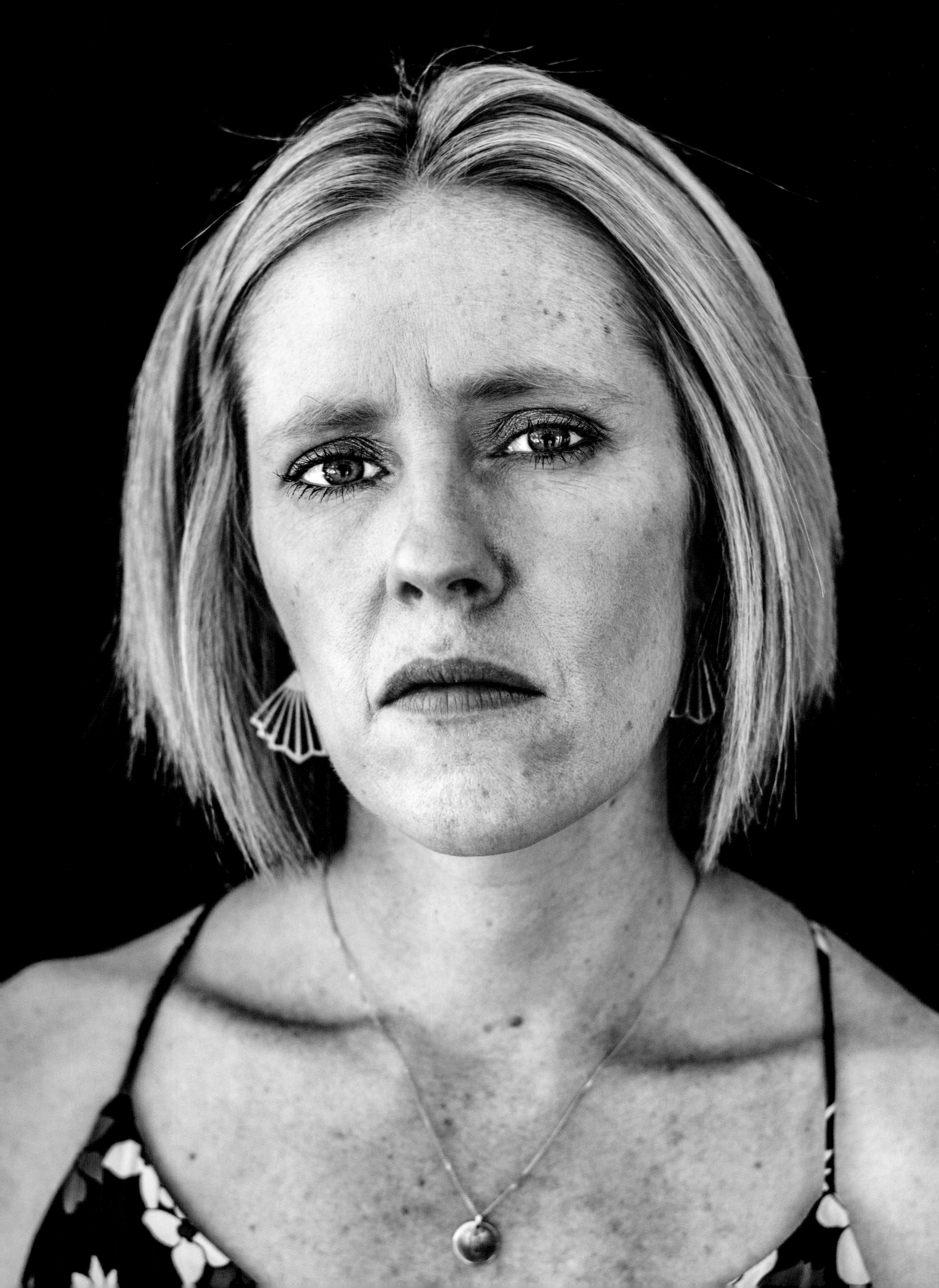

SHEILAGH, 64

DECEMBER 20TH, 2015, BOCAS DEL TORO, PANAMA

My grandmother's home was gorgeous. She would lovingly bake bread in her wooden oven each morning. She worked from dusk 'til dawn and was always content – the complete opposite of my mother, who was mean and moody.

My grandmother was a beautiful woman. She could turn small things big and make five dollars look like a million. When I was sick, she would almost magically bring me back to health, and she often told me stories of her life; like the one where she became pregnant at sixteen and travelled half the world by boat just to declare my grandfather, who knew nothing about her pregnancy, her love. Thanks to her, the word 'family' had a meaning. She had eleven children and eighty grandchildren. She was the clan leader.

Every January she would begin to knit Christmas presents so that she would be finished in time to give everyone their gifts. She gave each of her grandchildren the possibility to live with her for two years when they had new babies, so that she could help take care of the offspring. She was enchanting. My grandmother was my big role model. I wanted to be able to cook and bake as well as her, I wanted to work as hard as she did, and I wanted to live just as beautifully.

I was seventeen when I got married and twenty when I became pregnant. My husband at the time became an alcoholic, and upon my grandmother's advice, I left him before the birth of my second child. She wanted to be by my side but, shortly after, she passed away. My world came tumbling down – she was the person I always looked up to, and whose advice I so desperately needed.

My grandmother was the one person in my life who continually managed to encourage me, and now she was gone forever, but what she taught me I will always carry with me. I'm yet to see if a storm or a rainbow is approaching my life. She taught me always to look ahead even when finding myself in the eye of the storm. She taught me to be good-natured and to take care of others, and that that's how luck will also find its way back to me.

I strive for contentment and have a lot of dreams, and I try to infect others with my lust for life; regarding love, I've been happily married for 35 years now. My grandmother once said: 'Never go to sleep when you are angry. Always talk about everything because even if you can't resolve the conflict, you will still feel better after talking'. My grandfather wasn't always the best husband, but he was her best friend. It's easy to find new love, but only a true friendship remains forever.

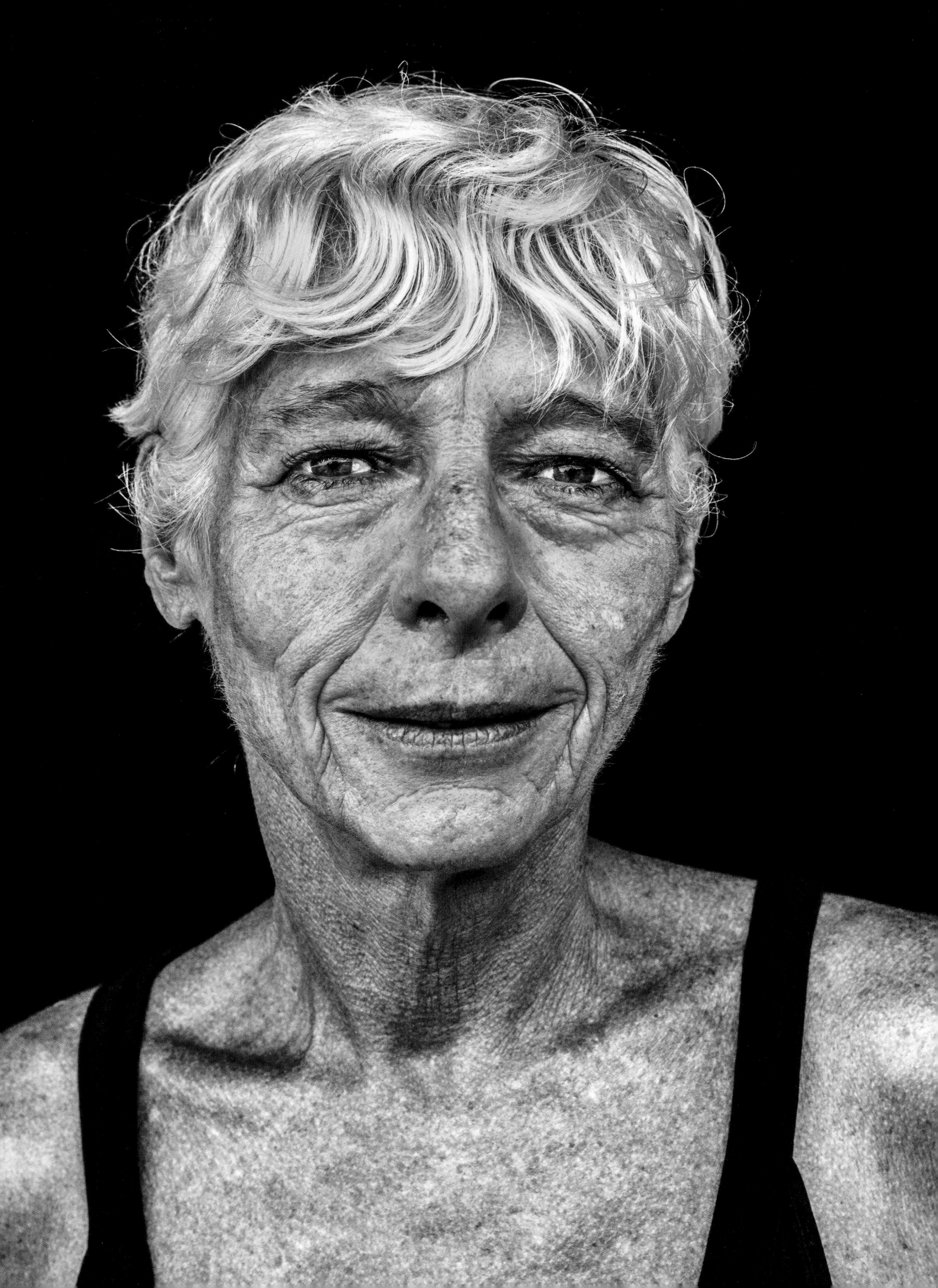

GERMAN, 31
NOVEMBER 14TH, 2015, POTOSÍ, BOLIVIA

The darkness down there is oppressing, the air is full of fine toxic dust. The deeper you climb into the mine, the more difficult it gets to breathe. The paths are narrow and often very steep, and the heat is unbearable. The tunnels are an inhumane, unpredictable and dangerous place to work.

In Potosí there are about 10'000 miners, and a bunch of them are kids. If you live here, you don't really have an alternative. Pretty much the entire population is dependent on the mountain Cerro Rico where we extract tin, copper, zinc, and lead. There used to be silver, and it won't be long until everything else will be pillaged as well.

A lot of people lose their lives in the mines from lung diseases or accidents. If you work here, you're aware that every day could be your last. My brother died in the pits a year ago. We always walked to the mountain together, put on our work gear and our protective helmet, a headlight and a cloth to protect our airways. We chewed on coca leaves to suppress our hunger and thirst and to be able to work for many hours. It was an exhausting day like always. I ended my shift before my brother did, as he wanted to keep working on the last bit of the tunnel.

I was already in bed when the phone rang: 'Your brother is in the hospital with heavy injuries'. I ran there as fast as I could, but I arrived too late. He had fallen into a ten metres deep hole; the 40 kilogram heavy machinery he was using fell with him and crushed his sternum. He was only 26 years old. I needed a few days before I could go back to work. My thoughts were unbearable, and I was afraid to go to the site of my brother's death, but I wanted to end the job he had started. Back at work, I heard screams while we were mining, thinking they belonged to a group working further down than us, so I went down to check if someone had been injured, but there was no-one there – just a deathly silence. When I came back up the cries erupted again, but there was no one else there. It was terrifying. The next day, at the same spot, I saw the flickering of a headlight before everything turned dark again. I searched for the light source but couldn't find anything. Suddenly the tunnel caved in, and I was buried beneath rocks for several hours, gasping for air, before another miner rescued me.

Looking back, I'm convinced that my brother returned to his place of death, that it was him screaming, that he wanted to bring me to him. I never heard his screams again.

We make crosses with our hands every day before we go into the mines so that God lets us out alive. Every Friday we give coca leaves and cigarettes to the devil as an offering so that he is occupied and leaves us untarnished. I work hard in the mines so that my kids can have a better future. I want them to study and do something valuable with their lives. It's their only chance to not end up in the mines.

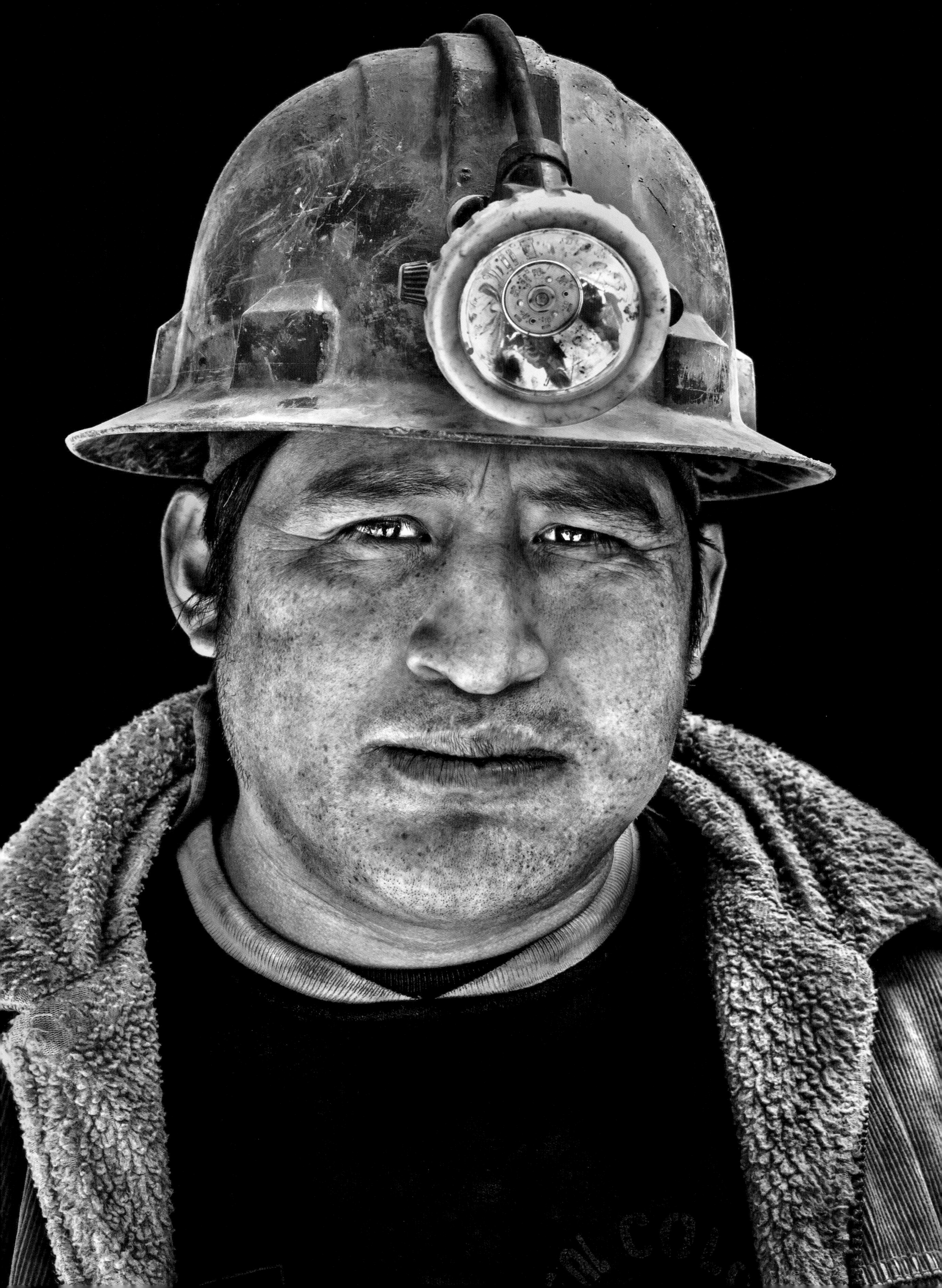

Putting on a diving mask, plunging into the water, becoming a part of another world and discovering its mysteries, fascinates me immensely. I love adventure, and my biggest one was with a great white shark.

In the late fifties, six people were killed in four months by sharks in South Africa, and panic ensued. Sharks became known for being unpredictable and dangerous man-eaters. To be eaten alive is a horror scenario and one of man's greatest fears. I never really had this fear, and yet felt immense respect towards these creatures. Ever since I was a child, I felt a deep connection to the ocean. I was fascinated by the marine environment, by its inhabitants, and by their behaviour. I spent most of my summer holidays in a bay close to Cape Town where, together with my two older brothers, we learned to spearfish and free dive. We explored underwater worlds and learned to understand and appreciate them. Our spearfishing often attracted sharks, so we would leave the water as soon as we could see them. As time passed, I began to get used to them, and I developed an inner trust and acceptance towards them.

When I was thirteen years old, I helped my brothers design and construct an underwater camera with a rubber exterior, and we experimented with it until we managed to get it to work ten metres below the surface. I discovered my big passion with the first underwater shots I took. In my high school years, I was head of the school photographic society. Later at the age of 20 years old, I was one of the first apprentices of South African television, training as a cameraman.

In 1984 I was commissioned to document the behavior of seals with an underwater 16 mm film camera. During the shoot, three great white sharks swam past me hunting the seals. I was one of the first cameramen to document the great white shark on film in South Africa. Thereafter, I was commissioned for further underwater shoots by television programs, commercials, and documentaries.

In 1992 I filmed, with the late Ron Taylor and his wife, the first international documentary about the great white shark in South Africa for Discovery Channel, and one year later we shot the sequel. On one of the days shooting, I experienced the most magical moment of my life; I was under the water and outside of our cage. The water visibility was about three metres, but through my lens, I was able to detect an image that was coming towards me. The image grew bigger and bigger, and I could hear screams from the boat above me. It was an unusually large great white shark, but I remained calm and tried to read his body language. He was gliding through the water serenely with ease and right towards me. I had never seen anything so gigantic underwater. He filled the viewfinder as he brushed against my camera and swam so closely past my body that I was able to feel him as if it was the most normal thing in the world. This moment maybe lasted for ten seconds – ten seconds I would like to relive forever. My fascination was too overpowering to feel any fear. I was overwhelmed. Back on the boat, my colleagues told me that the shark was larger than our six-metre-long boat. My adrenaline rush increased even more.

A few hours later, when the visibility improved under water, I went back in and secretly hoped to see the giant predator again, but he didn't return. This experience was magical, unrivalled and remains a one-off. An encounter with a great white shark of around seven metres is highly unlikely, and I was allowed to experience it without consequences – that's a real privilege.

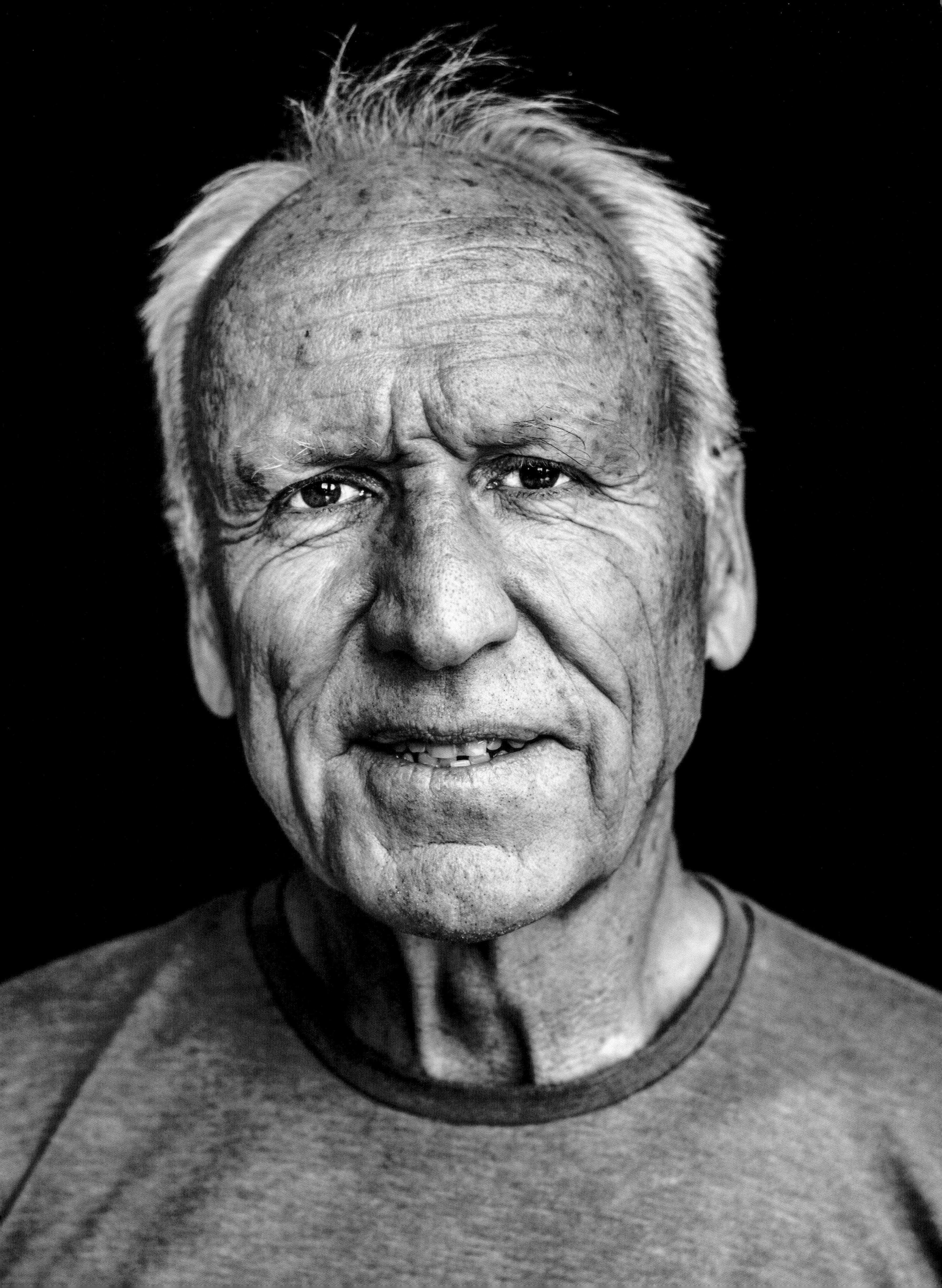

KATE, 26
JUNE 10TH, 2017, MANHATTAN, NEW YORK

Up until five years ago, I lived in an Amish community. My family lived a very simple life, refusing most technological progress. We had no television, radio, smartphones, computer or car. We didn't even have electricity, so I would read books by lit gas lamps at night.

I grew up in Myerstown, Pennsylvania, as the middle child of seven. Typically we would wake up at 6 am. I went to school until I was fifteen. Before going to class, I fed the calves and helped with other chores on the farm. After school, I helped with the crops or in the household. I went to bed around 9 pm every night, completely exhausted. We worked Monday through Saturday. On Sundays it was strictly forbidden to work – you weren't even allowed to make jello. During my free time on the weekends, I spent my time sketching, painting and reading. I was a creative individual living in a very structured environment, making anything artistic.

There are rules and procedures for everything, and the only connection to the outside world we had were newspapers. Fashion has no place in the life of an Amish – Makeup and jewellery are forbidden, men wear traditionally tailored black suits and hats, while women wear bonnets and simple dresses. The dress code was kept simple, with the intention to keep people's attention on more important things such as family, faith and work. While this lifestyle worked for most of the community, my creative spirit rebelled against the idea of conformity. I believed that the focus should not be on the little details of a dress code, but rather on the intentions and personality of the individual person.

After planning to leave for years, I gathered up my courage and moved to Florida for the winter, then to New York after being signed with a major model management.

Many photo shoots for fashion magazines and television appearances have followed since. I modelled at the New York Fashion Week, where the designers inspired me to create my own line while studying design at the Fashion Institute of Technology.

New York is loud and overwhelming, and it wasn't easy to adapt to this new lifestyle. I had to learn many things like being in relationships, what other people expect from you or how to communicate. I'm happy to be here and proud that I made my own decision. I gradually fell in love with the energy of the diverse population. Being surrounded by people from all around the world made me feel like if you have the drive, you can become whoever you want to become. It didn't matter where you were from. As someone from a religious community that is often misunderstood by people from other cultures, this realisation was exhilarating for me.

I visit my family twice a year. I tell them about New York but not about my job – my fashion shoots would not fit into their beliefs. They encourage me to come back, but that's not an option for me. Parents often have a particular notion as to what their children should do one day, which school is the right one, which hobbies fit the best, but every person should discover these things on their own. Perhaps the children's view on life is utterly contrary to that of their parents, but that's what we humans are like – we are individuals and change every day. I'm leading a completely different life now with new views and many goals, but nothing can take away that what already was, instead new things are always being added.

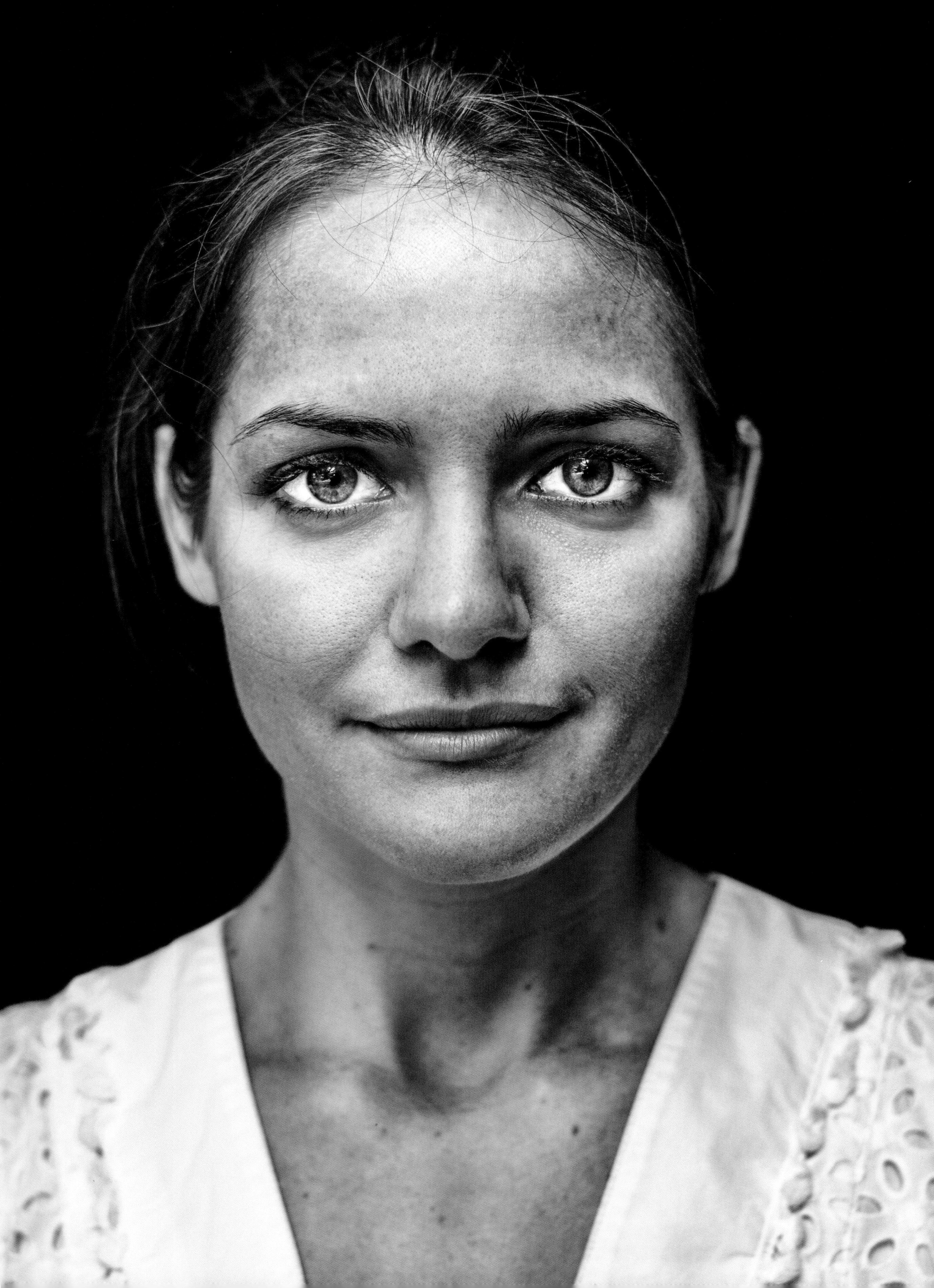

Forgiving and moving on. When someone hurts you, you try with all your strength to forgive the person who caused you pain so that you can let go, but sometimes forgiving can seem like an impossible task.

I was born in Philadelphia as a fragile boy with a lot of dreams. These dreams were taken from me at the age of seven when a neighbour raped me. I was eleven when I first tried cannabis and alcohol. That was the beginning of a turbulent adolescence filled with thefts and hard drugs, and that was only the beginning.

In 1981, in Delaware close to the border of Pennsylvania, a young woman was kidnapped, raped and stabbed to death. Four days later, in Chester, Pennsylvania, I was held up by the cops in a stop and search while driving a stolen car. The disputes between the police and I quickly escalated and led to an arrest. It was in jail that I read about the murder in Delaware and with the hope of mitigating my punishment I made a false testimony claiming I knew who the murderer was but the cops saw through me, and my situation worsened dramatically. Suddenly I was the prime suspect, and as this was before DNA analysis existed, I couldn't prove my innocence; my nightmare began.

In 1982 I was sentenced to death for the alleged abduction, rape, and murder. The jury called me 'white scum' and spat in my mother's face during the trial. My father lost his job. I couldn't afford to go to court again, and so I was 21 years old when I innocently received a life sentence. The prison in Pennsylvania which I got sent to was one of the toughest in America, known for torturing its prisoners.

I spent the first two years in complete silence. I was no-one, and society saw me as a monster. What happened in jail was inhumane: I was threatened, abused and almost beaten to death by the guards. My wounds from these beatings became massively infected, and I suffered unbearable pain. To somehow cope with this torment I began to tell myself stories, and I started to read up to eighteen hours a day. Reading changed my perspective, and I suddenly had a goal: I wanted to quote something beautiful on the day of my execution to prove that I wasn't a monster.

One day Jacky, a woman who wanted to know what it is like to live in one of America's most terrible prisons, visited me. I made clear to her that it isn't important where you are but who you are. She began seeing me regularly, and I fell in love. In 1988 I came to know that the first DNA tests had been carried out. That gave me hope. I was one of the first prisoners on death row to request a DNA analysis. It took five years for the test to complete and the results were sobering: not conclusive. In the nineties another shimmer of hope came my way: more DNA tests of pieces of evidence were carried out but to no avail.

Jacky stayed by my side for nine years. She dared to love me, and I will never forget this present but what could we do? We shared this incredible love, but she lived in an empty house full of legal papers. Eventually, I sent her away. I let her go, and it broke my heart.

In 2003 the DNA tests finally proved my innocence as the remains of sperm underneath the victim's fingernails did not match up. The guards put me into isolation as their fear of me taking revenge as soon as I was free was too big, and so I remained imprisoned for another eight months.

I was released from prison on the 15ᵗʰ of January 2004. I had been on death row for 22 years and I was no longer the same. It took a lot of effort to get used to being free. I didn't know who I was beyond the prison walls and I reacted allergically to the fresh air. After all those years spent alone, the world was too loud for me. I can't make up for the lost time, so I just have to let those years be what they are.

My story is terrible and hurts but I did the only thing that would make my mother proud, and I gave meaning to all her prayers. Today I take care of other people instead of complaining that I had no one. People ask me why I am not filled with bitterness and the answer to everything is love, especially the love towards myself. Even though others treated me as a monster, I know that I am good the way I am and I tell myself this every day. If I hold on to this opinion, no one can give me the feeling of being a monster.

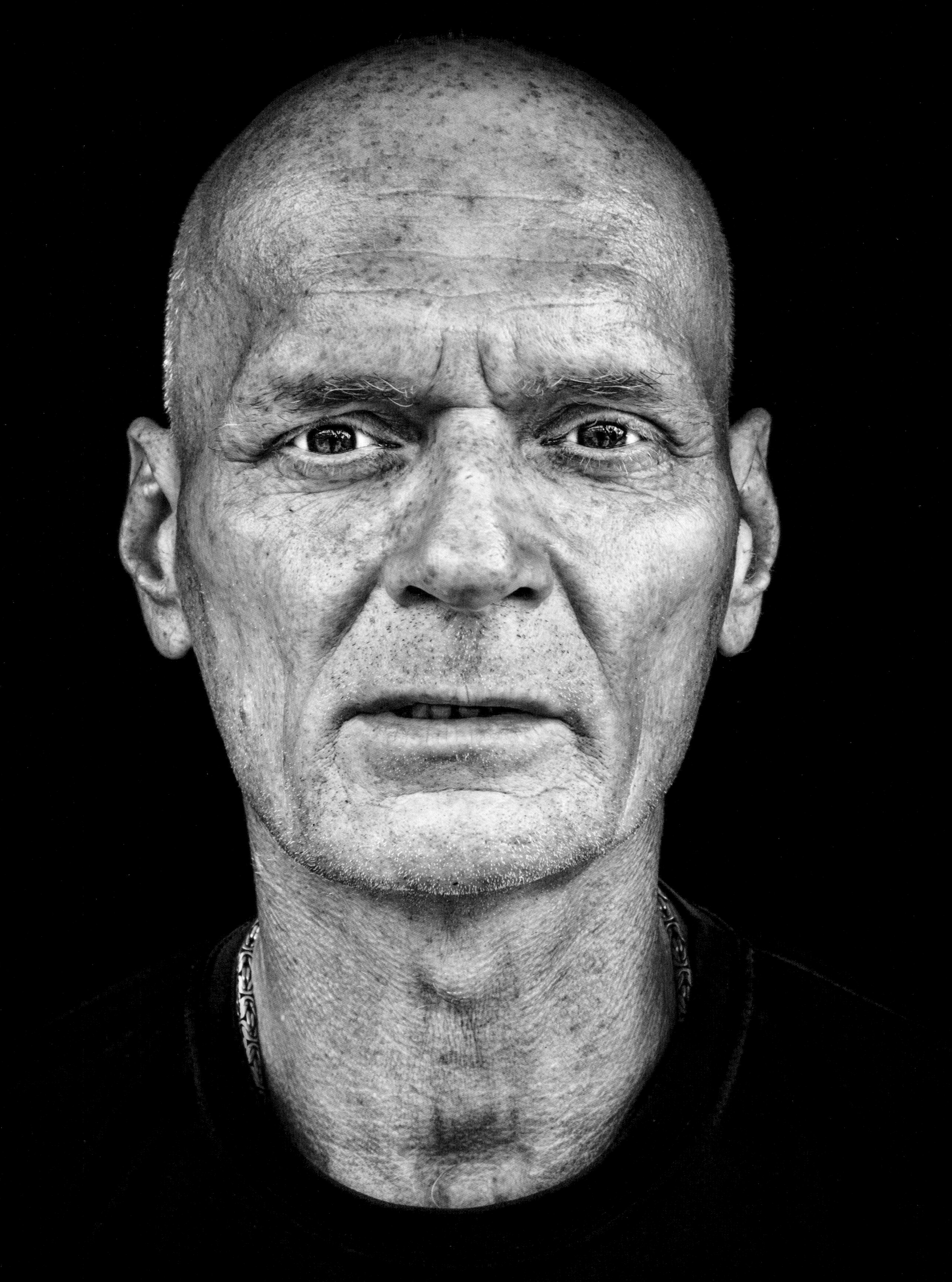

CHRISTINA, 52
NOVEMBER 5TH, 2015, WILLOQ, PERU

____

My biggest wish was to learn how to read and write. I really wanted to be able to go to school, but I had to accept that this wasn't my fate.

My mother died shortly after I was born. A few years later my brother left and never came back, so it was just my father and me, and I had to help him on the fields, take care of the animals, cook and sew clothes from early in the morning until late at night. I had to watch other kids make their way to school, and I stayed behind.

When I was ten years old my father died very unexpectedly, and a woman from the neighbourhood adopted me and promised to take care of me, but she would scream at me, insult me and used me as her slave. I had to sew clothes and make jewellery for the market; I worked until late at night and fell into bed every night completely exhausted. My wish to go to school remained unfulfilled.

I lived with this woman until I got married. Leaving the village I was from was never an option, as I didn't have the necessary money. I gave birth to two girls and a boy, and I gave everything so that at least they could go to school and have a better life than me, but my hands were tied and my husband, aggressive and emotionless as he was, made sure our kids couldn't go to school either. He let me and the kids do all the work, and there were times when we were starving and didn't know how we would survive the next day. He didn't care. Now he's sick and paralysed.

I often ask myself why I was given this fate? What's the meaning behind it? Maybe there is no meaning, and perhaps this is just how it had to be – there's no changing it anyway. I'm exhausted and have nothing left to give. If I could I would just give up and disappear into nothingness but my husband is sick, and I have to take care of my family. Soon he'll pass away.

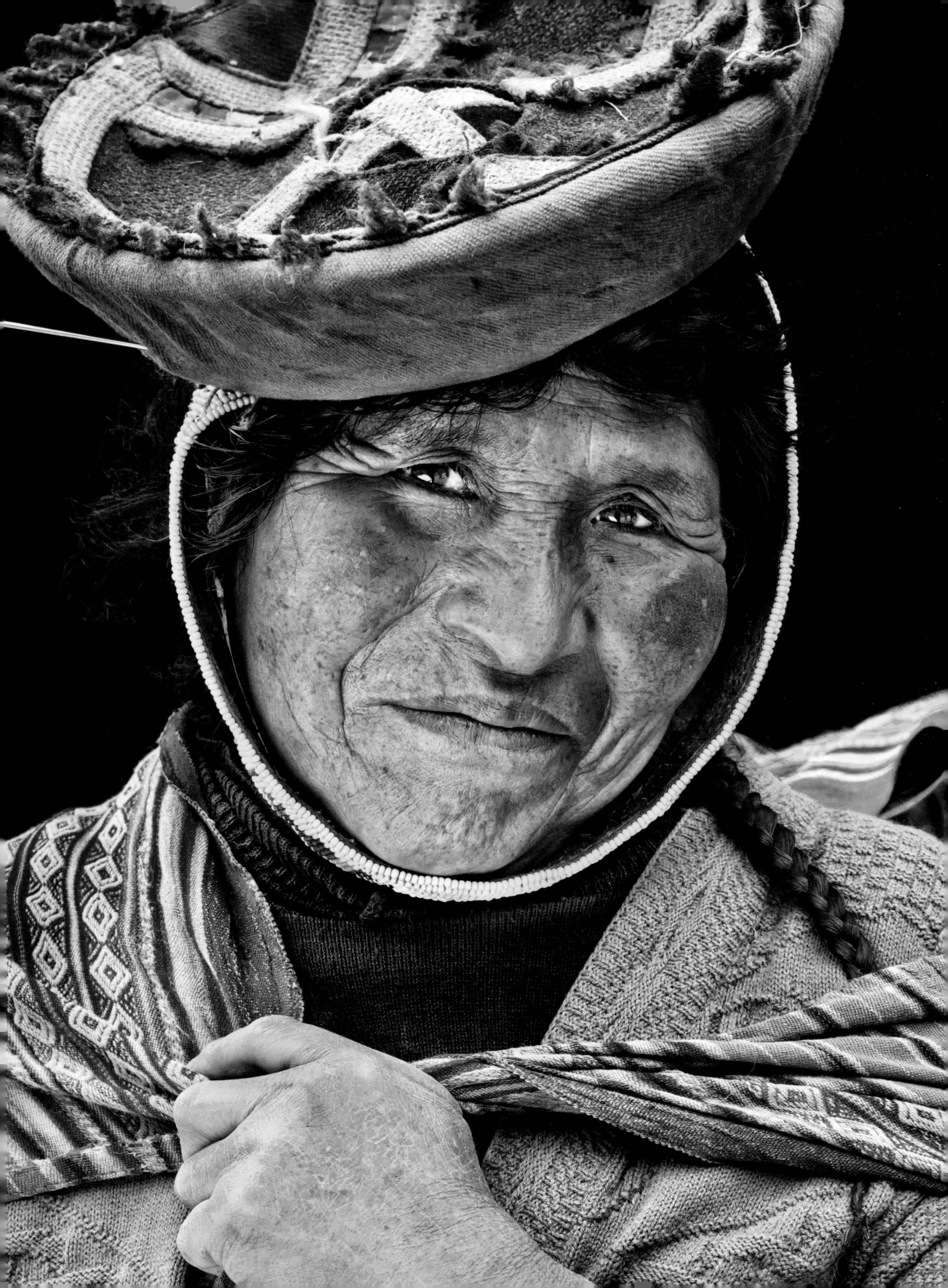

A lot of people are taken aback when they see me, some can't even look me in the eye. They find my looks abnormal, but what's normal anyway?

I love the endless possibilities of embellishing a human body. I learned how to make piercings early on, worked hard to improve my skill and got a job at a renowned piercing studio. Over the years I made a name for myself and earned good money. I was able to turn my passion into a job, highly motivated. I worked 16 hours and made up to 30 piercings a day. I fought to live my dream; perhaps I was too strict with myself, who knows. In any case, everything became too much for me. My body rebelled and hindered me from doing any more work. From one day to the next my life just came to a standstill – I had a burnout. I desperately wanted this high again, to feel the boundless energy my work gave me, and I was afraid of losing my reputation, scared that people would forget me. I discovered that cocaine, LSD and magic mushrooms helped me with these fears, and they were a reliable source of strength and inspiration. They made my life worth living again, but they also changed my personality, and I stopped caring about things, got into trouble and lost my job.

I got another job offer in Oregon, which I took hoping that new surroundings, a new apartment, and a new perspective would help me, but what I didn't know is that Oregon has some of the strictest laws concerning work licenses. A few months after I started working there, my temporary permit expired, and I was missing just one little paper that would allow me to work, and so, again, I lost my dream job. My hope and vision were shattered in an instant, and I was so angry at the system that I just gave up and hitchhiked to Salt Lake City. I lived on the streets there for several months using crack and heroin to numb myself. I was at rock bottom.

Then I met a guy who offered to drive me back to Los Angeles, and for the first time in months I felt a glimmer of hope and so I accepted his offer. I wanted to get away from drugs once and for all and was already imagining my new life. After being on the road for hours, I got out of the car at a gas station to get a drink for us, but when I got out of the shop, the car was gone. I waited there the whole day hoping he would return but he never did. My only belongings had been in that car: my clothes, papers, and phone. I didn't even know where I was exactly. How can someone do such a thing?

With the last of my change, I was able to make it to Los Angeles a few days later where I ended up in Skid Row, an area where thousands of homeless people, drug addicts, and veterans live. This place is terrible, almost unbearable. Every day I make plans that'll get me out of this hell hole. I would love to work in a piercing studio again, but I don't even have a passport. I don't want to give myself up – I'm god damn good at what I do, after all.

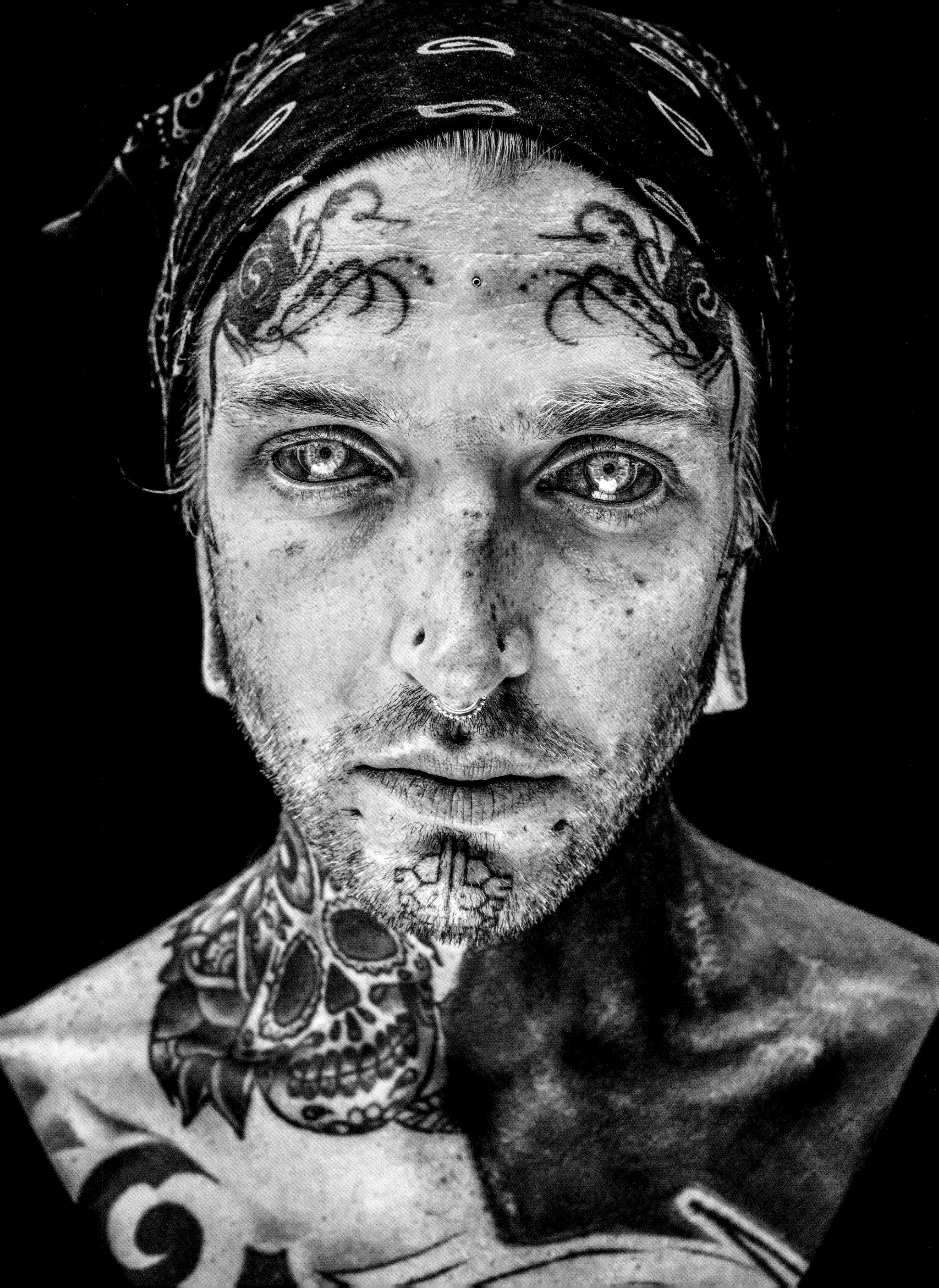

DANI, 43
MAY 25TH, 2017, MALANS, SWITZERLAND

I lived in a different reality as a child, a reality full of ghosts and magical creatures. My world was fantastical and versatile, but it's hard to live in such a world.

I grew up in a small village in Grisons, a place where people talk behind each other's backs and prejudices rule. My parents are lovely but they always cared too much about what everyone else was thinking, and I could never relate to that. I wanted to be myself and live my own life. I longed to break free but didn't know how. I was always on the lookout for something, without knowing what I was searching for. I wanted to push boundaries, experiment and be free. Once I died my hair, then I shaved it all off; I drank and smoked weed. When I was 21, I discovered speed, ecstasy, cocaine, and LSD. I lived in a parallel world without sleep from Thursday to Sunday. When the high I felt from the drugs decreased, I just doubled the dose. I was on a rollercoaster that was taking me up high and dropping me down low. I reached my limit at 23 and found my way out of the hell I had created for myself.

I used to be an atheist. I didn't believe in transcendental powers or life after death. I didn't believe in anything yet suddenly I was once again able to see things other people were not able to see. The sensibility I had had as a child to perceive other realities had returned: while looking at an apartment, I saw a man hanging in one of the rooms. Later on, I discovered that the previous tenant had hung himself in the apartment. Shit! I didn't want this ability and tried to suppress it, but it wouldn't go away. I saw dead people, was able to feel spirits and could sense when something was off. Whatever I was able to perceive, was in accordance with what had actually happened and this was proven again and again. I was angry and scared to be alone.

I sought out a shaman for help and travelled a lot. I discovered cultures unknown to me and studied different religions and began to question life. On a journey to find myself, I went to many different regions in Asia to meditate and ended up in Goa with a blind Himalayan yogi. It might sound odd, but he was able to see a lot more than most people with perfect eyesight. I met a lot of people able to see 'more', and they all told me that I had a great gift with a lot of potential. I discovered this with time, and today I know what they mean. I was at rock bottom and danced with my demons, but I returned to the light and learned that there's more light than darkness in the world. I believe that everyone is the creator of their own life and its content. Whatever you focus your thoughts on, is where the energy will flow to. In the past, numb and high on drugs, I gave more power to dark energies, but today I choose love – unconditional love.

I'm a family man now, and love to be in nature with my son. Fairies and spirits exist for us there. Once, he told me that he was scared of a dog only he could see. I went with him to say to the dog that he should leave him alone and it worked. My son sees fantastical beings like all children, and that's incredible.

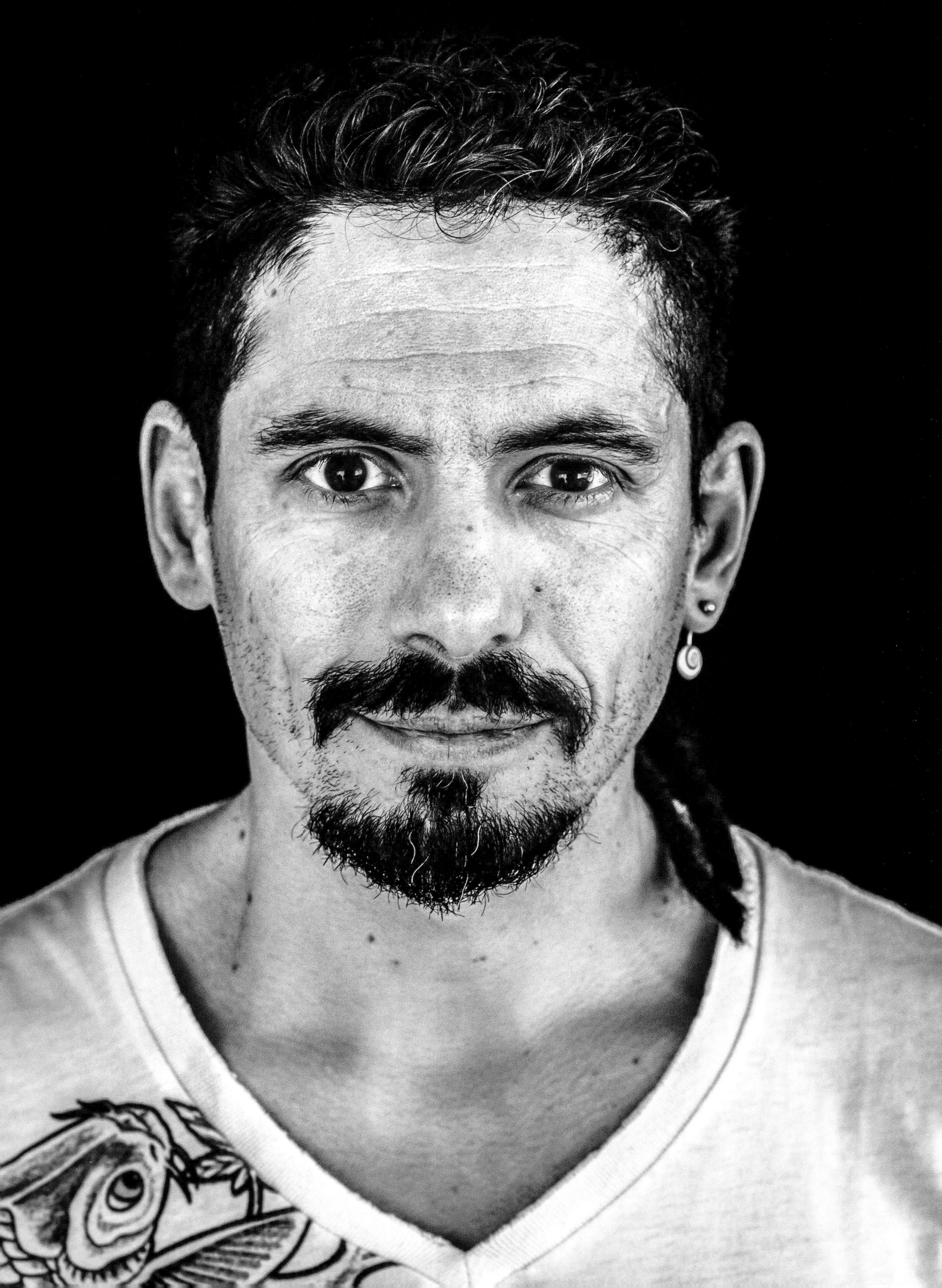

I was a priest on Praslin, an island belonging to Seychelles. It was 1975, and I had just gotten married. A few weeks later, on the 12ᵗʰ of August, I had to go to Mahé for a church meeting. I took a sailboat, which took around four hours back then.

It was early in the morning, and a massive storm was making the ocean especially rough. We were 22 souls on board of 'Ero' and it didn't take long for me to become seasick, so I went beneath the deck to relax. We were about half way when I heard water rushing into the boat. The extreme intensity of the waves had ripped away a copper plate on the bow of the boat, allowing more and more water to slowly enter the vessel resulting in the motor eventually turned off.

'The boat will sink!', Luc, our captain, yelled. He handed out swimming vests and began to make rafts out of empty canisters. We had about one hour until the boat capsized. I was scared, but I tried to calm myself and began to pray.

Before we had to jump from the boat, a five-year-old boy was taken by a wave and sucked into a hatch, but we were able to pull him out by his hair at the very last second before jumping into the water. Everyone tied themselves to the raft with a rope, but a strong wave undid my line and I started drifting away. Frantically, I tried to swim back to the others but the current was too strong, and I was too weak. Luc swam in my direction and risked his life to get me back. The view was blurry, the ocean was relentless, and after hours of being in the cold water I was fully depleted and had lost almost all of my hope. I prayed to God and asked him for help.

The little boy, the one whose life we saved, said to me: 'Father, back on the shore can you give me some money so I can buy ice cream?' Even though we didn't even know if we would make it out of the ocean alive, it really cheered us up. And then something strange happened: I saw a yellow, flickering light on the water. It was gentle, yet it had an intense and commanding presence. I felt that it was a sign from God, letting us know he was by our side. At that moment I knew that we would be saved. I was totally overwhelmed and began to cry.

We drifted on the open ocean for six hours before a small airplane saw us and sent for rescue boats. We were saved just before the sun went down. In the following night my entire bed kept swaying back and forth, and gradually I began to realise what had happened – and what terrible things could have happened, but everyone on board had survived. The sinking of 'Ero' happened over 40 years ago but I still, each year on the 12ᵗʰ of August, thank God for protecting us.

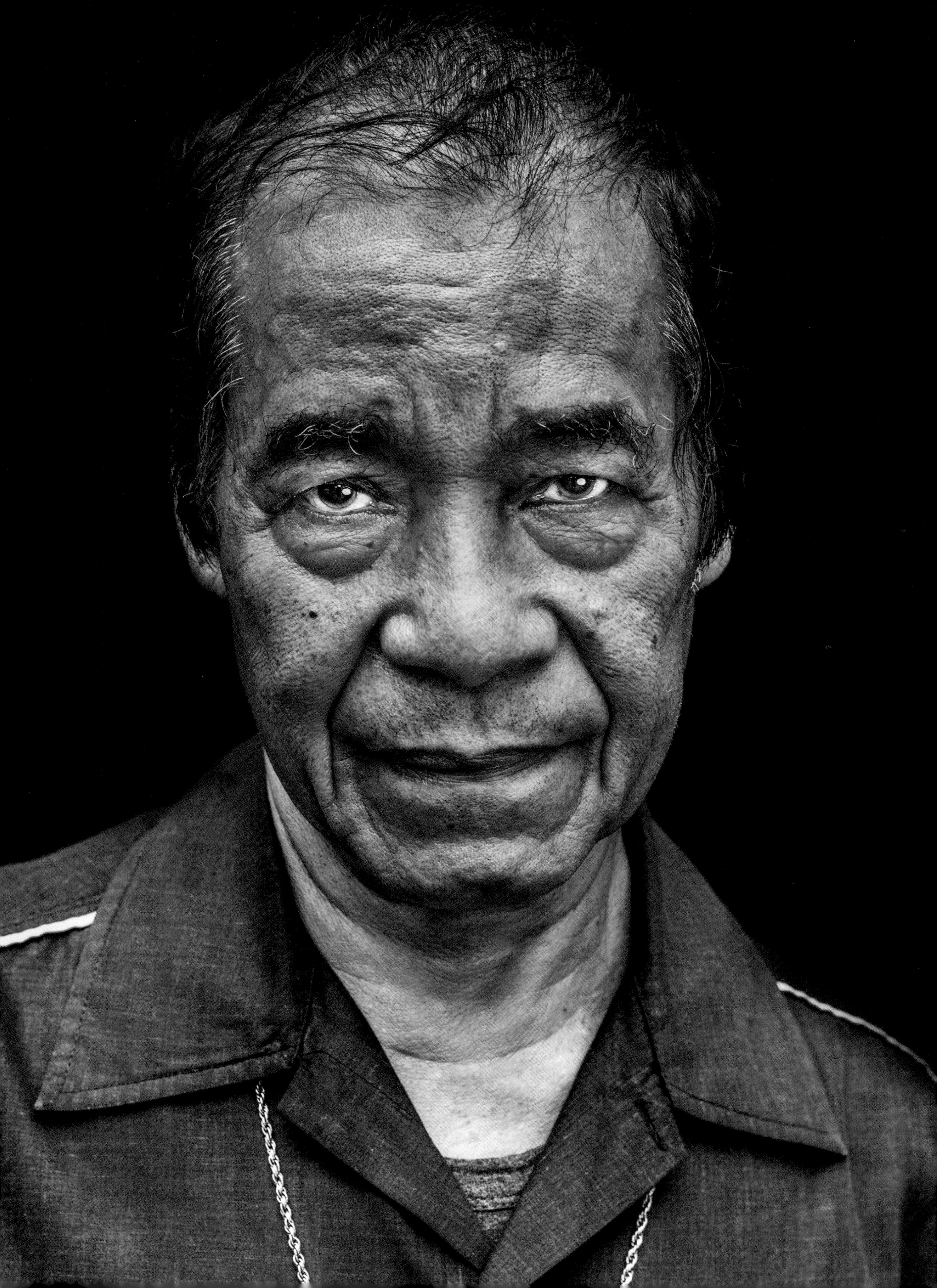

MARTIN, 62
SEPTEMBER 13TH, 2017, STEIN AM RHEIN, SWITZERLAND

I was happily married, had two healthy children, was a home-owner, had an exciting job in television and at some point, I even had my show called 'Time Out'.

This show was essentially my third child; for one whole year, two of my colleagues and I suggested topics to the director of the channel on a weekly basis, so he could see what our show would look like if it existed.

In 1990 we were finally allowed to produce it, and it was the best and most exciting time of my life. We had a million viewers during the show's peak. After eleven years the show was discontinued, as the head of the channel wanted our slot back. Our opinions weren't taken into consideration at all. People who didn't even view the show decided that it would discontinue. The decision was made on a political level.

I lost a part of my identity when the show ended. All of a sudden, I no longer had a precise function. I missed working with a team and having daily discussions. I needed discourse with other people, as that's the only way I can come up with good ideas.

My marriage ended in the same year the show did. I didn't want to give up, but I was putting up a fight on my own, and so we finally divorced. I got custody of our children, and so I had to take everything on on my own; job during the day, single father at night. That darned 2001! Everything I touched that year went to pieces. I once even managed to break my right wrist and sprain my left wrist within ten minutes. That's pretty representative of how I am: when something goes well, everything goes well. When something goes wrong, everything goes wrong. In soccer they say when you're doing good you can just kick the ball and it'll fly into the goal, and when you're doing badly you just hit the post.

The loss of my marriage, family life, my show and lastly my apartment was so painful that I didn't know what to do anymore. I sought out help in the form of therapy and learned how to reflect my actions and how to be honest with myself. I began to understand that I had difficulties letting go. It was unbelievably hard for me to accept when something had come to an end. I learned to not hold on to things that are out of one's control. If you resist you just waste your energy in a hopeless battle – after all, one's whole life is a process of letting go. Nothing in life is forever. Only by letting go you can be free again.

When I look back on my life, I have to say that these losses were significant experiences for me and my personal development. I only realised through these events how much luck I had had in my life. My life used to be too easy; everything worked without having to think about it. Then those losses taught me not take happiness for granted. You can never assume that the good will always stay in your life.

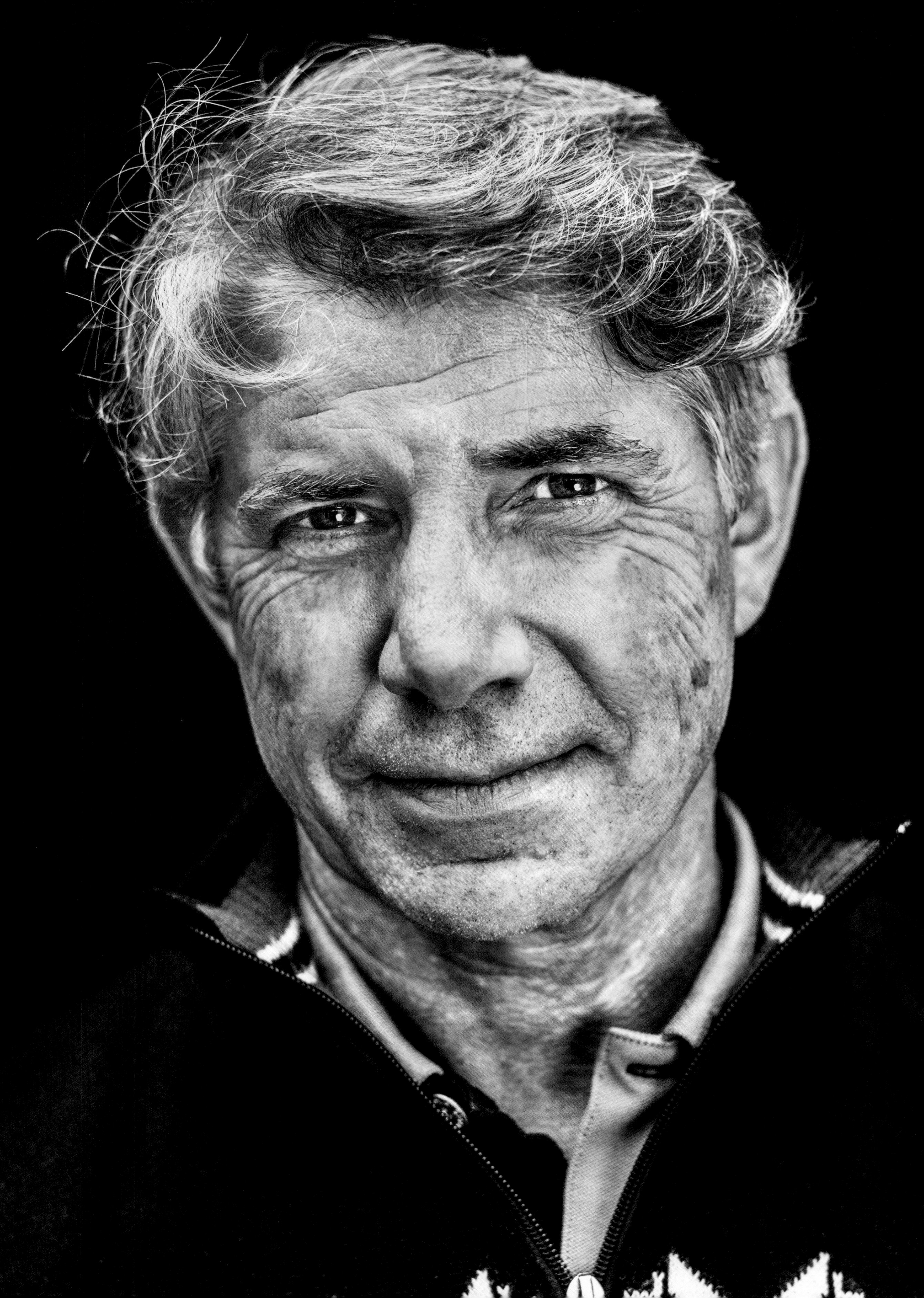

JANINE, 44
JANUARY 23RD, 2015, ZURICH, SWITZERLAND

I have too big a heart, so big that it makes me sick, as islands are created in the inner walls of my heart, making it hard for my blood to flow. The medical data of my body predicts my death.

My prospects have been miserable for years, and just the tiniest amount of activity exhausts me. I'm out of breath when I comb my hair, I can hardly leave my house, and my constant companion is a defibrillator, built into my heart to give my heart a shock each time it stops beating. Science is at its limit and thus only a donor can save me, but should someone die for me? I can't stand the thought of putting myself on the priority list and lying in the intensive care unit full of cables. I won't do that voluntarily.

Loneliness is the worst part of my illness. My therapist warned me a few years ago: 'Your family members will be the only ones left by your side'. As a teacher, I had had a large social network and was very active. I had a group of friends who were always there for one another – or so I thought. I said to myself: 'My friends will be there for me, they'll visit me'. A romantic thought, as people are scared of ephemerality. How does one deal with a terminally ill person? There's only one friend left by my side. Suddenly everyone had a fear of contact and felt overwhelmed. My best friend said: 'I love you so much that I can no longer be by your side'. I was so disappointed. People are defined by their environment. If you're isolated, you don't ex-

perience any appreciation. I lost my equilibrium when nearly all my friends disappeared; I fell without a safety net and started getting suicidal thoughts. I felt too weak to deal with all of it on my own. Even though it might sound paradoxical, it was euthanasia that helped me continue living in the end. I've had a prescription for these drops of death for several years now, and it's the power of self-determination they gave me that has unburdened me.

My suicidal thoughts have ceased, and I've learned to be on my own. Books and computer games distracted me. I visited workshops for the terminally ill, received psychological help and began to restructure my days. Qigong helped me above all. This Chinese meditation technique taught me to value things differently. I stayed active until I was no longer allowed to leave my sofa, but I've succeeded in seeing this as a form of relaxation.

Often we perceive our own circumstances as unbearable but what about all the people who have to fight for their survival on a daily basis? Humans are able to adapt to the most horrible living conditions. I realised that I'm not in complete control of my life, yet I want to be self-determined for as long as possible. My inner fire is alight and I want to enjoy each moment and not just wait around. Every so often I allow myself to imagine my future, but I also don't want to live in a dream world.

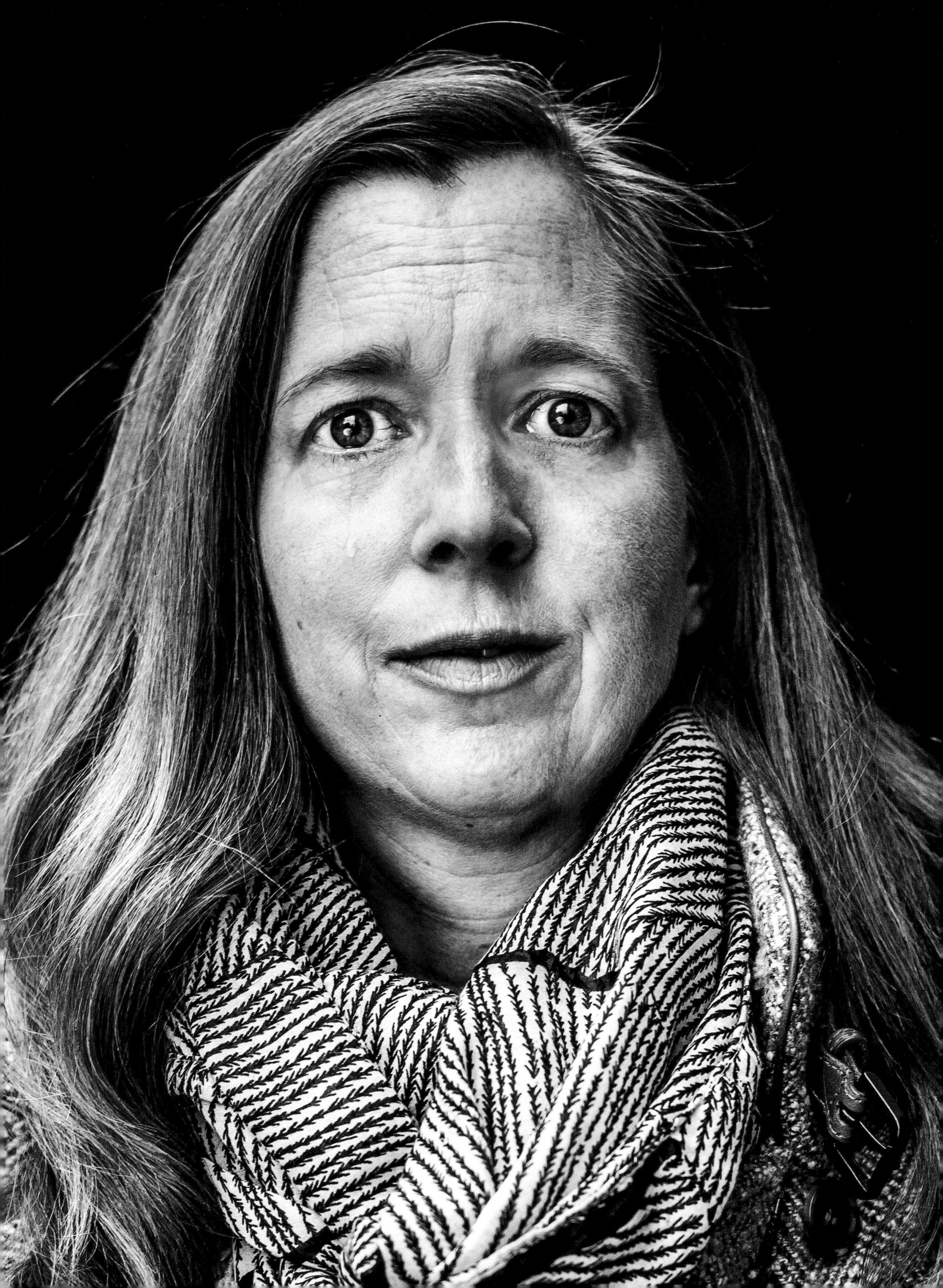

JADE, 32
OCTOBER 15TH, 2015, HOLLYWOOD, LOS ANGELES

I was Howard, trapped in the wrong body and raised in an uptight suburban environment under poor conditions. To be able to go to college in America without taking on the burden of lifelong debts there was only one option for me: the US Army.
I was 18 years old when I signed up. I had to go to Iraq and Afghanistan where attacks and death confronted me. What was I doing there? I felt horrible and wanted to give myself up. I was 21 years old when my time at the army was over. My body hadn't suffered any injuries, but I was profoundly traumatised. No one had warned me of the war's bitter repercussions, and I was left to fend for myself with no help to process all that I had endured. I lost myself in my wounded inner worlds. I used drugs and alcohol to numb my thoughts and to blend out the horrible images flashing through my mind's eye. College was no longer an option, and years passed yet the images remained. Nothing had changed.
Alongside my post-traumatic stress disorder, I was fighting another inner and unconscious battle against myself and my body. Everything felt wrong. I felt wrong. When I looked into the mirror, I saw a stranger. I had to get out, out of that body and finally leave Howard behind. I dared to take the first step by starting a hormone therapy, and when I was 31 years old, I began to undergo gender-transforming operations. After this, I finally saw myself when I looked into the mirror, for the first time in my life – I saw Jade.
Leaving Howard behind also meant leaving a significant part of my past behind. Finally, I could free myself from the war trauma and from my internal struggle of being trapped in the wrong body.
I hope others can see that my decision is more encompassing than that. I want them to perceive me as I am. I am not a man wearing women's clothes. I am Jade, who is on the right path to leading a good life, and if I am to stray, I know now: life provides different options, and no matter what will happen, I will always find the way back to my path.

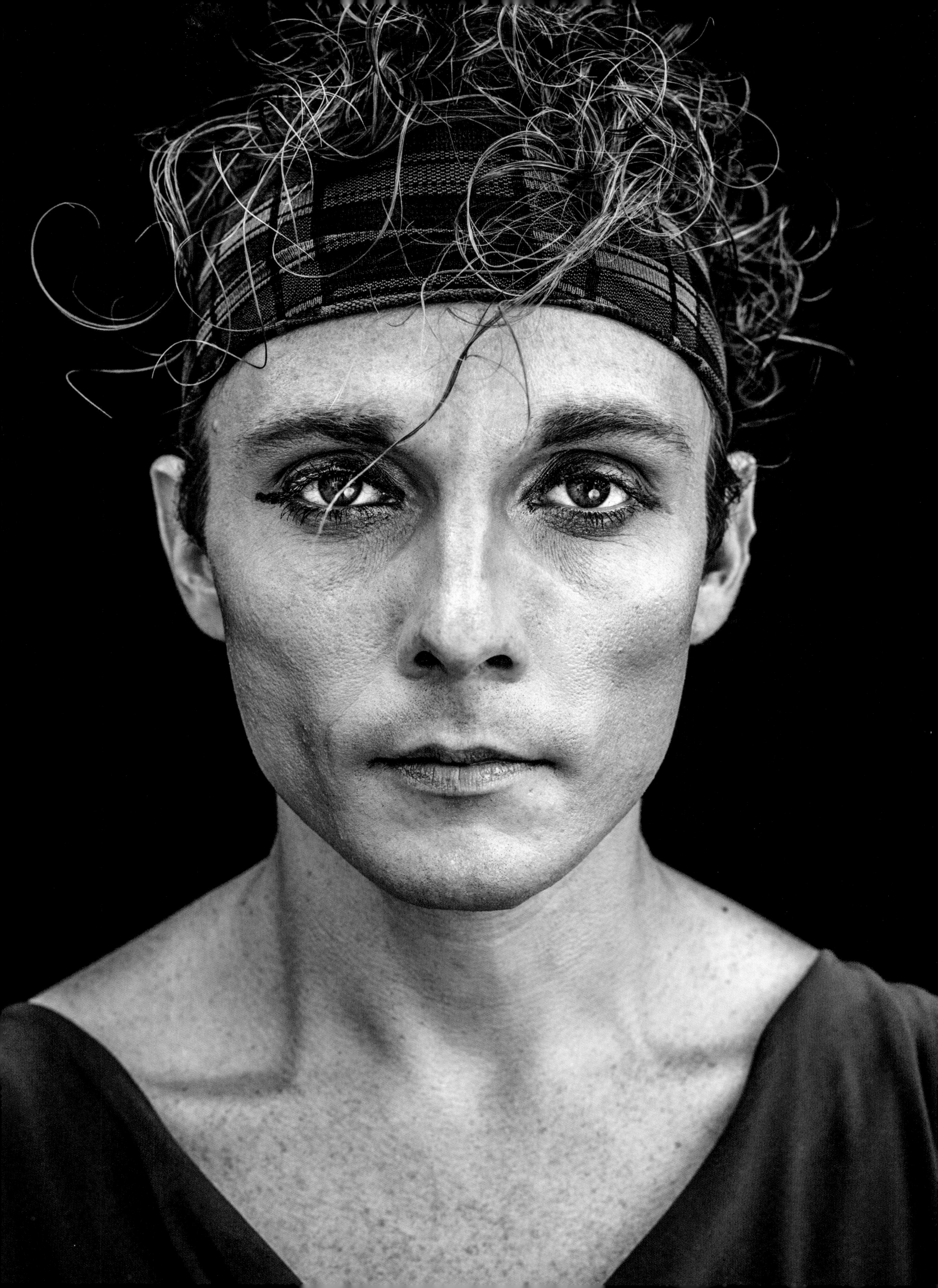

BRYN, 27
NOVEMBER 7TH, 2016, HOUT BAY, CAPE TOWN

Basketball has always been an essential part of my life; I was already playing at a reasonable level when I was thirteen, and four years later I was the captain of my high school team in Zimbabwe. I travelled a lot to play in national tournaments and dreamt of a professional career.

Political crisis in Zimbabwe at that time forced closure of many of schools because of hyper inflation and political conflicts when I was nineteen years old, and though I could have sat around at home and let my mom feed me, I decided to take matters into my own hands and moved to my aunt's place in Hout Bay, close to Cape Town. The living conditions were horrible in the neighbourhood I moved to – the kids smoked, drank and were high on drugs. They fought each other with knives on the streets – I saw ten-year-olds stab each other. They were all kids without a future. I wanted to help, and so, three years ago, I founded the 'Hout Bay Snipers Basketball Club'. I aimed to get the kids off the streets, keep them busy and create a safe space. Giovanni Freeman, an American co-founder of one of Cape Town's help organisations, financed balls and mobile baskets for my initiative so that I could turn a parking lot into a basketball court every evening. I founded teams and taught kids to play.

Politics, religion, and race don't play a role in basketball – everyone is welcome no matter who they are. We are a team and a family at the same time. Everyone takes care of one another even beyond the confines of the basketball court. I also teach kids to be disciplined outside the game. I want them to be role models for others, and I want to show them that they can reach big goals through being respectful. We train four times a week. Friday night is for doing homework, which the players need to show me on Mondays – this way I can make sure that they are on top of their school work too.

Thanks to sponsorships we were able to partake in our first away game last year. It was the first time the kids stepped foot onto a real court, in front of a big audience, and played against a strong team. They were speechless and giddy from all the excitement. Unfortunately, their enthusiasm was immediately followed by disappointment as they lost and were very upset. But the next day, the number of children at training doubled. They were full of hope and motivation to fight and win. We only just lost the following game, and that made them very proud.

Recently we had our first home tournament – cheerleaders and singers turned the event into a spectacle. The crowd was cheering and my kids won! It was a fantastic success. We even managed to make it into the local paper.

I had many sleepless nights and a fear of failing. Retrospectively, there were many obstacles that I had to overcome, but it was worth it – the kids are hopeful thanks to me. A lot of people on the streets call me 'Basketball'.

I do my work wholeheartedly and out of complete conviction. When I started, many kids didn't even have shoes and knew nothing about basketball – today they wear all the attire and made it to the regional semi-finals alongside a solid team. I love to watch the kids grow to form a team, observe how they individually realise their dreams through hard work and see how their surroundings begin to support them.

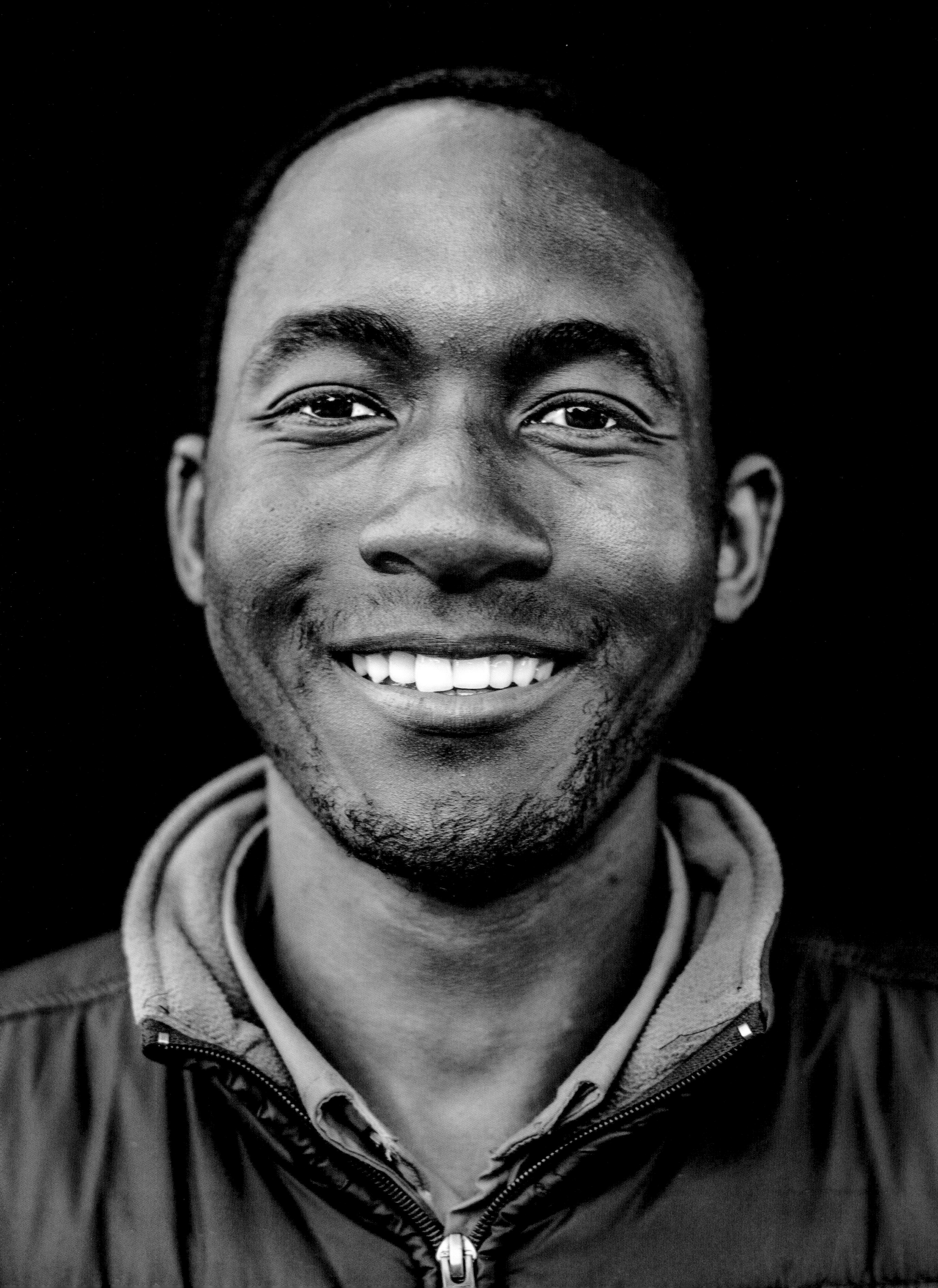

SIMON, 42
OCTOBER 28TH, 2015, GLENDALE, LOS ANGELES

I work in the dream factory and let fantasies to life. Sometimes, I pinch myself to make sure I'm not actually just dreaming.

I loved Disney movies, as most kids do. My favourite was 'The Aristocats'. I loved the animated characters in this movie so much that I wanted to draw them myself, and so I began to sketch all the time and everywhere. I already knew that I wanted to work on making an animated movie when I was twelve years old. I built dream worlds in my imagination and dreamt of working for Disney one day, but I was told that this job, in Switzerland, was unrealistic, abstract and financially insecure. My career advisors were frustrated – I might as well have said to them that I wanted to be an astronaut. For the sake of my mother, I did an apprenticeship at a bank, but I quickly knew that this was not for me, and I wanted to follow my dream. I was 21 years old when I applied to an animation school in Paris – 900 applications for 20 spots and I was given one of them.

After a two year course, heads of American animation studios knocked on my door and offered me a job for 'The Prince of Egypt'. I was baffled. USA, Hollywood, DreamWorks! My childhood dream had become real – so real that I still have difficulty to comprehend it today.

I had a culture shock when I first arrived. It took me six years to find my footing in this vast city, yet I worked hard and was full of ambition. Then I celebrated my first big success: I created the main character in the movie 'How to Train Your Dragon'. I brought the dragon called 'Toothless' to life. He's a mixture of other cartoon characters and my cat. He's a combination of a lot of things I love, and he means a lot to me. I throw myself entirely into the technical world of making an animation movie while I'm creating. Four and a half seconds of film footage requires 150 drawings and the help of many animators. Using thousands of controllers, I manipulate the gestures and mimics of the digital characters thus giving them emotional depth. It's during this intense phase of the animation production that I lose myself so much in the figures I create that I find it difficult to navigate in the real world at the end of a long working day.

On average, I work eighteen months to prepare the characters and fourteen months to produce the movie. Once the movie has been finalised, I begin to separate myself slowly from the project and have to accept that my work is done. It's almost like a period of mourning, and to get some emotional distance from the movie I usually go on a trip.

Then when the premiere arrives, I feel as if I'm intoxicated. When the soundtrack fades in, I am overcome by such strong emotions that I completely lose myself. It's an indescribable feeling!

It takes months to process all the highs and lows of such intense work. You need the right mentality, a lot of stamina and the ability to assert oneself. We always have to reinvent ourselves and search for that special something; after all, we are all creative dreamers.

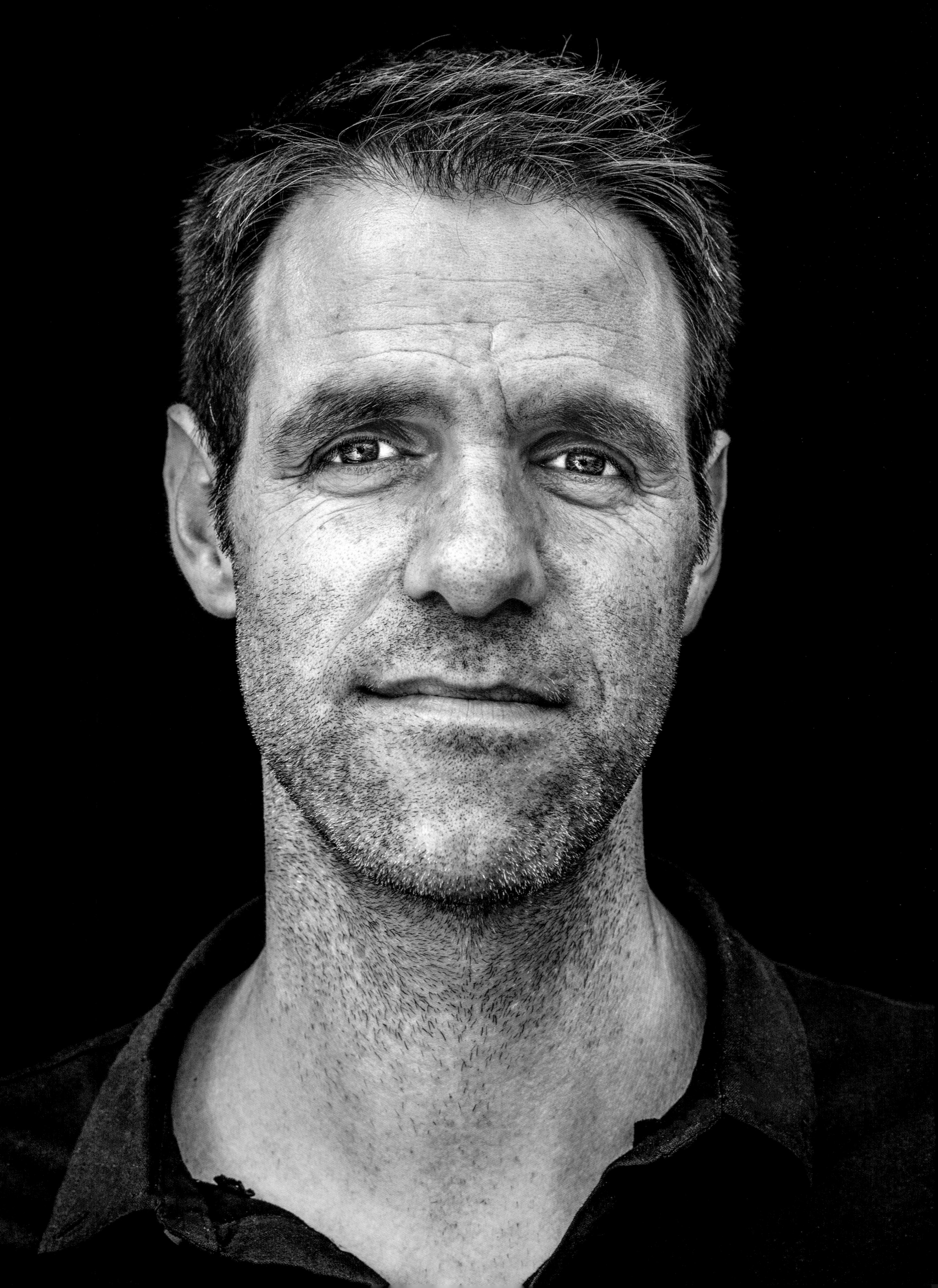

The cult brainwashed me to believe that there are no victims, that I am responsible for my own fate, that my soul has created everything that happens to me so that I can learn.

My dream as a child was to become a teacher and live in France. I spent my early childhood on a farm in Bavaria with my younger brother and parents. The world was ok, at least within my microcosm. Then my parents' marriage began to crumble, and they turned to spirituality to find meaning in life. A seminar about saving the world by Arno Wollensak promised them happiness, and so within months, they sold every single thing we owned. I screamed in fits of anger but to no avail: I was ten years old when we moved to Austria and joined Arno's cult called 'Light Oasis' with 40 others. My brother and I were crammed into a room with other kids, and someone else started taking care of us. We weren't allowed to address our parents with 'Mum' and 'Dad' any more. Arno told the grown-ups that their role as parents was unimportant because kids are also just 'old souls' and that they should concentrate on communicating with the spirit Ramtha. Doing this, said Arno, could transform the members of his cult into light beings and thus save them from the end of the world.

In the beginning, we were all showered with love. We would sit in a circle and speak about our emotions for hours. Sharing their fears and desires with Arno was profoundly freeing for many, and the grown-ups cried, screamed, cheered and laughed as if they were on drugs.

We became more and more estranged from our parents until we lost them but we weren't even allowed to mourn this loss, and that was the worst thing about it. We were only allowed the 'everything-is-good-attitude'. This was meant to heighten our frequency. We weren't allowed to think negative thoughts or express doubts towards our guru.

When the Austrian media started paying attention to 'Light Oasis', Arno fled to the jungle of Belize and took his members with him. There, far from any civilisation, he was able to be in complete control over us. He gave us commands that included who was to sleep with whom. I was eleven when I first had to kiss a grown man; later on, I had to sleep with him. I was fifteen when Arno promised Christoph, a man my father's age, that I would be his. I was scared to death, but I had to pretend that I was in love. The borders between being a child and an adult were dissolved. Girls had to undergo rituals to increase their spiritual growth but these actually just prepared the girls for future abuse. Parents didn't defend the kids, as that would have disrupted their mission to save the world.

I hated myself. I loathed my body, and I despised being a woman. Falling asleep was the worst as suppressed thoughts and fears crept to the surface. I was living in hell, and it was impossible to flee.

Arno regularly changed the code of behaviour, and if we didn't follow his rules we were punished. At some point, I really believed that I was unworthy and that only Arno could save me. I took on his insane ideas and was convinced that my inner being didn't belong to me and that I wasn't worthy of any privacy whether it be about owning a toothbrush or closing the door when I used the toilet let alone my own body, which, by all means, didn't belong to me any longer anyway. If he had told me to, I would have killed myself.

The psycho terror lasted for ten years, until one member was able to flee. Arno was scared that he would be arrested for child abuse, so he fled the country; taking some members, including my mother, with him. Others stayed in Belize like my father, and I first moved to the US before going to Switzerland. My brother went back to Germany. We have a good relationship with one another, and he's helped me process the whole thing. He's confirmed that the things I remember actually happened and that they were terrible. I needed this confirmation because there were times where I thought I was the crazy one while others had a good time there.

It was challenging to return to normal life and to erase the brain-washing after ten years of being in the cult. My self-hatred was immense, and it was impossible to turn off the belief that I wasn't allowed to do anything wrong and, as destructive as the cult was, it was hard to lose the communal aspect the group had given me. I first had to recognise that the world wasn't as Arno had said it was and that I had a right to live and love. I had very low self-esteem and was full of fears until one year ago, but I've now learned to understand my own emotions and to trust them, to let anger out and give space to my sorrows. I know now that no one can provide you with happiness, not a guru, a loved one or your own children. Being happy, to me, means to understand one's self, not be scared of one's own feelings and to feel good in one's skin.

And Arno? His murdered body was found in Uruguay one year ago. His arms were tied up, he had a plastic bag over his head, and his body had been thrown into a river. That's how it all ended – finally, I almost have to add.

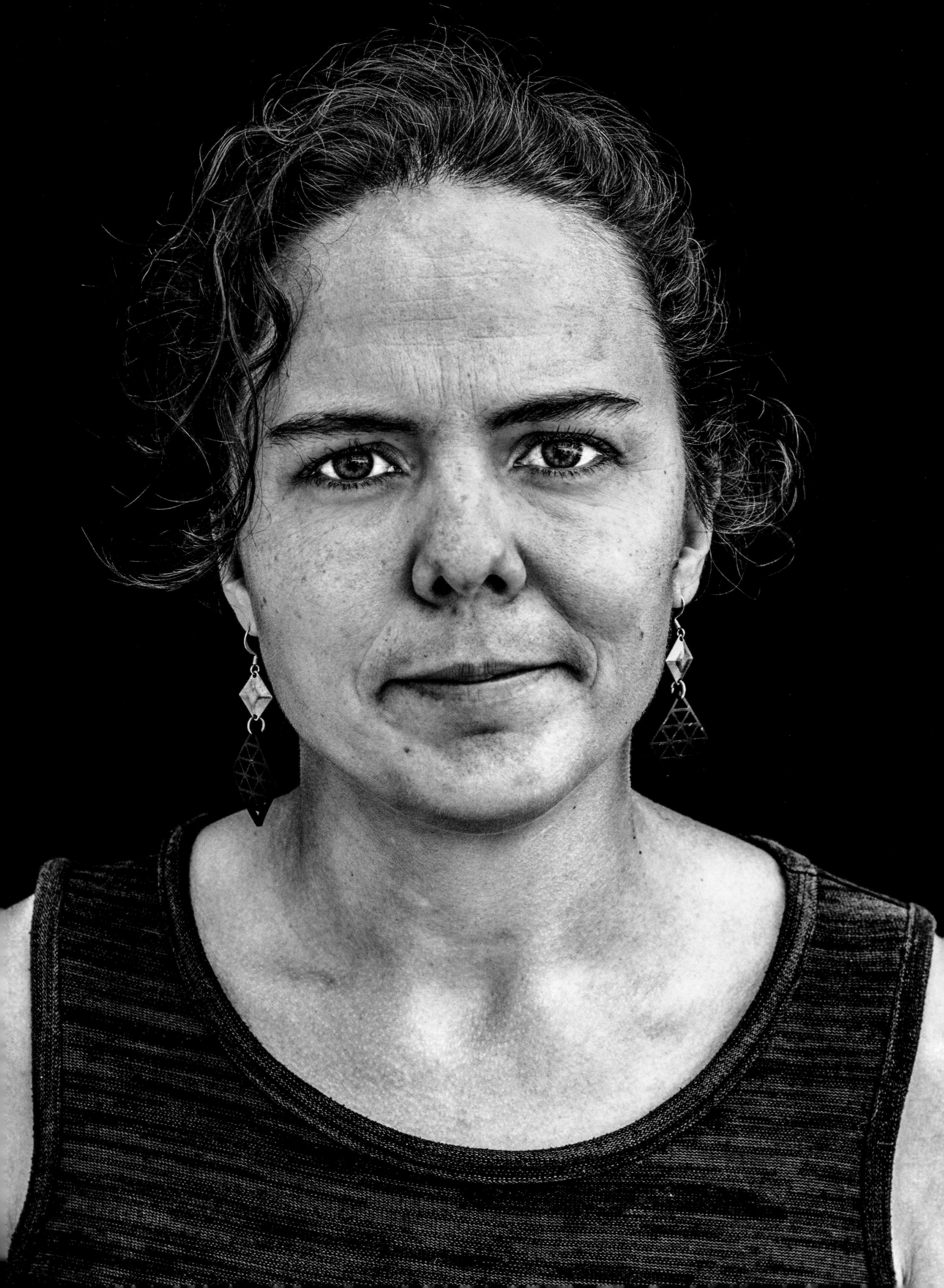

We care about certain people, yet we let others down. We admire the Earth while simultaneously destroying it. It's my task to inform people about the planet they live on, the people they live with, to generate awareness, and show the truth, and maybe that will sensitise and mobilise people so that they want to act.

I grew up in a farming village in Ohio where no-one in my family had gone to college. We knew of no significant national newspapers. I was eight years old when I read a book about Nellie Bly, a pioneer in early journalism. She lived in a time when women did not yet have many legal rights or voices, yet she managed to uncover and write about how society treated the disenfranchised – the poor, the insane, its women and children and animals. And those stories changed society. When I read the book, I knew that this was my calling!

I began to write whenever and wherever possible, for school newspapers and the local newspaper. And when I turned seventeen, I went to college in Los Angeles, California. A year or two later – back when the Los Angeles Times didn't have so much security – I was able just to enter its mighty headquarters and ask the local news editor whether I could cover stories for free, as a college student. Shortly after I graduated college, a full-time job offer followed.

At this point I had no idea what the future had in store for me: That I would come to be a Los Angeles Times Reporter and then a news columnist, that I would host public television and radio programs, write a bestseller and receive awards for my work, including six Emmys for my TV work and a share of two Pulitzer Prizes for my newspaper work. Getting there was hard, and sexism in the seventies and beyond was immense, putting up with the dirty jokes, the provocations, and the 'glass ceiling' limitation and the paycheck that went with it. As women know, we had to work twice as hard for what felt like half the recognition.

My career, like my education, helped to open up my world view, and the more I learned, the more I understood just how complicated the world is and how different the range of human experiences had made the world's people. I travelled and reported on people, events, and places ranging from the streets of rural Mexico to the interviewing the former President of South Africa. I encountered power and prosperity as well as despair and misery. So many of these stories touched me as they did readers. One story touched one specific reader – my story on a disabled three-year-old girl whose new leg braces and crutches were stolen from the family's car. That reader was Frank Sinatra, who called me the morning the story appeared and said he'd send money to help the girl. That's a perfect example of what a single newspaper story can do.

Newspaper stories are a kind of travel machine, like a time machine. Reading correspondent's stories can show people who live in safety and prosperity what it's like to be poor in the slums of India, what it means to be a victim of corruption and violence in Guatemala, what it feels like to have survived the nuclear catastrophe of Fukushima.

I want to share stories about the world with the world, because those stories implicitly ask readers: What would you do? Would you still shower for half an hour if the people who have to fight for their drinking water were standing in front of you? As a journalist, I can try to give a voice to everyone, and I can ask those in power what effect their power has on others, and how responsibly they are using it.

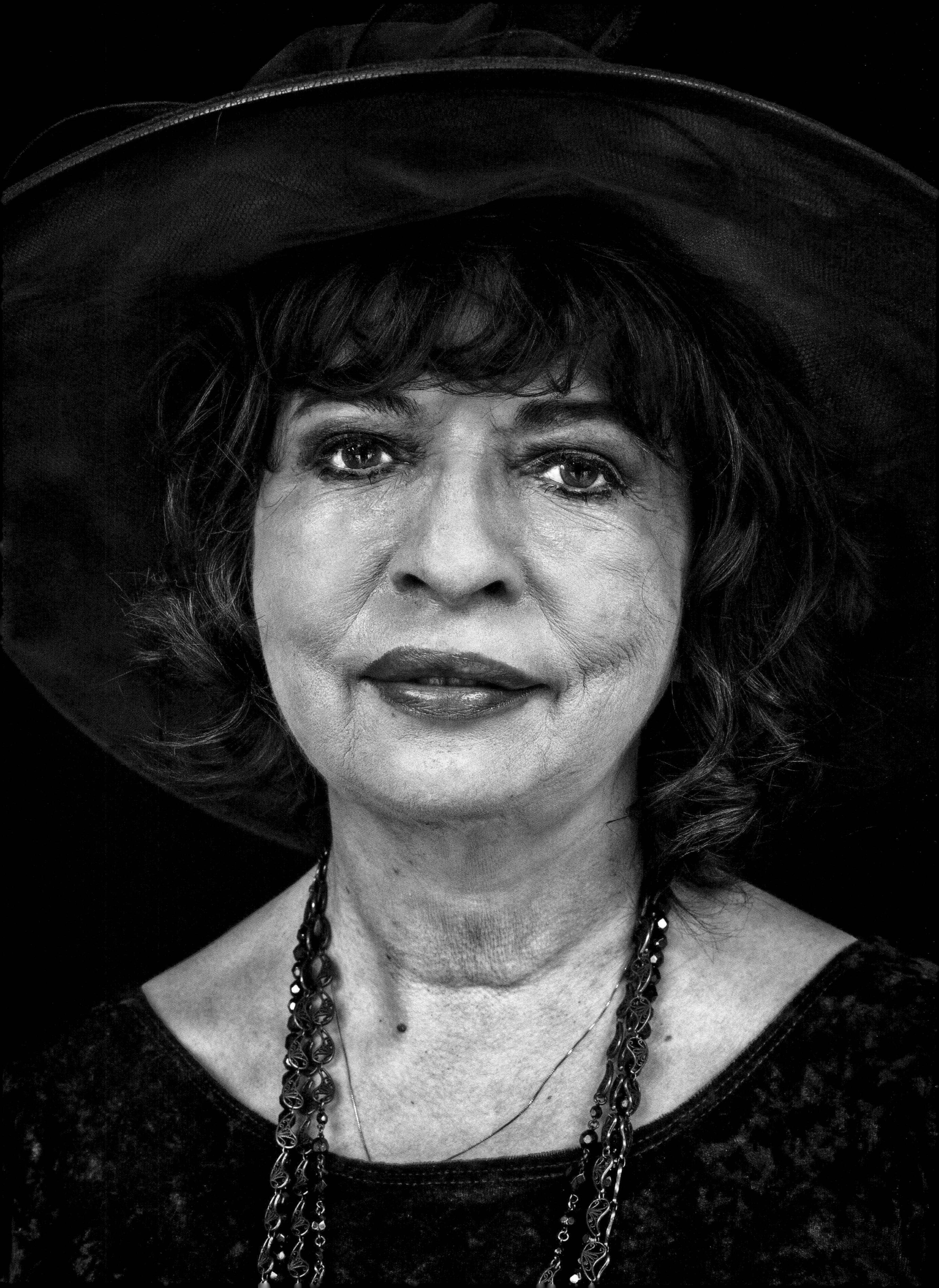

WENDY, 23

NOVEMBER 11TH, 2016, KHAYELITSHA, CAPE TOWN

My father died when I was two years old. My mother, it seemed, had never wanted me. For a long time, I tried to fight for her love by cooking, cleaning, complimenting her, making her laugh; but it was all in vain as she just cared about getting drunk. She always found something to complain about, she always found a way to degrade me. She would yell at me, throw her empty alcohol bottles at me and once she even attacked me with a hammer – the scar is still visible on my head today. Sometimes I had to escape her and would sleep outside. When my brother began abusing me, and my mother wouldn't believe me, I had had enough and told one of my teachers about all the abuse at home. That's how I ended up in a children's home when I was fourteen years old.

I had a great time there. I had a lot of friends, and the caregivers tried hard to make sure we had a good home there. After two years I was put into a foster family, even though I would have rather stayed in the home. I was speechless when I first saw the home of my adoptive parents as it was gigantic, but I quickly noticed that I was just a means to an end; I was put into a tiny room with seven other kids, and we weren't allowed to use any other place in the house. Our foster parents got 800 Rand (in 2009 this equated to 67 British Pound) for each child. We had to eat in the room we were sleeping in; through the walls we were able to hear the TV next door. They had three children of their own, but we weren't allowed to participate in their family life at all. I was the eldest of the foster kids, so I felt responsible for making sure everyone was alright. During the day I went to school, and in the evening I did women's nails on the streets to make a bit of money with which I bought bread for us. Our foster mom didn't take care of us at all; she was indifferent towards us.

When I was eighteen years old I became pregnant. How was that supposed to work? I had no support system, no one who could help me raise a child. I panicked and tried to commit suicide by hanging myself, but it didn't work – my child and I survived. I wasn't meant to die then.

After the birth of my son, I looked for a job and moved into a township with my boyfriend. We've been living in a little hut for four years now and are working hard towards having a good life. It's not always easy, but when I feel like I'm at my wit's end, I look at my son, turn up the music and dance with him. He gives me strength, and ultimately I know that I'm able to survive anything because I'm strong.

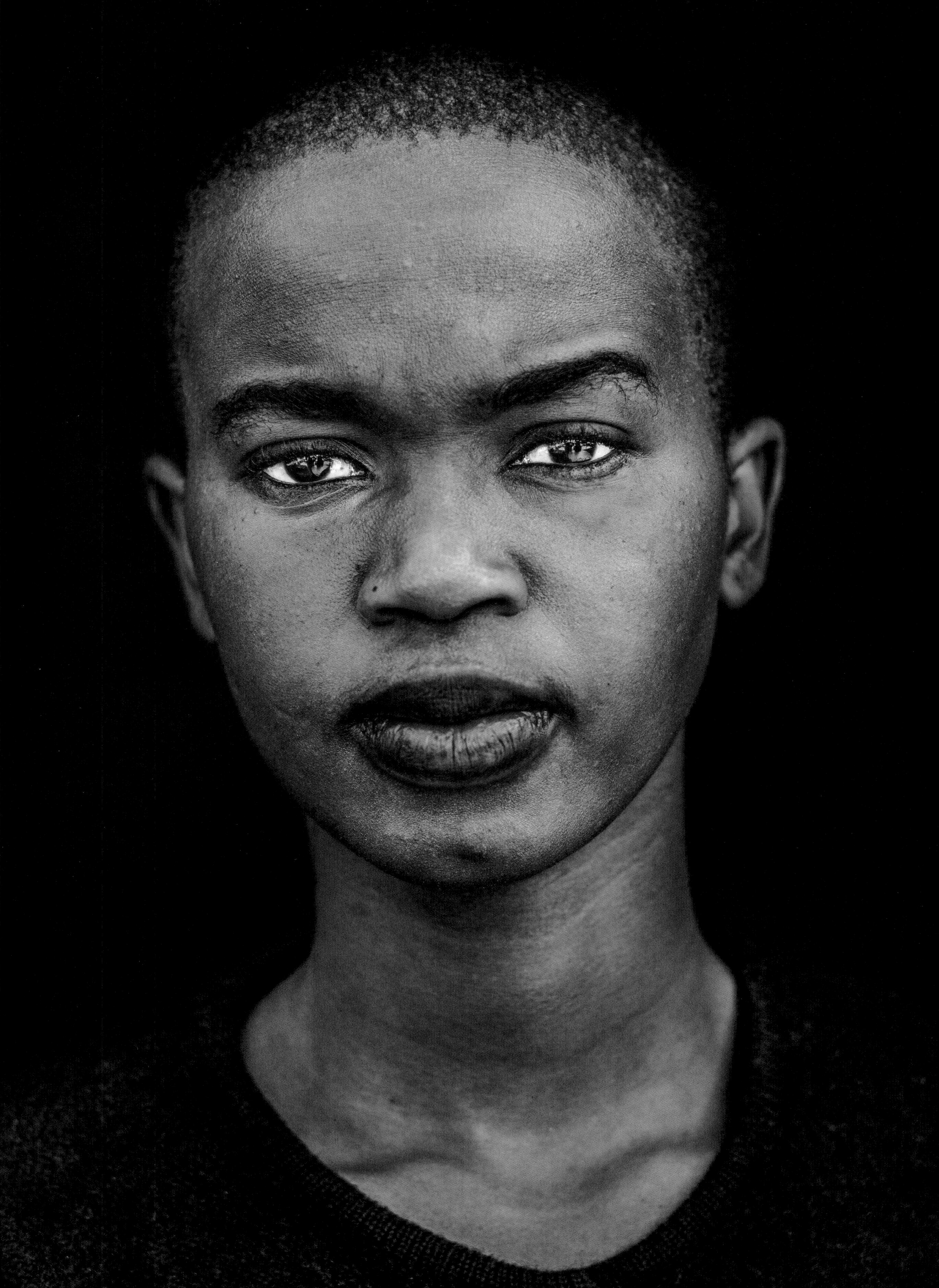

TERTULIEN, 37
OCTOBER 15TH, 2015, HOLLYWOOD, LOS ANGELES

Growing up, I was part of the cult 'Assemblies of God' – a Pentecostal denomination. My parents were very devout, and believed that the church's rules should be strictly followed.

There were clear guidelines on how I should behave and dress. For each service men had to wear suits and white buttoned-up collared shirts and be perfectly clean-shaven. All men had to sit on one side, all women on the other. I had to go to church on Tuesdays, Fridays, and Sundays, and every Saturday morning I had to fast and pray. I was only allowed to date in the church, and it was made clear that I had to marry within the church and continue the tradition.

My biggest passion was music, but I was only allowed to express it in limited ways. I was told to only sing Christian songs, and so I began to participate in the church's music group to make the most of my situation. My Father did not want me to sing 'worldly' music and said that it wasn't for me. For a long time, I tried to explain to him that music is an art form that doesn't require rules. I could never comprehend why my parents would want to suppress my personality by imposing their belief system on me. I hated the endless regulations and limitations. At school, this way of life felt wrong too as I was always asked why I wore such funny clothes and behaved weirdly. These kind of questions were difficult to answer, as it simply was the way my parents had raised me. As a teenager, all I wanted was to just fit in. So I began to lead a double life; I would change my clothes at school to feel free, and I would lie to my parents to meet friends in the evenings. It was almost impossible to merge these two worlds. It became all too clear to me that I did not want to live like this for the rest of my life, and I prayed for a sign to show me the way out.

One night, years later, I had this dream: I saw a large hand tear a sheet of paper from my diary and write the name 'David Kelsey' on it. I put this name into an internet search engine the next day and clicked on the third result – my favourite number. It directed me to a man in Los Angeles, so I contacted him and told him about my dream. We talked on the phone for almost an hour, and this call planted the seeds for my new life. A few days later my mother asked me if I was planning on going away – she too had had a dream in which she had seen me go West where I found a new home and was happy.

The time had come for me to spread my wings and fly, and so I left Stamford at the age of 23 and moved to LA to unapologetically pursue my dreams. I had decided to put all my hope and energy into music, but first I had to find the music deep within me. I had to shed my self-limiting beliefs and fears and learn to listen to myself – that was the only way to build up a trusting relationship with the art form I loved so much. That's how I discovered to be true to myself.

I want to spread love and hope with my voice, experience pure joy and forget all that surrounds me when I sing. I undergo a journey and enter other worlds. It feels as if I am floating and melting into the music until we become one. Music is a gift and the best expression of my soul. Where it will take me is always a surprise, but what counts is the moment. Every second of every minute.

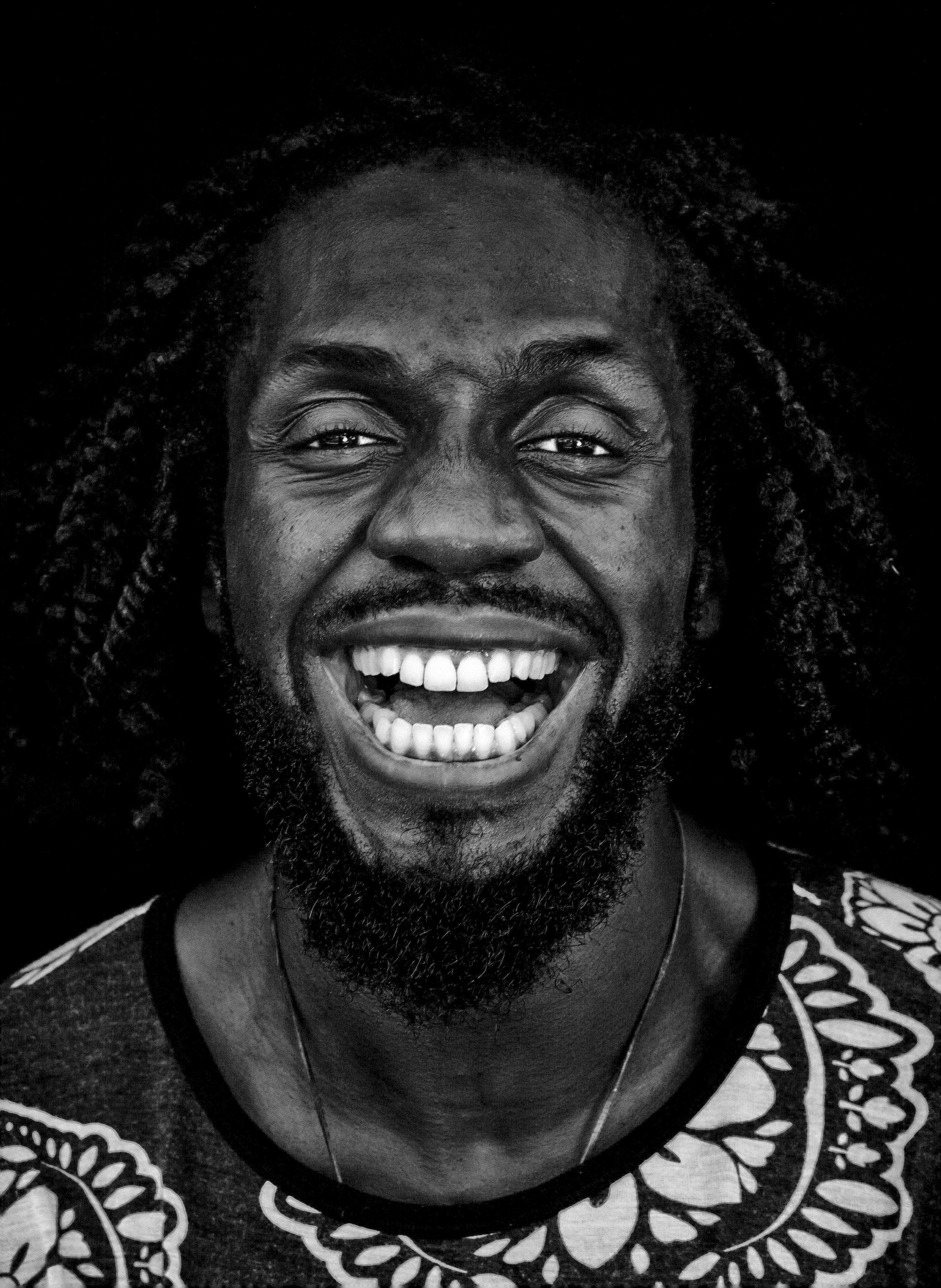

DEWI, 29

DECEMBER 4TH, 2017, NUSA LEMBONGAN, INDONESIA

I was at work when suddenly an unpleasant feeling overcame me. Tears shot into my eyes and I knew something wasn't right, but I was unable to understand where my emotions were coming from. When I came home, I found out that the bridge connecting the island of Nusa Lembongan and Nusa Ceningan, which was in dire need of renovation, had collapsed, injuring 30 people and killing eight. My sister-in-law and her son were among the dead, leaving my brother without a wife and child from one moment to the next. That was just over a year ago.

My sister-in-law and her son were born on the same day in the same month, on a Wednesday, and now they died together. My nephew Wayan was only three years old when the bridge collapsed, the same age as my son was at the time. I stayed at home for one week and cried uninterruptedly. The burial service, a Hindu fire ceremony, followed shortly after their death. This ceremony is one of the most important moments to happen to a person as, according to our beliefs, the cremation frees the soul and allows it to reincarnate.

This type of ceremony is elaborate and costs around 100 million Indonesian Rupiah, (circa 5600 British Pound) which equates to around three years of salary. We have a huge family, and everyone gave what they could to help pay for the ceremony. The service began early in the morning and went on until midnight. The whole family got together to say farewell. We filled a coconut bowl with their ashes and scattered them into the ocean.

As Hindus, we each have a small family temple and a priest. After the cremation, we brought our offerings to our temple and prayed for their souls. During our prayers, our priest went into a trance to connect with the ghosts of the deceased. I could feel that my sister-in-law and nephew were present and indeed the spirit of Wayan took over the body of our priest. He told us that he and his mother were in a good place and he asked us where his milk is. I had to cry when I heard those words. I knew that it really was Wayan speaking to us. He left after a short while, and later on the priest explained to me that the ghost had entered his body as a sort of energy that simultaneously feels hot and cold.

The words of my nephew helped me to accept his death, and the death of his mother. I can feel that they are still very close to us and Wayan comes into my dreams almost every night asking for his milk. I now have added a glass of milk to the daily offerings I give.

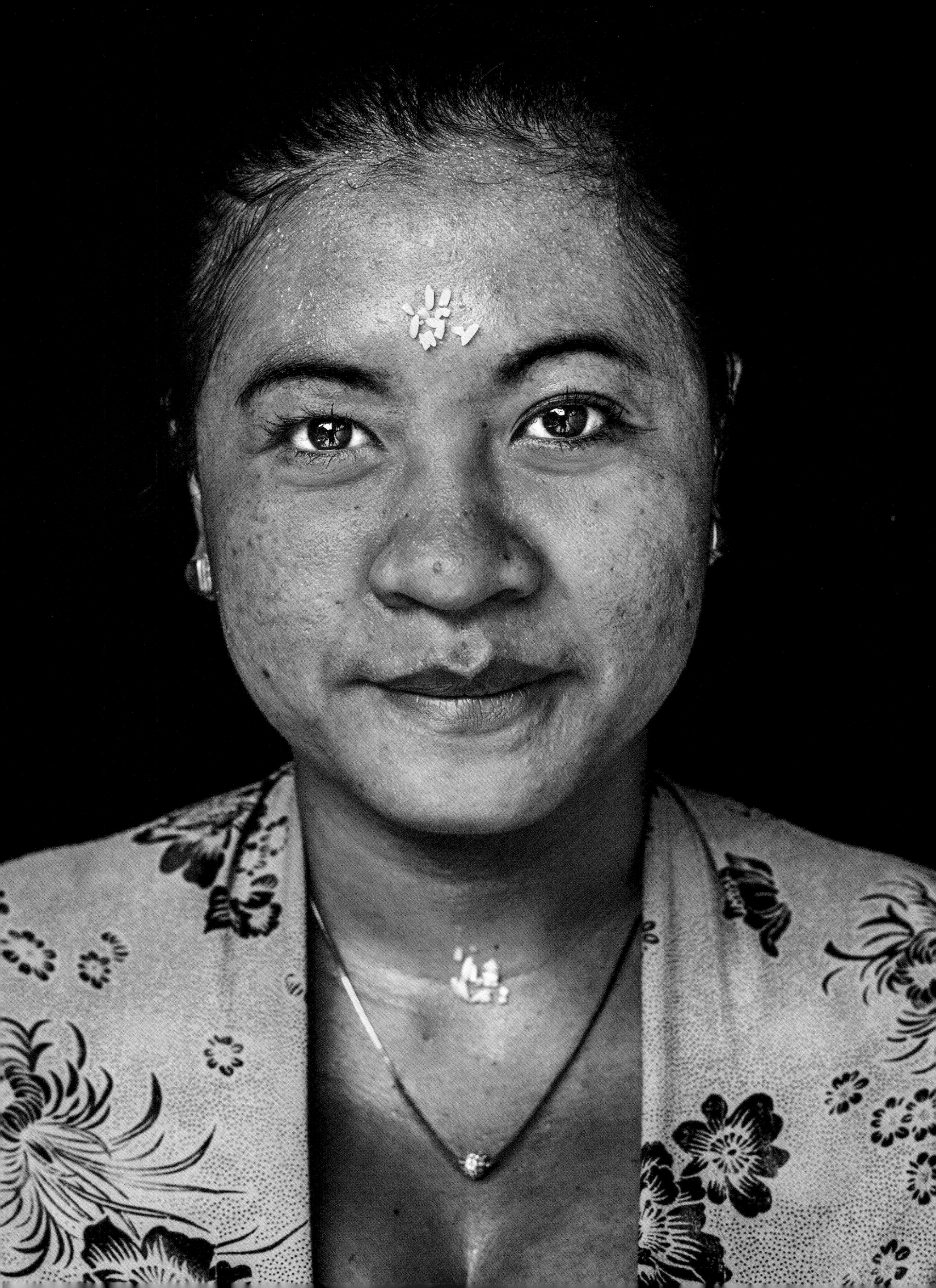

GÁBOR, 87

JANUARY 19TH, 2017, ESSLINGEN, SWITZERLAND

June 26th, 1944. Up until this date we, the Hungarian Jews, were spared from the industrial killings of the Nazis. My mother and I were deported from our home in Békéscsaba to Auschwitz. They split up men and women, tearing me away from my mother.

The German officers selected who was able to work, and I was one of the chosen, which saved me from dying immediately. They shaved me, cleaned me and dressed me in a striped prisoner's uniform. I slept in old horse barracks with thousands of other people not far from the crematoriums. I spent many moments observing the glowing lightning rod and the smoke seeping out of the chimney not knowing of the horrors happening inside. For a long time, they told us that these were bakeries.

Auschwitz had an extermination camp, a transit camp, and a labour camp. Every day people were taken away, murdered, destroyed, extinguished. Twice I was deemed incapable of working during the selection process, twice I was able to dodge my death sentence at the very last moment. During the first selection, the camp doctor Mengele fixated a bar at the height of 1.5 metres, and everyone who was able to walk beneath it was to die. A lot of those too short tried to cheat his test by putting stones in their shoes. We were 600 moribunds, all of us too short, but an additional selection followed and me and 21 others were lucky and were sent back, escaping death. Fifteen days later, another selection process; hundreds of us were locked in a barrack. Some tried to escape through air vents, but were unsuccessful. We were deported to Crematorium V, and at this point, we knew that it was a death factory awaiting us. We had to take off our clothes. With the last ounce of strength in my emaciated body, I forced myself to do push-ups, and seeing this the officers decided there was still some use for me after all. I left the crematorium, wearing the clothes of those who had to stay behind with 51 others, and returned to the wooden barracks.

As the Red Army was approaching, the Nazis decided to dissolve Auschwitz – they blew up the gas chambers to hide the traces of their mass killing machine and sent us on a death march.

I was so beyond famished that I was unable to move and stayed behind. Ten thousand died on the way towards freedom. They broke down, froze or starved to death, or were shot by the guards.

27th of January 1945. It was a bitterly cold winter when the Red Army ended the horrors of Auschwitz. I was fifteen years old and only weighed 27 kilograms. I had a sack of bread with me, which I dragged behind me as I was too weak to carry it. It took me seven months to return home where I met my father, who had been forced into the military work commando of the Nazis. My mother didn't come back. I only found out that she had died in 1944 at a concentration camp when I was 69 years old. That's all I know.

More than one million people were exterminated in Auschwitz. I was one of 7000 survivors. Why I survived when so many others didn't, is a question that has plagued me my whole life. I was with smarter, stronger, prettier and more devout people and they were all eliminated. It wasn't my faith that protected me but luck, sheer luck.

It's been over 70 years now that these terrors occurred yet I still have nightmares, though they have decreased over the years. That something like this could have happened is unimaginable. It took me nearly 50 years to be able to speak about my past. It was difficult, but I wanted to work through it. I researched, went through the archives bit by bit and wrote a book. I made it my mission to hinder the forgetting of these events.

Our generation loudly yelled 'Never again', but again marginalisation, racism, and strong right-winged radicalisation occurred, and again there were wars. It alarms me to see what is happening in the world out there. I'm afraid of the consequences. People think in categories and deliver judgments based on religion, origin or skin colour. People forget to encounter other people as humans.

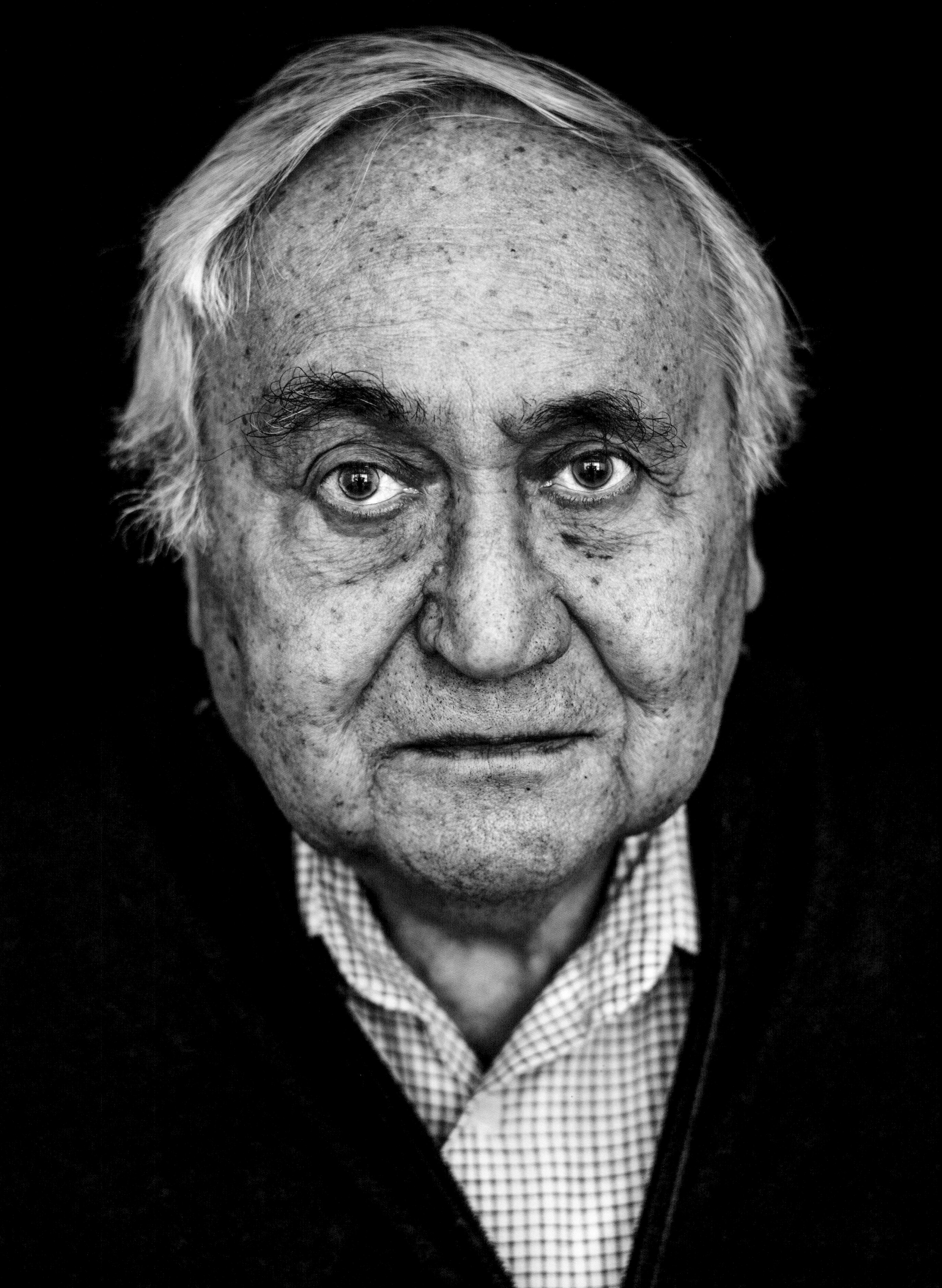

EMILIA, 74
NOVEMBER 5TH, 2015, WILLOQ, PERU

____

It was my dream to have a larger family. I gave birth to eleven children, but only two are still alive today.

I inherited a small house, without a kitchen or bathroom, from my mother. Here in the mountains, we live in deplorable conditions. There's no water or electricity, but we've got the basics. In this community, everyone is on their own; even when something terrible happens. Here, fathers choose husbands for their daughters. I was lucky as my father picked a man who owned land and animals and was able to teach me things like how to make textiles out of wool. Our friendship eventually turned into love.

I was twenty years old when I gave birth to our first son. More kids were soon to follow, and I was overjoyed as we had our family, and that's all that matters. Our sons helped my husband on the fields, and my daughters helped me turn the wool into fabric. Our youngest son was my favourite, as he was intelligent and learned how to read and write; but he became ill and had to endure a slow, agonising death as there is no medical care in the mountains, and the next city is too far away. I had to watch him die unable to help him.

After his death, I was emotionally absent for a long time and unable to take care of my other family members. But that wasn't to be the worst: my children were stricken by cases of flu, parasites, and colds, and each illness ended fatally so I lost eight more children. They died between the ages of six and twenty. I felt powerless against these harrowing diseases that were taking my children away. The pain of loss I was feeling overwhelmed me, tearing me apart from the inside but my husband kept fighting. He gave me strength and motivated me to once again participate in life. After all, I still had him and two healthy children by my side.

Having a family is the most important thing in life. Without that support, one will eventually be alone. I'm Catholic, and every evening I pray for my children. One day, I hope to meet them again. I learned to accept my losses as fate. Now I'm old, and my eyesight is dwindling. I only have the bare necessities, but I'm happy because I know that my family will always be by my side. My husband remains next to me. He's my rock.

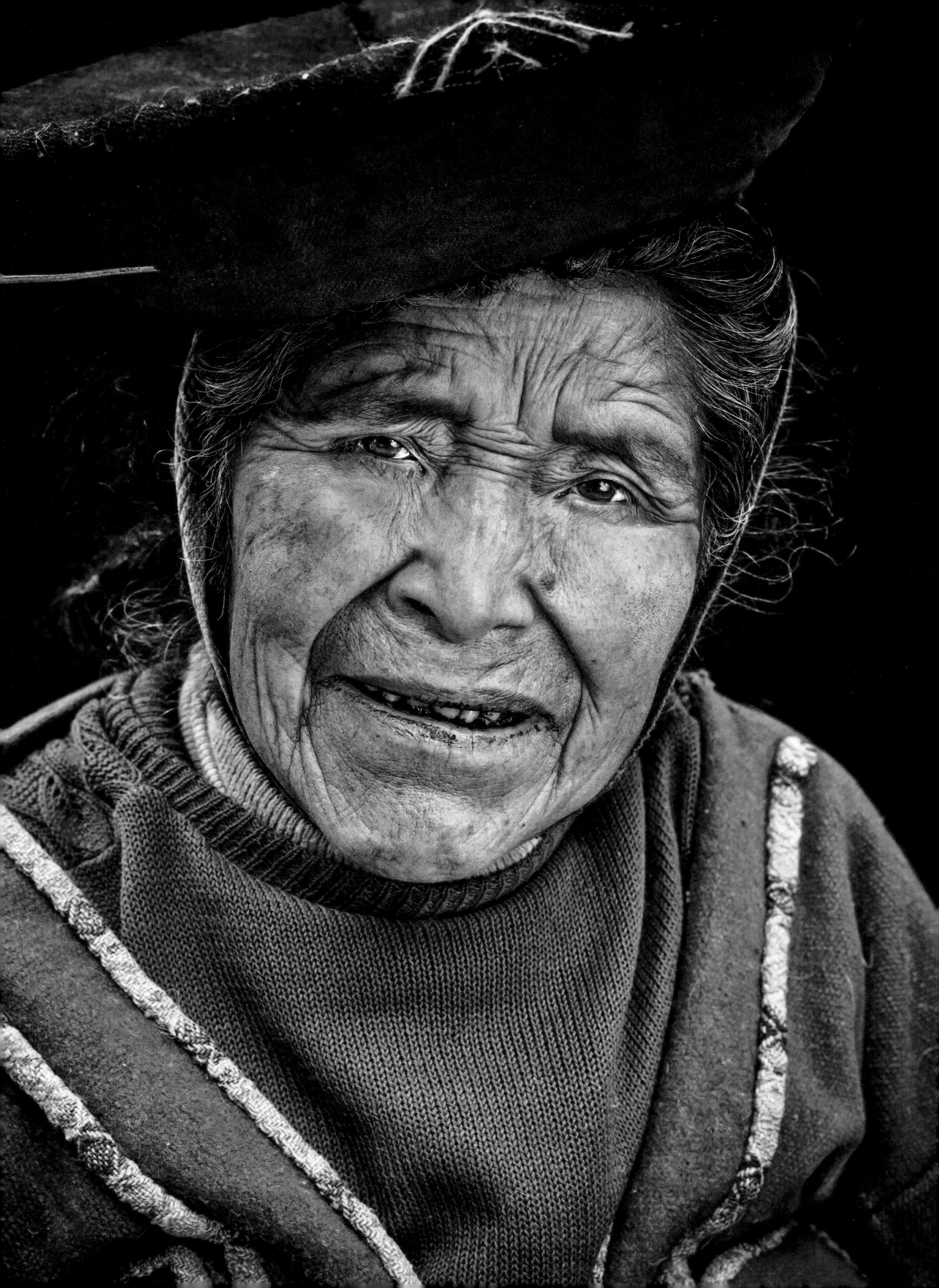

DENISE, 54

JUNE 8TH, 2017, MANHATTAN, NEW YORK

It was the coldest day of the year in mid-January, and the streets of New York were covered in snow. After my business meeting in New York, I headed back to La Guardia to return to Charlotte. On my way to the airport, US Airways notified me of my flight's delay.

When we were able to board the Airbus A320, I sat in the second row. I observed the other passengers, who boarded the plane after me. I guessed that a lot of them were on business trips like me, but I also noticed a four-person family who were going on vacation. The person sitting next to me was one of the last to board. He introduced himself as Mark.

I enjoyed the view of Manhattan once the plane took off but only about 90 seconds into the flight, there was a massive bang and the aircraft thrust back and forth. My first thought was 9/11 – was this another terrorist attack? We later found out that the plane had collided with a swarm of wild geese, but no one knew this at the time and panic spread throughout the aircraft. Many people were screaming and praying out loud. The cabin filled with a slight smoke screen and a strange, unidentifiable smell. Then it became silent, and I strained to hear the noise of the motors but there was absolutely nothing – you could have heard a pin drop. Both engines had shut down, and the plane started to sink.

One second felt like a minute, and a minute felt like an hour. I focused on three people: Mark, a gentleman sitting across the aisle, and a pilot who was on the way home from another flight. I tried reading her facial expression and asked her if we would be okay – she negated, and at this moment I understood that we would die.

The airplane neared the ground as I quietly sat in my seat while my thoughts went to my father, sister, and friends. There was so much yet to say and do. I just hoped to die painlessly and quickly, and not be dismembered beyond recognition.

Suddenly I heard the warning system through the intercom: 'Terrain! Terrain! Pull up! Pull up!' Mark held my hand, and we prayed. Then the pilot spoke: 'This is your pilot speaking; brace for Impact!' The flight attendants began giving instructions: 'Brace, brace, brace, heads down, stay down!', again and

again without interruption. I put my head between my legs while simultaneously trying to look around so I could see when, how and where I would die. The instructions became louder and more high-pitched, and it was impossible not to hear the shakiness in their voices.

The airplane crashed into the Hudson River at a speed of 270 km/h. It passed several blocks as it glided down the river. The pressure of the water ripped the left engine off the aircraft, causing the aircraft to spin to the left until it suddenly stopped dramatically. Captain Sullenberger managed to successfully emergency land the massive Airbus. I was still in my seat and felt paralysed. 'Evacuate the aircraft!', Sullenberger yelled. People ran past me down the aisle, and Mark took my hand and led me to the exit. We slid down the emergency slide into the cold water. Adrenaline pumped through my body as I swam to the life raft, where I began to help others. Some faces were painted white or blue by their fear of death and the cold. We were 155 people on board, and we all survived.

Two days later I was back at the airport carrying with me just a toothbrush and toothpaste and all I wanted was to get home. I sat in the second row again, this time filled with terrible fear. Once I was finally at home, I cried relentlessly. I suffered from flashbacks for months, and I had to learn to control my anxiety in therapy. Keeping in touch with other survivors helped me to tackle my trauma bit for bit.

Not one day passes without thinking of flight 1549. I get nervous easily and panic when I can't perceive any escape routes. I still suffer from a feeling of guilt – why did I survive when so many others died on planes? Why did I survive when friends of mine lost their thirty year-old daughter in a plane crash? I still find it difficult to talk about all these feelings, as I don't think I have a right to them when, after all, I survived.

Now I volunteer for air safety and help people who have a fear of flying, or have lost loved ones in airplane crashes. I want to support these people while they go through difficult times and I want to make the most of the second chance I was given through the wonder of the Hudson River.

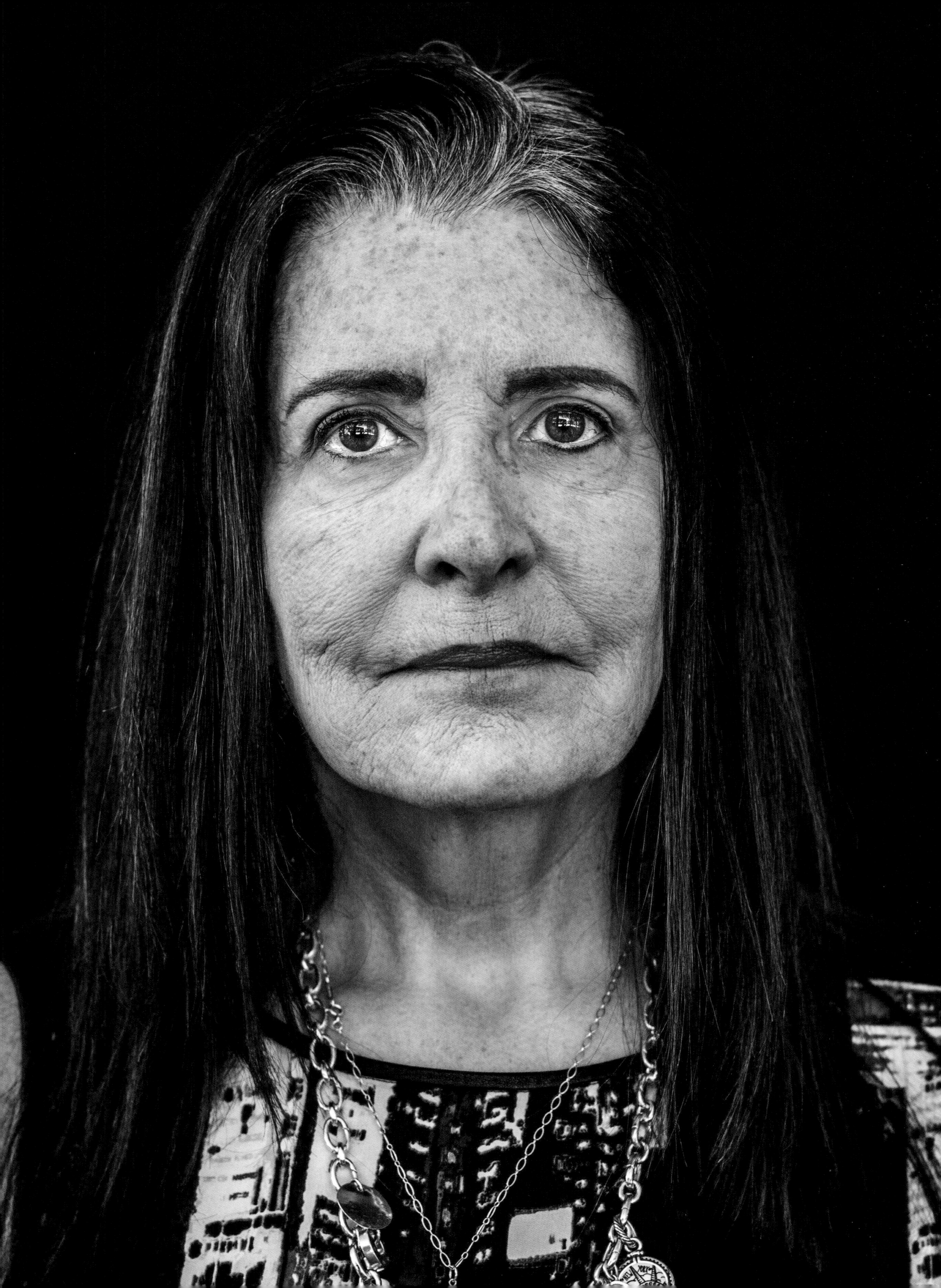

NICOLE, 20
APRIL 11TH, 2015, ZURICH, SWITZERLAND

I'm in the hospital, though I want to be at home. I eat but would rather starve. I fight myself despite liking myself. Anorexia has taken over my life.

It started in high school. I didn't feel right in my body, as I thought I was much larger and less attractive than the other girls. A feeling of hate towards everything and everyone, especially myself, began to grow inside of me. I started to eat less and weighed myself daily. I came up with meal plans, counted calories and exercised intensely. There was an inner voice that gave commands, provoked, insulted and tortured me. The voice played a ruthless game with me and wouldn't stop. It became especially loud and mean right after meals. I drank as much water as I possibly could – cold or fiery hot. In the winter I stood on the balcony wearing light clothes so that I would freeze and my body would be forced to burn more calories. I took laxatives and medicine to stimulate my kidneys. Comments like 'You're too skinny', satisfied me because it ensured me that people noticed I was skinny. I convinced myself that I had to be thin to be loved and accepted. I lost all self-control, and my self-perception was distorted.

My addiction made me ruthless. I lied and cheated just to give the voice in my head some satisfaction. I became introverted, sluggish, isolated, whiny and depressed. Sometimes I'd be aggressive and irritable. Deep down I knew that only I was responsible for my state. My body was at its end. My health deteriorated with each passing day as my bones poked out of my body more and more. My appearance and behavior became unbearable for those people around me. I mistrusted everyone and wouldn't let people near me until I reached rock bottom: I weighed a mere 36.4 kilograms, and my body temperature had sunk to 35 degrees celsius. I was cold and shaking. My heart rate was at 22 beats per minute on the day my parents brought me to the hospital – that's the heart rate people have right before they die. The doctor told me that I would die if I didn't start eating, but I still didn't feel like I was sick; on the contrary, I felt proud as I had read that many anorexic people didn't manage to get their weight down to 36 kilograms.

Perhaps I would have had one or two more days before my heart would have stopped beating. I was only able to admit to myself right before the end that I needed help but I was afraid of being fattened up.

My eating habits were the only thing I could still control. I was split between the bad, fat, no good Nicole and the affable, sweet and loving Nicole. I fought against the evil and robust voice but felt ambivalent – one day I wanted to be healthy, the next day I tried to lose weight.

Getting healthy was much worse than starving, but slowly I gained weight. It took a lot of strength to fight my way out of that vicious cycle. I wouldn't have found my way back into a regular life without help and support. I learned a lot about myself and the human psyche. I discovered how to share myself with others and not bottle up everything I feel.

My road to recovery was a long and painful ordeal, but I am much better today. It still takes quite a bit to overcome myself to eat, and I guess my weight will always play a role in my life. Today I see the sickness as a chance to live a more conscious life and to appreciate my health more. It wasn't a pleasant experience to go through, but the most important thing is that I survived.

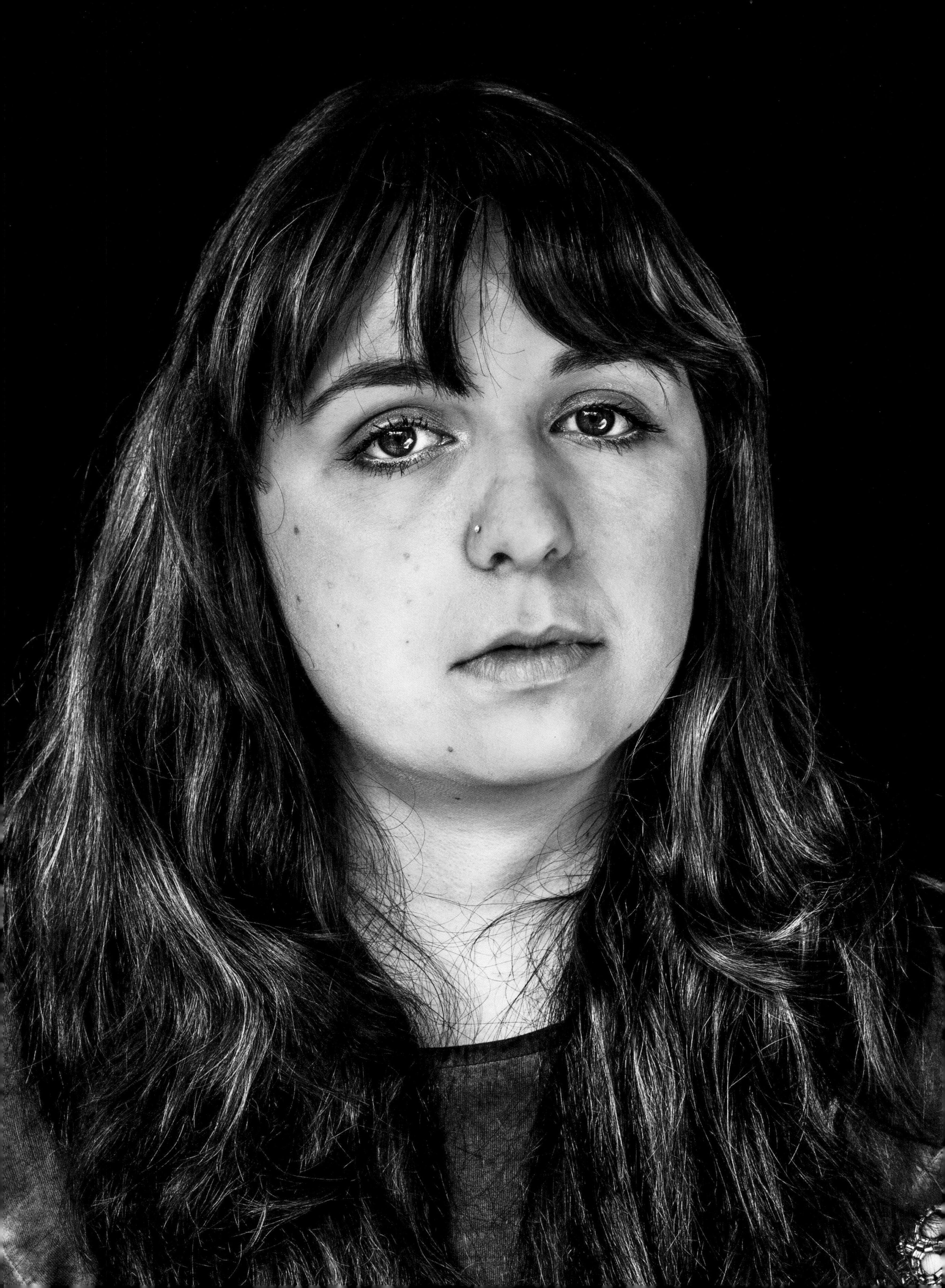

DAVID, 25
SEPTEMBER 28TH, 2014, BERLIN, GERMANY

Out of the office and into the big, wide world.

Up until two years ago, I was working as a software developer for an international company in Ireland. I have a Bachelor of Science degree, my income was excellent, and my career was looking promising – my life seemed to be perfect, but increasingly I was feeling the urge to do something meaningful with my life. I became fidgety and nervous at work as my fear to miss out became overpowering.

In June 2013 I left my job, my family, and my girlfriend behind. I felt I had to end our relationship to be open to whatever might come next. Then, with two friends and a camper van, I played music on the streets to finance our life on the road. I've always had a talent for music – I learned to play the piano when I was five, and a few years later I bought myself a guitar. I never took any singing lessons. After just a few days I was addicted. I played the guitar, wrote lyrics and sang for hours with no end in sight. The audience applauded me, and I never wanted to look back.

To leave was the best decision I've ever made in my life. I never thought that my life could change so drastically. Until now I've played in twenty different European cities, I've performed on the streets, in concerts and at festivals in front of thousands of people. I produced my album, which I sell on the streets, online and in a few shops. I don't make much money with music, but it is the freedom it gives me that is my actual pay. I made my dream come true, and I find new challenges every day. In my eyes, it's not about everything working out perfectly, but it's about trying in the first place. I don't know what's ahead of me and if I should believe in my big breakthrough, and even though I earn half of what I made two years ago I wake up every morning with a smile on my face and that's real success, isn't it?

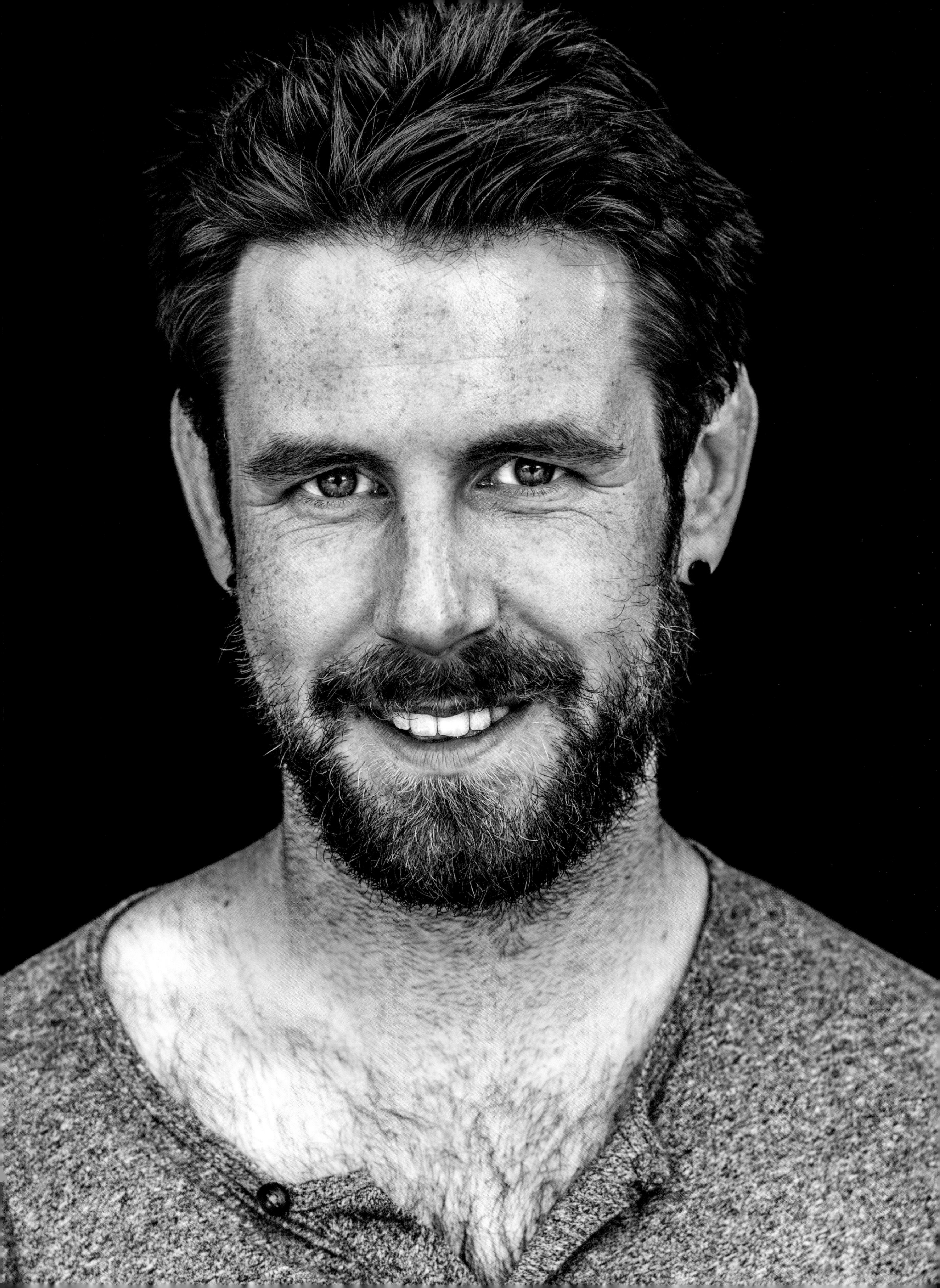

SOTHY, 49
FEBRUARY 16TH, 2018, LUCERNE, SWITZERLAND

It was the 17th of April 1975 in Phnom Penh, I was six-years-old when the guerrilla army forced us out of our homes with guns and cleared the entire city.

Those working for the dictator Pol Pot drove thousands of us into the countryside for weeks. We were separated like a flock of sheep again and again, but I managed to stay with my grandmother, mother and both my brothers but it was in Phnom Penh that we last saw my father. He remained missing forever.

Through the terror reign of the Khmer Roug, Cambodia rapidly turned into a massive slave camp. Their goal was to create a radical, communist farmer state. We built huts out of wood, and some fabric, collected rainwater for drinking and washing and the only thing I had to wear was a grey nightgown, which I also had to wear while working.

I had to wake up at five every morning to go on the rice fields with about one hundred other girls. We had to plant seedlings barefooted in the mud while armed soldiers were watching us, screaming at us and demanding we work faster. Quick work was rewarded with a watery rice soup, whereas otherwise there was no food all day. We were only allowed to return to our huts once the sun had set. I heard my mother whisper to my grandmother: 'We're not even allowed to take rice grains with us, or else we'll get killed'. The soldiers killed everyone who dared to break the rules or defend themselves. Intelligence was seen as a threat and was punished by death. We were forbidden to speak, show emotions or express pain. One day, I ripped out my toenail by stepping on a sharp piece of metal; the pain was excruciating, but I had to keep on working, and I still have scars of leeches sucking on my legs.

Once a little girl fell head first into the water. Other kids ran to her rescue, but the soldiers intervened and let the girl drown. I was a few rows behind her and had to watch the whole thing, realising just how careful I had to be. I spent the evenings with my family on the floor of our hut, but often we were separated for long periods. I tried to visit my mother, but a soldier caught me and tied me to a post for an entire day. The Vietnamese started fighting against the guerrilla movement of the Khmer Rouge in 1979, and so we were forced, by Pol Pot's men, to flee in the direction of Thailand – they needed us as human shields. We had to march for weeks, and this took a toll on my grandmother who became so weak that we had to carry her; but at some point, we no longer had the strength to and were forced to leave her behind. To lose her tore me up inside but I had to keep functioning as a puppet. We arrived at an abandoned hall where we stayed for months squished together like sardines. Suddenly shots were fired meant for the Khmer Rouge, but we were all there together, and one-fifth of us died that day, including my older brother. My mother, my other brother and I survived but the fight wasn't over yet, and we had to continue marching towards the border to Thailand, through the jungle, and over minefields. There were explosions every day and so with every passing day we were fewer people marching. My brother, mother and I walked hand in hand with death close behind. At some point, we weren't aware anymore of the things happening around us. We were only fifty people, traumatised and starved, once we arrived at the Thai border and entered a refugee camp before we could register with Red Cross. Eventually, we were brought to Switzerland.

About one-fourth of Cambodia's population was killed through famine, forced labour, murder and torture during the four-year reign of Khmer Rouge. My childhood was over. Coming to Switzerland felt like I had been given a second life and though I couldn't repeat my childhood, I was able to see life through the eyes of a child when I became a mother. This allowed me to see and feel what it means to lightheartedly enjoy little things. Every chance I get to go down a slide with my kids, I take.

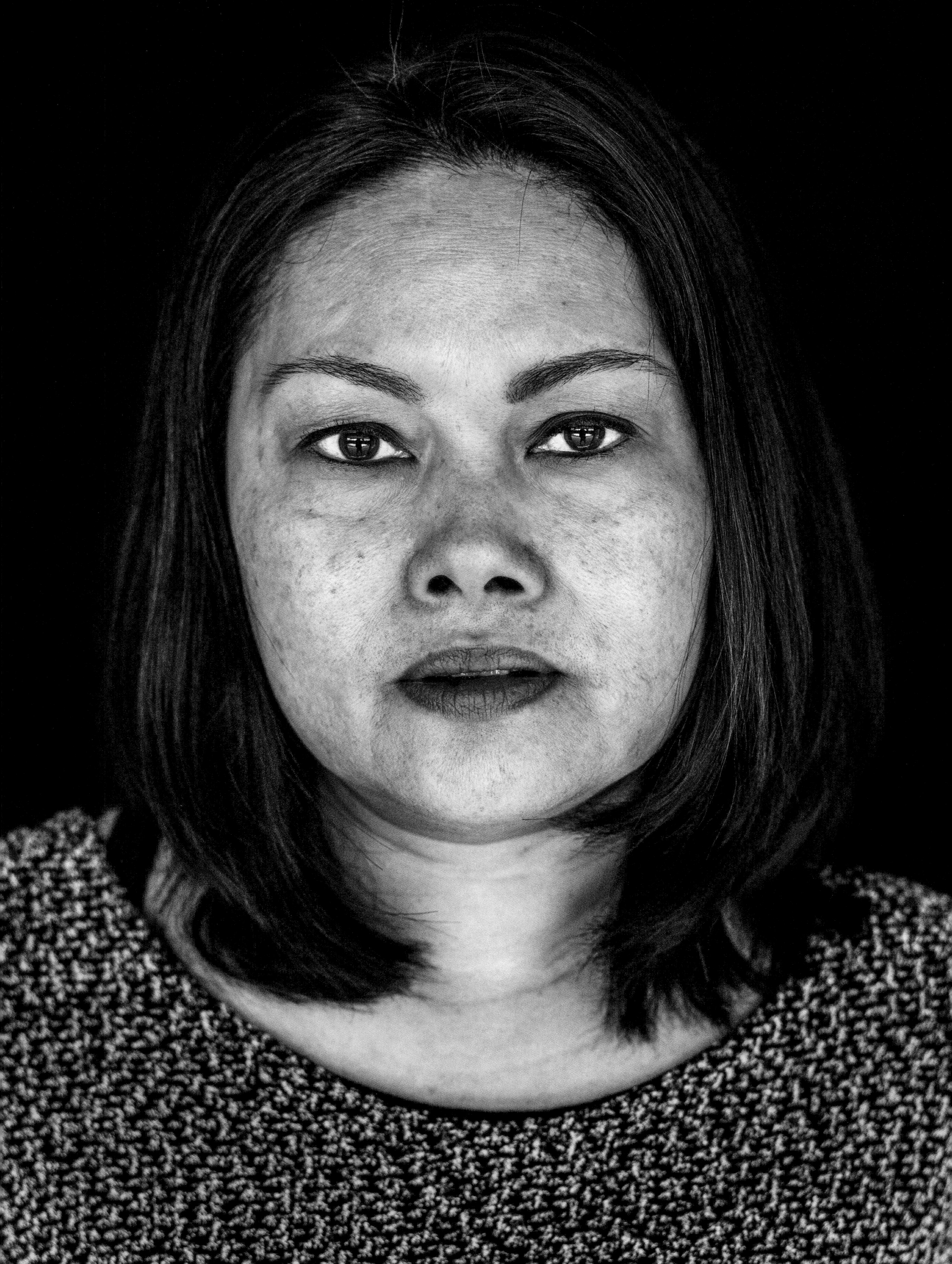

RICHARD, 56
NOVEMBER 8TH, 2016, KOMMETJIE, CAPE TOWN

'Look at the stars; they belong to you. Reach out and touch them – you can reach everything you put your mind to!' My grandmother believed in me. Even as a child I knew that I wanted to fly one day. We lived close to an airfield, and I watched the airplanes fly over my head every day. I wanted to know everything – from the construction of a plane to aerodynamics. Once I finally had my flying license, nothing was able to hold me back.

I met my former wife at the airfield, and we moved to Zimbabwe together. We lived on her parents' estate, far away from civilisation. Her parents owned hectares of fields, and I had the idea to use new technology to spray pesticides on vermin plaguing the fields from the air. We made a family business out of it. Later on, I began to question this practice as I read reports about the multinational agricultural biotechnology corporation who produce this. I realised how bad the chemicals are for humans. I also began to engage myself in the national parks to help stop the poaching of rhinoceroses. I would fly over the Savannah, fascinated by nature's beauty, the shape of the cloud's shadows on the ground and the power of the sun – the freedom of flying had me captivated.

I loved the vastness, experiencing different dimensions, and all the other priceless feelings one gets from being in the air. I enjoyed observing the animals from above, seeking out rhinoceroses and, through that, doing good. I was able to seek them out well from the sky. The park rangers would numb the animals to carve a V into the soles of their feet – a sign for the poachers that there was no horn left for them to hunt. I thought the animal was only desirable for the poachers with the horn intact, but I was wrong as I found out that even the ones without horns get killed; the poachers want to increase the value of their already existing loot by eradicating the entire species. What I found out next was even worse: the cut off horns from our mission also ended up on the black market, as the national park was bankrupt and the government had no money to support it. The entire system in Zimbabwe collapsed; the currency suddenly and drastically lost its value, and unemployment increased. Farmers lost their properties to the corrupt government, as everything fell to pieces including my marriage.

Zimbabwe is a marvelous country and the people I met there are incredible, but I felt foreign and isolated under those dire conditions. I left Zimbabwe after five years and rented a garage in Cape Town to build an airplane for myself just I had done in Zimbabwe. I missed my daily flights and wanted to return to the sky as quickly as possible. It took me six months to build my plane.

I don't fly over the Savannah on a daily basis any longer, but I sleep with open curtains to wake up by the sun. I want to grow my vegetables here, and run everything on solar energy. I want to keep bees for my honey and chicken for my eggs. Caring for my own healthy food provides me with a feeling of freedom. I go for walks and observe the mountains. I stand still and listen to the ocean. And if I have a bad day, I get in my plane and press my 'happy button'. I enjoy the solitude and vision up there, and how that combination has the power to let problems appear small.

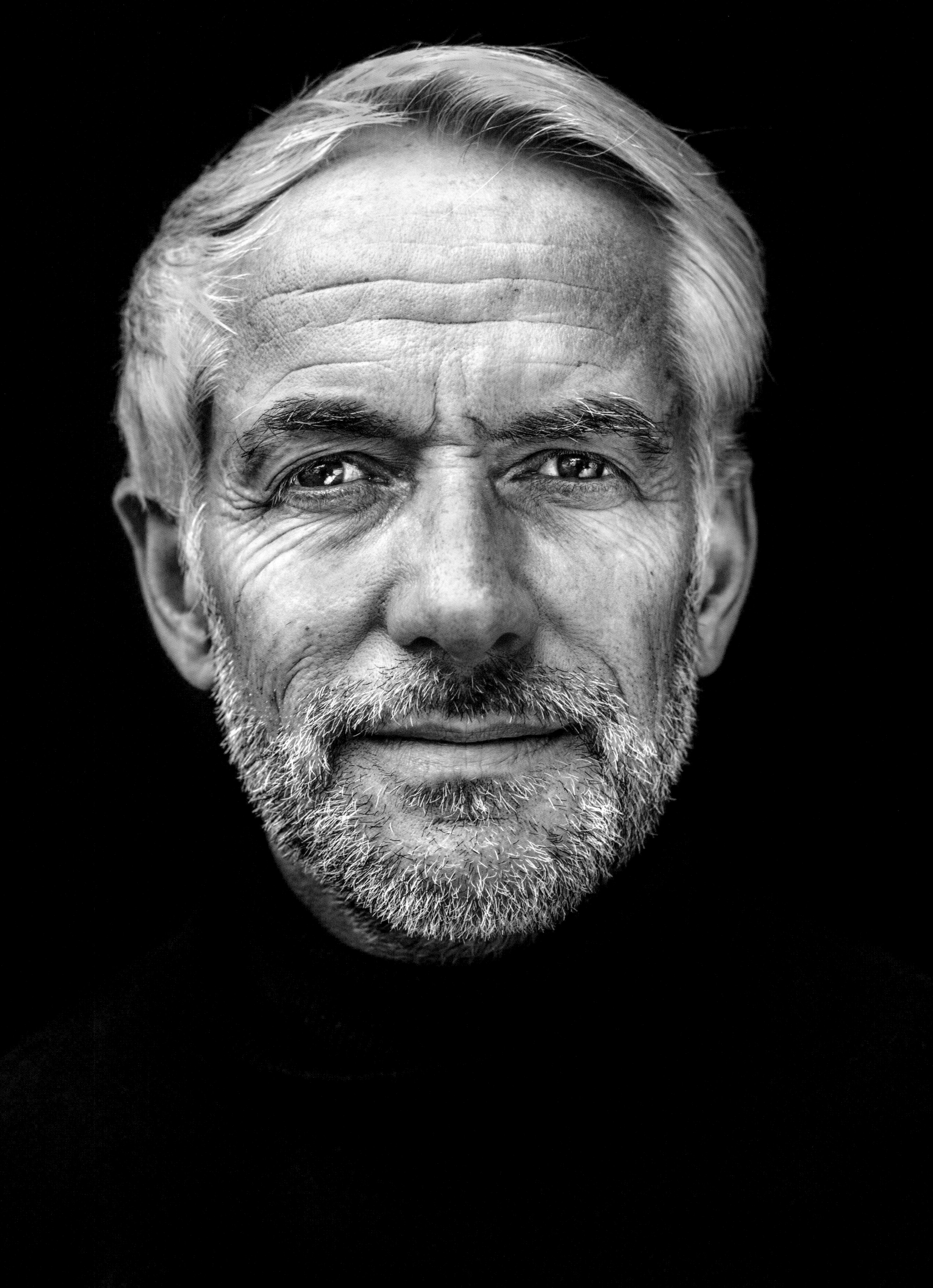

JIMMY, 56
DECEMBER 7TH, 2017, BANGKOK, THAILAND

———————————

My body is my canvas. I started getting tattoos when I was twenty, and by now most of my body is covered. Sure, it becomes an addiction, and all the colours and shapes changed my appearance. I never had a concept about what I wanted to look like but, I mean, is there such a thing as a concept for life?

People change every month. Each tattoo of mine tells a story about my life, they sketch the stories I experience and mirror my character. They are a collage of moments that influenced my life.

Four of my tattoos are especially meaningful to me: the tears underneath my eyes are dedicated to two people who were very close to me. The left tear is for my father who died from an illness when I was twelve years old. The right tear is for my best friend, who was killed ten years ago here on this street. We were on our way to a bar, he got into a little fight; suddenly shots were fired, and he was dead. Until this day I'm unable to understand how something like that can happen. To understand and accept the death of a loved one will always be challenging, I guess.

One year ago our King Bhumibol died after serving our country for nearly 70 years as a symbol for national unity. He touched me and others profoundly and so, as an homage, I tattooed 'We love the King' on my forehead. My absolute favourite tattoo is on the top of my head, and it's a peace sign, the symbol of freedom and peace, the two holy words.

Humans should be free in that which we want to do, we should be able to let our intuition spontaneously guide us, enabling us to do the things we feel like doing, the things that make us happy. We have to learn to accept others as they are, listen to others, exchange ideas, be attentive and open – that's the only way we will be able to leave in harmony with one another. That's what I wish for.

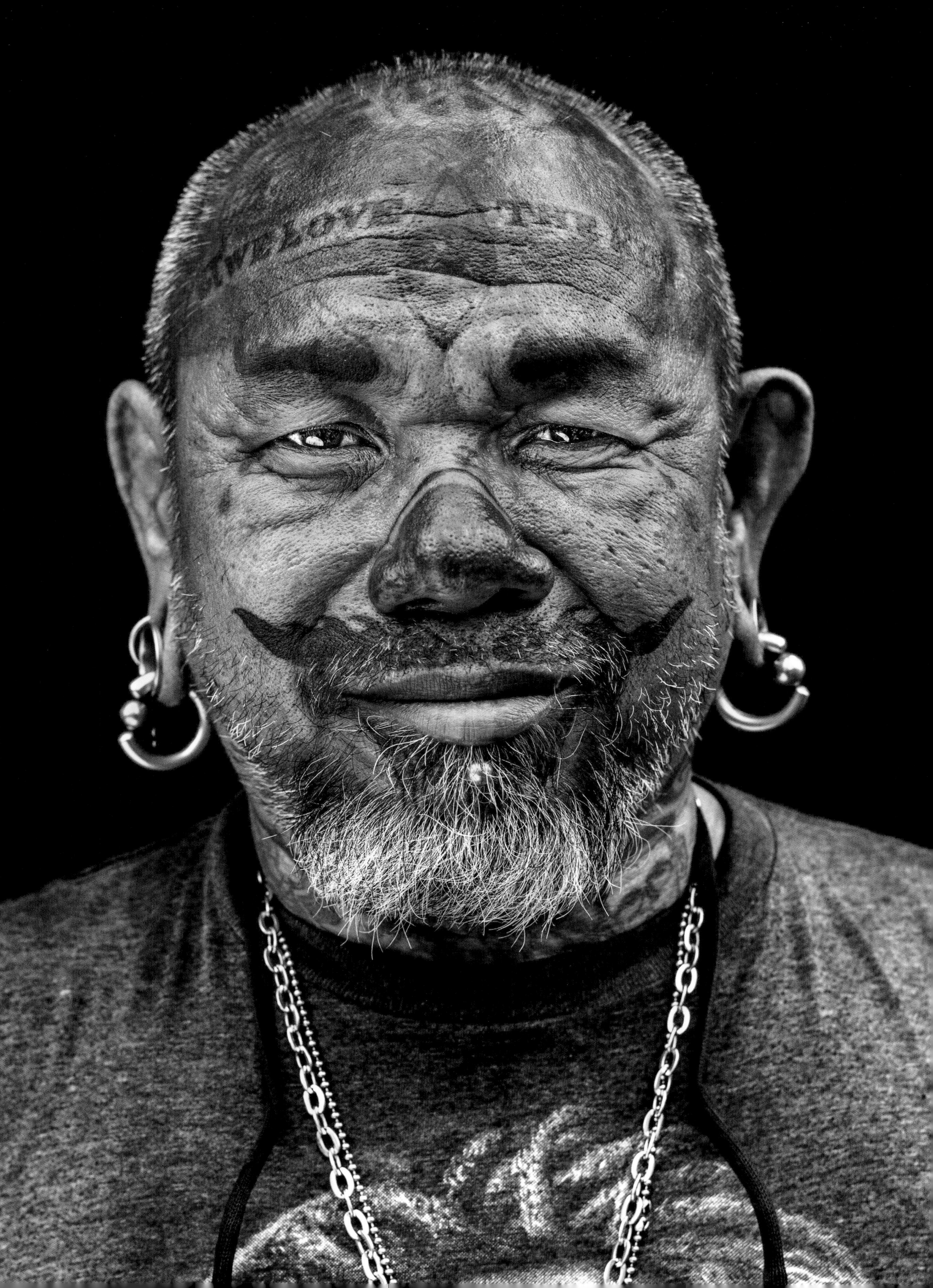

I'm not able to run fast or stretch very far as my arms and legs are too short in relation to the rest of my body. I'm 4 foot 2 – I'm growth restricted, but that doesn't mean I have to lead a limited life.

My parents found out two days after I was born. They had never heard of achondroplasia, as no-one in my family is affected by it. I was told from the beginning that all though I was different, I wasn't alone and that there were many other vertically challenged kids. My parents put stools everywhere for me, and light switches were made accessible for me with strings. My family made a significant effort to make sure that I didn't feel different. I got the same treatment as my three siblings, so I wasn't spared from being scolded when I did something wrong.

My parents explained to the kids in my kindergarten that I am smaller because my bones don't grow as fast as theirs and with that, the topic was closed. I only really understood my condition when kids around me had growth spurts and when my younger brother became stronger than me. I was overrun by others in my school because I was unable to open the door, I was slower than everyone else on field trips, and any type of sport was a challenge. At times, I lost the will to go to school as I felt helpless and didn't want to burden anyone. I didn't want any special treatment.

Puberty was the worst: all my friends started to have boyfriends but I stayed single, and I thought I'd always remain a virgin. I was terribly angry at my condition during this time and thought it was unfair, and that I was worthless and unlovable. I was emotional and aggressive, which made everything even harder. A lot of people told me that I should find a partner with achondroplasia but a functioning relationship has to fulfill more requirements than just one's height. Later on, I came across a lot of men who believed I would take anything I could get and made me cheap offers. Often they would belittle me and treat me like a little girl – that happens to this day.

A lot of people have the prejudice that 'small equals stupid'. When I started my university degree, many people asked me if that was even possible for me to do.

There are days where I want to hide and be able to disappear in a crowd of people like everyone else. I might be overlooked and accidentally run into a lot, but I always stand out. People turn to look at me, some point their fingers at me, sometimes I hear insulting comments like 'You're an eyesore'. or 'Watch out, dwarf coming our way!' This kind of thing used to make me angry, and I would fill my diary with thoughts that I kept to myself as I didn't want to burden my parents as they were my base. My friends were also there for me. They don't care how big I am, and through them, I was able to develop self-confidence.

There are days where I forget that I am different. I don't know what it feels like to be of normal height, but what I do know is that I am a woman who has good and bad days like everyone else. I have the same dreams and longings like others my age – I think about my career and if I want to have children in the future. There's a big chance that they too will have achondroplasia. I'm scared of being asked things like why would I make them go through the same fate as me. I often ask myself if I would have the necessary energy to endure the accusations.

I've been in a relationship for three years now. My boyfriend didn't have any experience with achondroplasia, but he unconditionally accepted me and took me for who I am. He made me realise that I am great just the way I am.

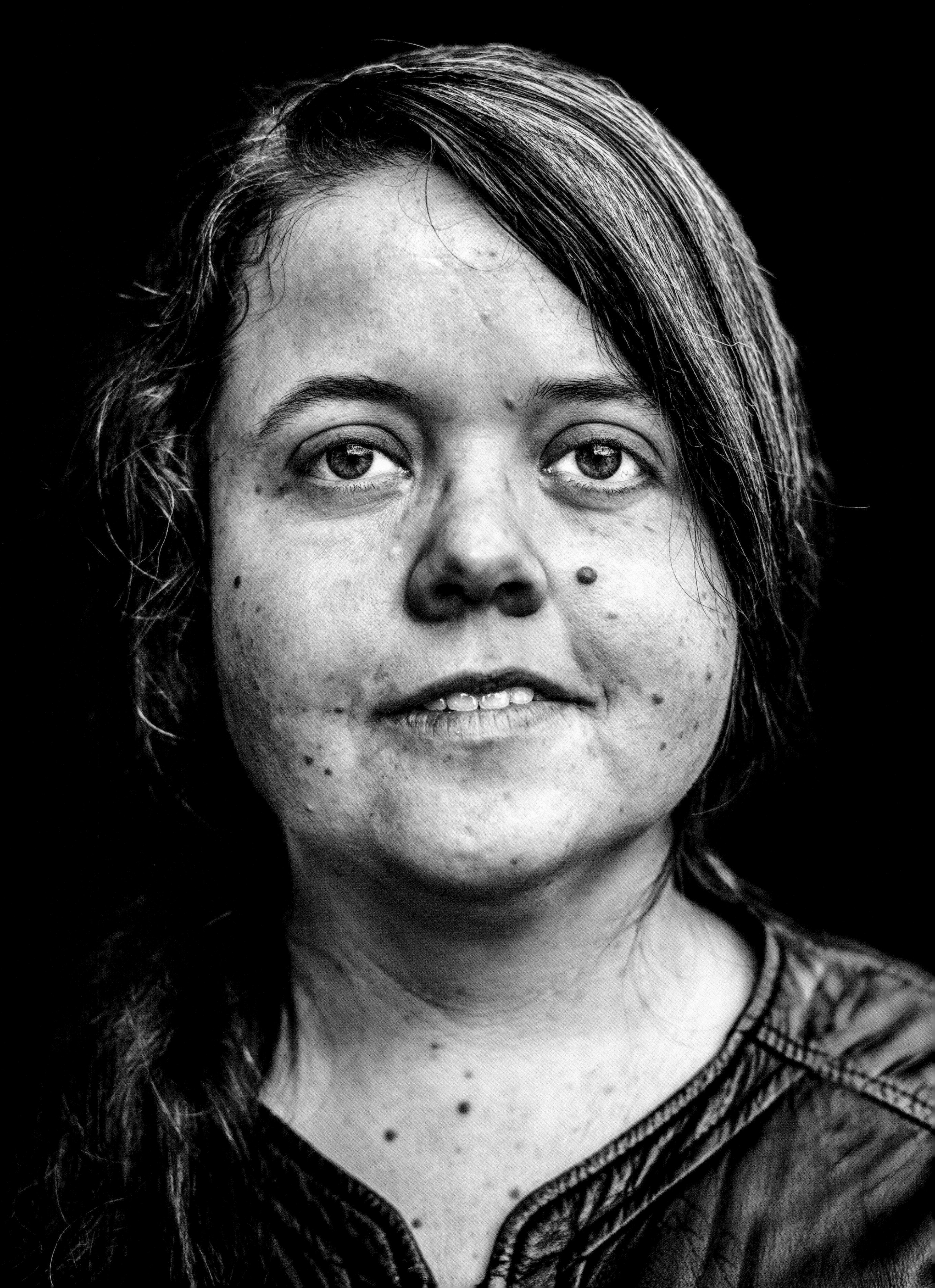

DENNIS, 64

OCTOBER 13TH, 2015, HOLLYWOOD, LOS ANGELES

Everything I own in this world is in this shopping cart right here. I've gotten used to life on the streets; I've gotten used to my situation as much as I possibly can, but no one wishes to be homeless, yet a lot of people have no other choice.

My life was good, and I was happily married until my wife was diagnosed with cancer. We used all our savings to pay for her treatment, and we even began to sell our belongings to somehow make ends meet but the cancer was too aggressive, and my wife died. I was broke and landed on the streets.

It was especially hard at the beginning. A lot of homeless people steal from one another instead of supporting each another. It's ironic, but sadly it's true. Once I got a severe lung infection and was lying in the middle of the sidewalk as it was storming and raining. I felt that my body was about to give up when a stranger walked past, handed me a blanket and a magazine that had the word 'AWAKE!' on its cover. In it, I read of a just society and pure earth, of love and harmony and reading it a wave of warmth spread through my body. This magazine, by Jehovah's Witnesses, gave me purpose and strength.

I interpreted this encounter as a sign, and so I was introduced to my God, Jehovah. He changed my life and the lives of many others. What I read about Jehovah's Witnesses gave me a good feeling, and by now I've even met some personally. They taught me how I can use my skills to do good in the world.

I collect trash from the streets and help make my surroundings clean. I raise money and donate it. Even if I can only obtain a small amount it makes a difference, they told me. I do what I can to support them. Jehovah's Witnesses provide disaster aid in Asia, Africa, America – everywhere. My donations go to Nepal.

There's a lot of suffering in this world, human and animal suffering. We treat our planet and its inhabitants without care. I say to everyone: if you collect trash then pick up two pieces and don't immediately throw another three pieces on the ground. Everyone is able to make a contribution, and together we're capable of change.

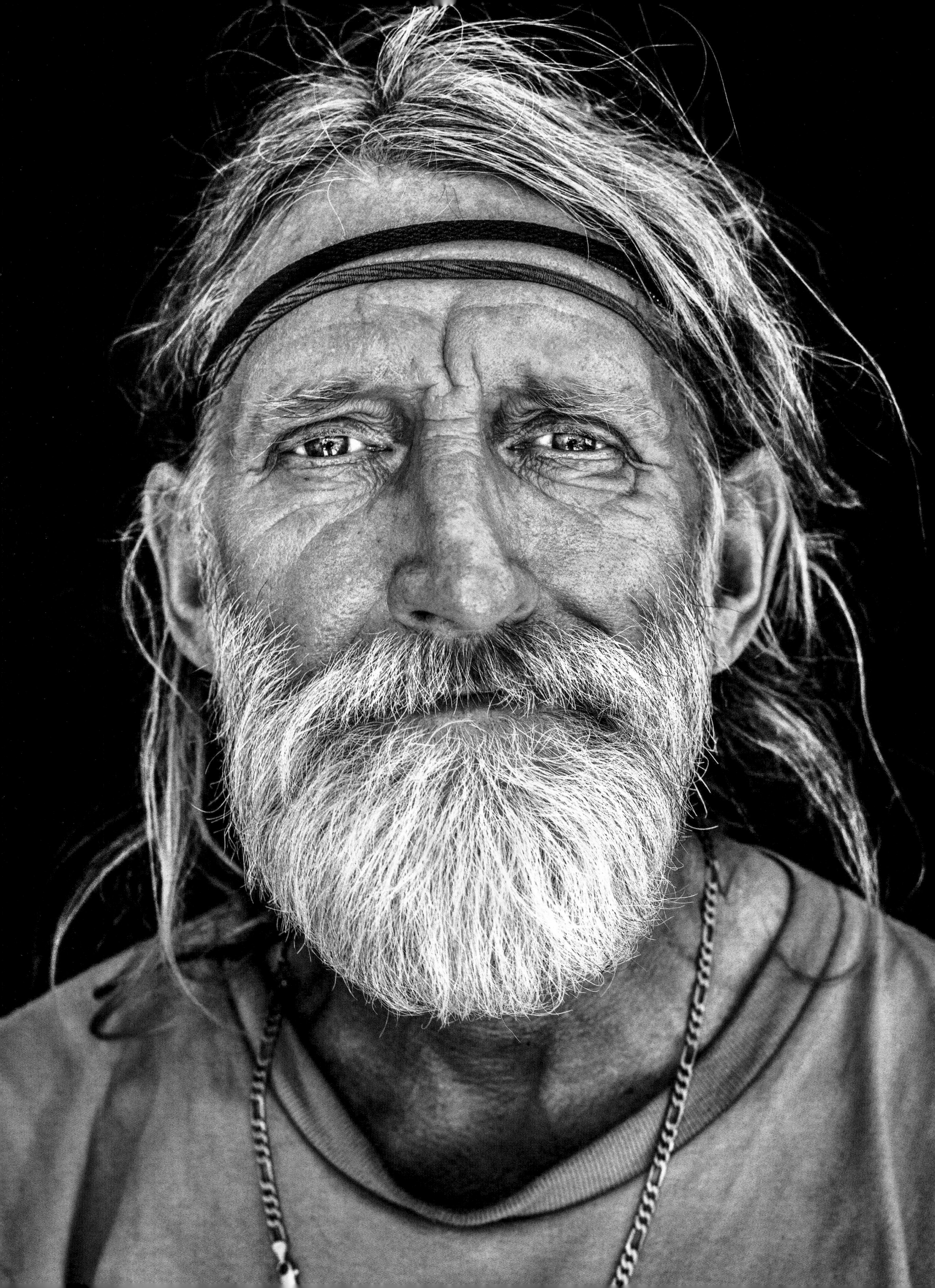

STEPHEN, 42
APRIL 20TH, 2014, MANHATTAN, NEW YORK

____

Elvis Presley was the best. He had a massive influence on my life. Inspired by his music, I travelled to Graceland when I was 30 and decided to step into the footprints of the rock'n'roll king.

What I saw and discovered in Graceland brought me to tears. Elvis was an unbelievable artist and philanthropist. His engagement for the deprived was huge: he paid off the debts of strangers, bought a family a whole house after their father died in a war and purchased a handicapped man a wheelchair. I aspired to be just as generous, socially engaged and interested in the greater good as my role model had been.

I lived in Las Vegas for a few months, and every morning I would pass by two homeless men collecting money for food, the sight of which pained me. I never understood why wealth is distributed so unfairly, creating a deep divide between the rich and the poor. I brought them food almost every day as I believed that everyone deserves a second chance to get their life in order. Elvis always said that we all come from the same source and when we disregard others, we disregard a part of ourselves. I became friends with the two homeless guys, and I took them with me to New York when I left Las Vegas. I let them stay with me until they were able to afford their own place – that was the deal. I helped them get a job and took their matters into my hands. I earned money as an Elvis double on Times Square and was also struggling to make ends meet, but making others happy was my absolute priority.

After some time I noticed that my goodwill was being abused as both my friends were lying to me and stealing money to buy drugs. I was so naive and disappointed! I repeated the same mistake several more times trying to help others, but every time I was manipulated and used. Everyone just wanted to profit off of me, and at some point, I had had enough.

People still ask me if they can stay at my place, but I tell them that their problems aren't mine even though this doesn't correspond to my beliefs. I feel lonely a lot and would like someone to live with, but I'm no longer willing to be deceived. I live in a hotel now, but I still dress and move like Elvis on Times Square in an attempt to spread good vibes, yet I'm no longer as good-natured as I used to be. I'm no real Elvis.

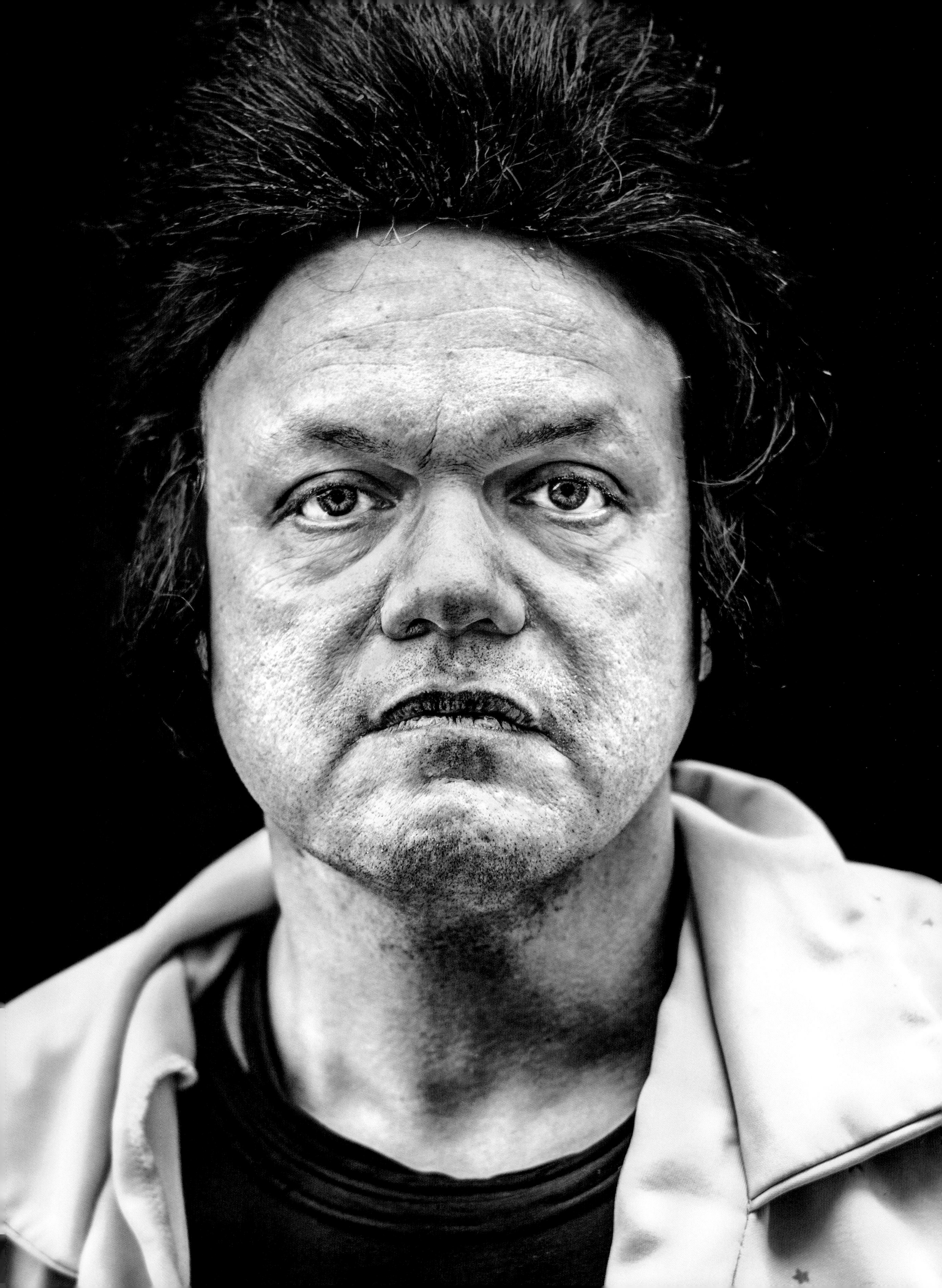

REGULA, 53

FEBRUARY 2ND, 2018, BERN, SWITZERLAND

I was the only one wearing glasses at school, my bike had a rearview mirror, and I had to visit an eye specialist often; but other than that, I was like everyone else.

While my brother would laugh outrageously while watching television, I had a hard time understanding what was happening, and if I accidentally knocked a glass over because a lack of contrast made it hard for me to see, he belittled me for being clumsy.

It got worse when I started going to school; I could hardly read what was written on the board, so I had to be very concentrated and had to learn everything by heart. I would memorise the numbers of the different coloured pens in art class – number 160 blue, 210 green. Geography class was especially hard as I couldn't differentiate climate zones and bodies of water. When I told my teacher, he just said: 'Girls don't get colour blindness!'

I was always the last one to be picked for a team in PE, and I would often get balls thrown at my head because I was unable to see them coming with my limited field of vision. Instead of playing I became the referee for volleyball games in class as I had told my teacher about my limitations. But it was impossible for me to see the ball from a distance, and so I had to count points according to the cheers I heard.

My teachers never noticed how bad my vision was. They called me a minimalist and my fellow students said I was clumsy. I had developed a lot of strategies to not stand out. I became the class clown to downplay my visual impairment, and outside of school, I feigned disinterest to keep away from activities. When my friends started going to parties, I pretended that I preferred staying at home to read. Clubs were too dark and loud for me to orientate myself. I often felt lonely and lost. And my family? They didn't notice anything.

I was eighteen years old when I was diagnosed with RP – retinal degeneration that can lead to blindness. I gave birth to my son six years later, and thankfully he was an easygoing infant. Seeing so little was strenuous, and going outside became more and more difficult, yet I kept riding my bike with my son sitting in the baby seat and sometimes he would yell: 'Mom, you can't go there!' I wasn't able to see the street signs.

My field of vision kept shrinking and my ability to see worsened. I could only see very little when my daughter was born four years later. I was a single mom and forced to learn a lot of new things: braille, using a white cane and using a computer with an audio function. At some point, Cleo, my guide dog, joined the family. I lost my eyesight at 30.

The worst thing was that I hadn't told anyone just how impaired I was for a long time. I couldn't and didn't want to admit this to myself and was scared of losing my independence. As absurd as it may sound, it was a sort of relief to completely lose my eyesight, as it was something final and clear and more comfortable to deal with than an unclear situation.

What I see is hard to describe. It's not just black but comparable to a grey, dense fog. I had to learn to just do one thing at a time, live with a lot of structure, not lose my cool in unpredictable situations, take the time I need and to be happy about the small things in life. The most important thing of all: I have learned to accept help and to use humour to tackle difficulties. People are helpful, yet I can't choose who I want to speak to. I've asked a ticket machine for help in the past.

I met Andreas, my partner, when I was forty. I immediately felt drawn to his deep voice. We often ride a tandem bike through nature. Once he explained to me that we were passing by a field of sunflowers. I turned to the right and said: 'Wow, how beautiful!' The field, though, was to our left. My imaginative powers enable me to 'see'. To know what something really looks like can be sobering, like when Andreas and I rode through Thailand on a tandem and I imagined the place to be tropical, idyllic and full of blossoming flowers but he said it was actually a forest like we have at home; just full of metal huts, a lot of trash, and poverty.

Sometimes I am angry or sad especially in the summer when I can't just go swimming in a lake or take a spontaneous walk alone. If I were granted the wish to see something once again, I would ask to see my kids as I only see them as children in my mind's eye.

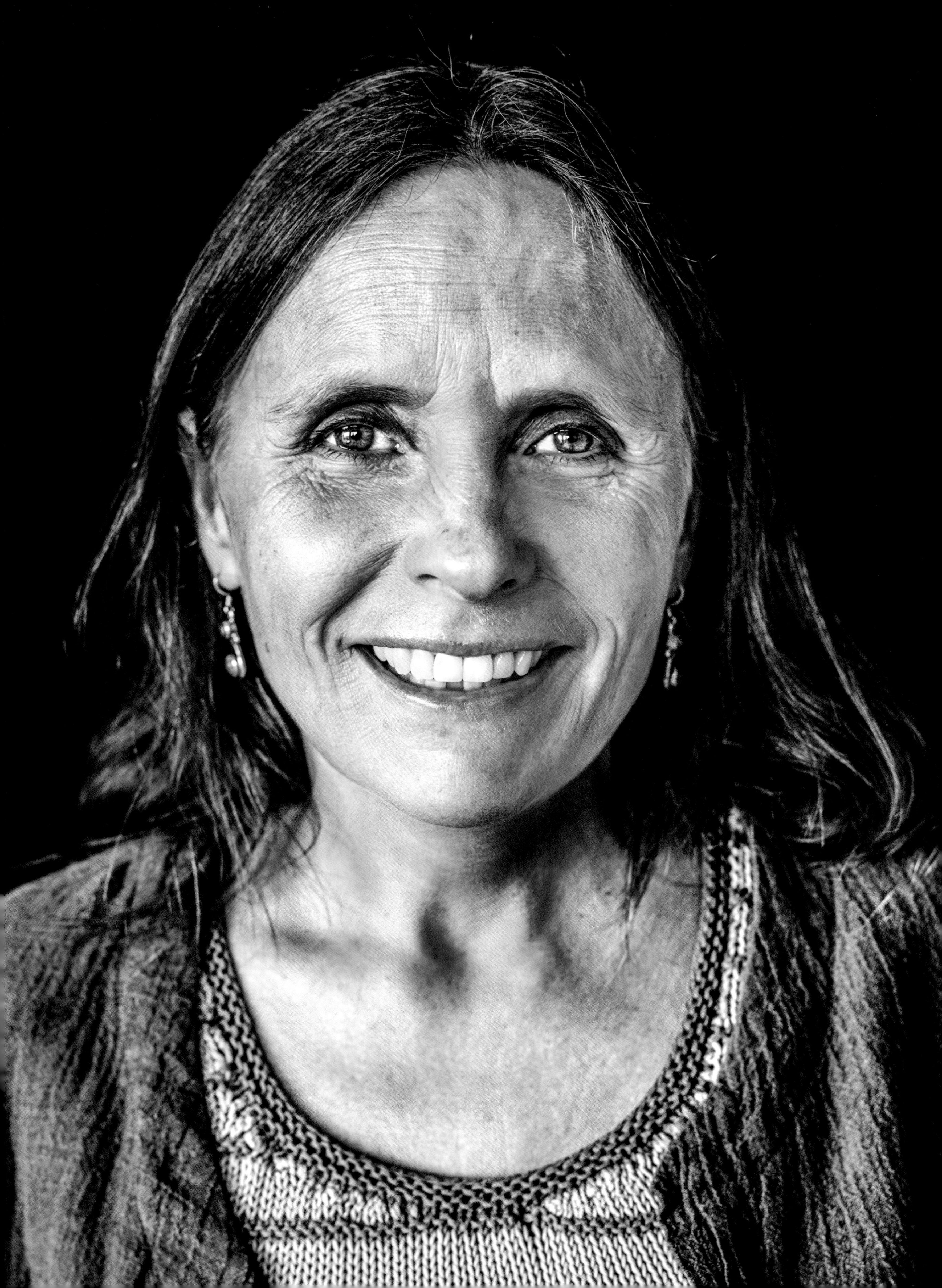

If my childhood were a movie, alcoholism would be the setting, the parents the main protagonists, and I would be an extra.

It was rare for my parents to be sober. They continually shouted at one another, threw plates through the house, got physical and degraded each other and eventually me as well.

I notice how my heart starts racing and my mouth goes dry when I speak about it, even after all these years. This suppressed anger is still with me, and it's hard for me to talk about this time in my life. The most important thing for my parents was never to have an empty liquor cabinet. They didn't care if their behaviour would give me a lifelong trauma. Each drop they consumed took a part of their personality until there was nothing left of it. In the best case scenario, they would react to about half of the things I tried communicating with them, knowing that they would remember nothing the next day.

They went out at night and left me home alone, not caring how scared I was. I hid underneath my blanket until I heard their house keys slam on the table and only then could I finally fall asleep. I was dependent on myself throughout my entire childhood and had to teach myself everything. I had no one to show me what was right or wrong. School only teaches you the bare minimum; it doesn't prepare you for life at all.

I left home at eighteen. It was incredibly challenging for me to trust others and to let go. I was a lone wolf. I didn't have a girlfriend until I was 45 years old. She was the first person I ever trusted, and after five years of being together, I bought an engagement ring. When I proposed she told me that she was leaving me as she needed a wealthier and a more educated partner.

My dream of starting a family imploded, and I began to drink mimicking my parent's behaviour. I drank so much that I was fired, eventually losing my home.

I'm homeless now, and those passing me ignore me. People look away because it's an emotional strain for them to see me. I wanted nothing more than to start my own family. I've stopped drinking now, but while I am living on the streets, my dream won't come true; for what woman would be interested in a homeless man?

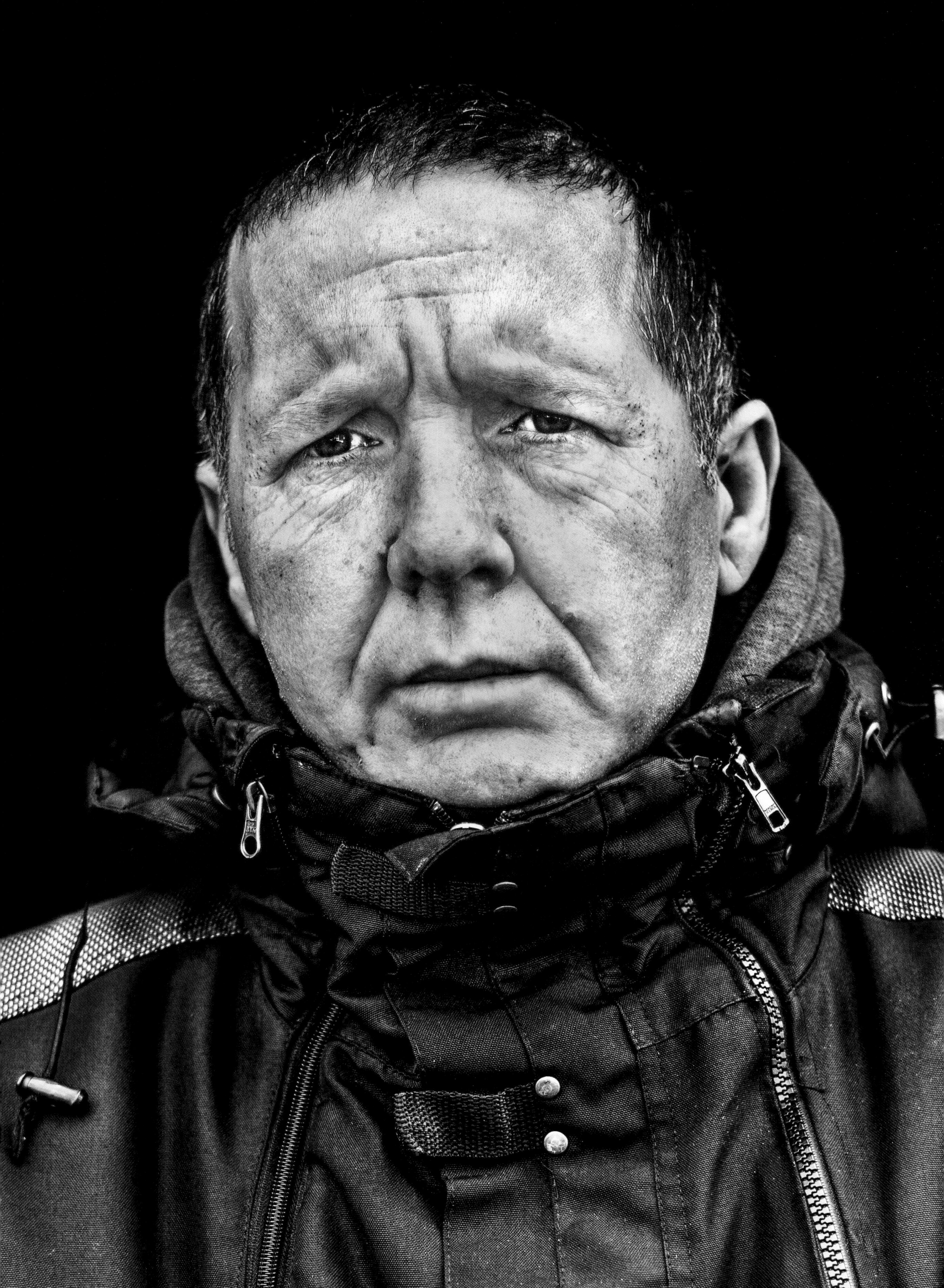

ELISABETH, 25
NOVEMBER 13TH, 2017, JAKOBSBAD, SWITZERLAND

Even as a child, I would share my secrets, worries, and fears with Jesus. I was Angela – shy, withdrawn yet still open towards others and the world. I grew up close to Hannover and had a very sheltered upbringing. My mother would read Bible verses out loud to my sister and me, but she had no idea that I would end up living in a convent one day.

I had a Christian upbringing, but could choose how often I wanted to visit the church. Sometimes I hardly went, other times I went very often. As time went on, I felt more and more how my belief in God strengthened me. A lot of my friends weren't religious, and when they went partying on the weekends, I mostly chose to stay at home. I wanted to wake up early, enjoy the morning atmosphere, take photos and get in touch with Jesus. This didn't make me an outsider though.

When I was younger, I had the dream to become a baby nurse as I loved kids. My father thought I could make a good cop or doctor, but as time went on thoughts of one day moving into a cloister became more prevalent. I was eighteen years old and almost done with school when I found the convent 'Leiden Christi' in Jakobsbad over the internet and got in touch.

A lot of my classmates made fun of me when they found out, but I didn't care at all, as I knew what I wanted and stood by what I felt. I was more worried what the nuns would say about an eighteen-year-old joining their cloister but they gave me a positive answer, and this really surprised me. At first, I had planned to only go for one year to try it out. My father drove me to Switzerland, ten hours away from my home, and shortly before we arrived he said that he knew I would stay there, he could just feel it. I didn't know the place or the nuns, but when I first laid my eyes on the convent, I was sure that I had finally arrived home.

My relationship to the sisters was amicable and natural from the beginning. When conflicts arose, we spoke openly about them and tried to help one another. The age gap is big, but it wasn't a problem for me. What I had to get used to though was the silence. I liked the daily routine from the start as everything, the meals and the seven daily prayer sessions, were clearly structured. My relationship with Jesus became ever more personal and intimate. He knows where my strengths lie, what I can do and what I should stop doing. He is there when I need him.

Life in the cloisters is easy. The clothes are simple. When I was younger, I liked dressing up – girly with a lot of lace and high heels, but the habit makes it clear where I belong, and I like that. I wear my lovely dresses underneath, for myself. I also chose a new name for myself to symbolise this new stage of life: Elisabeth. I flourished as Elisabeth, and I feel free. My family though still calls me Angela. They hoped that I would return; especially my sister, who is entirely different than I am. She didn't understand how I could have possibly given up my old life, but today she understands that I am happy here.

I've been here for five years, and a few months ago I took my vows to fully commit to Jesus. It's comparable to the bond of matrimony. I said 'yes' to Jesus and to the cloister.

A lot of people ask me how I can be so sure of wanting to live a life without a partner or children and perhaps, I would have chosen to be in a relationship if I had met someone before going to the cloister, but I had never had the urge. I am convinced of the path I am on and trust where it's taking me, but I am aware that, just like in any marriage, life can also get difficult in the cloister. Happiness is never a guarantee. In case I feel unsatisfied with my life there one day, I'll have to see how to deal with it. Life is full of challenges, and you can accept them and work on yourself.

I hope that in the future, I can give people what they are often missing, I want to provide them with peace, thoughtfulness, and love. A lot of people are blind towards each other and don't listen. They forget to regard one another and to be loving. Humans are all connected at the end of the day. In my eyes, a Christian can be with a Muslim because what does it really matter? Why can't we accept one another and treat each other with respect? Our time on earth is limited; love doesn't cost a thing but gratifies us immensely. To me, Jesus is the embodiment of love, and so he's my role model.

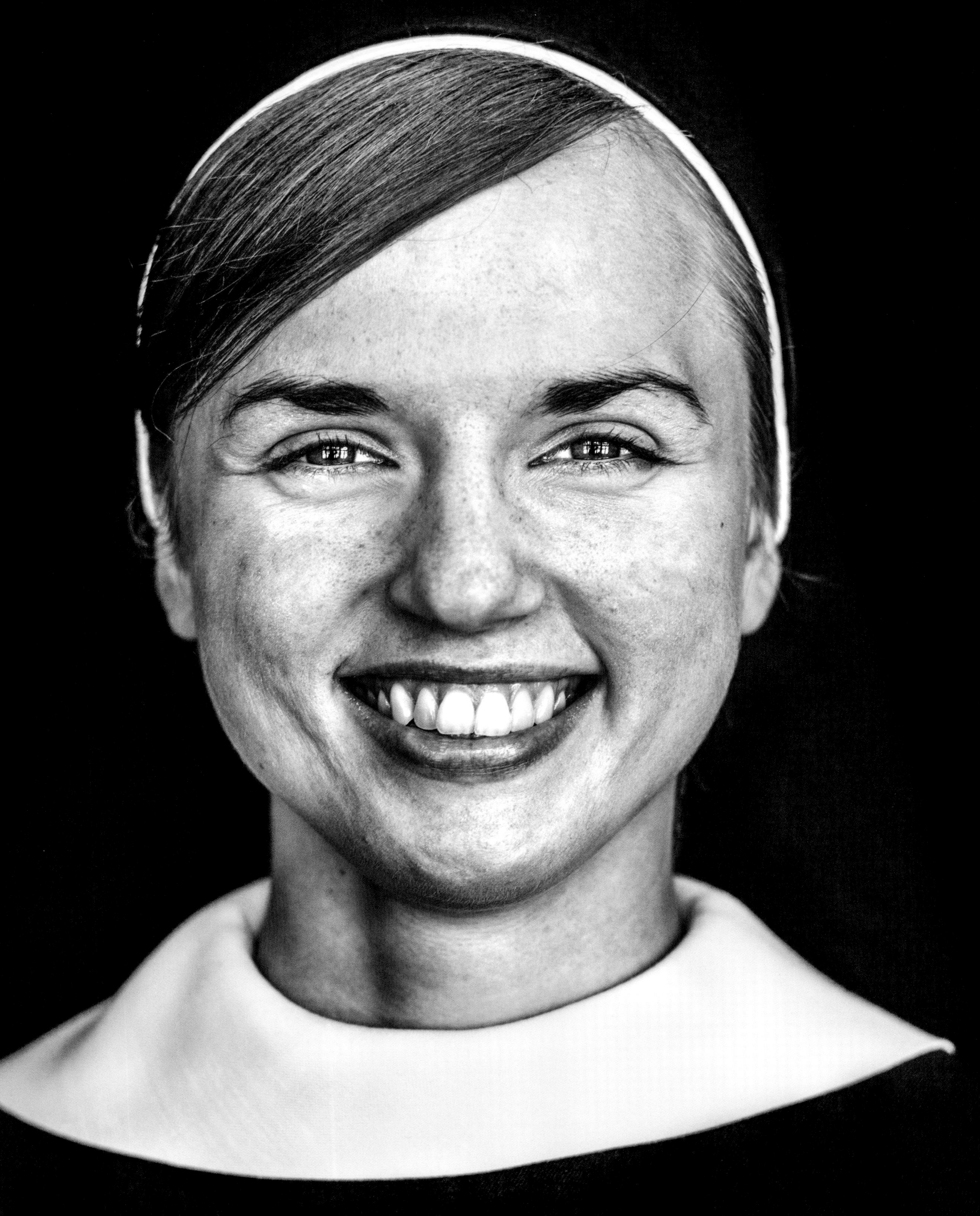

ROGER, 40
OCTOBER 25TH, 2015, WESTWOOD, LOS ANGELES

Finally self-employed!

This decision was the most significant turning point in my life. I'm a piercer and am so passionate about this work as, to me, body piercings are more than just body art or a craft – they can be an expression of a way of life. More and more people have piercings, and so it's important to perfect this craft. Driven by the idea to improve the reputation of the piercing studio I was working for, I wanted to offer courses. I presented my employer with innovative plans, but I was never taken seriously. At some point, I realised that I had to go my own way if I wanted to express myself, so I quit. No-one found out about my plans to open my own studio. I tried to come up with something entirely different, and I wanted to do it from scratch and on my own.

I opened my own studio called 'Ancient Adornments' three years ago. In the beginning, I hardly had any customers, which meant hardly any income. I had existential fears and was scared I'd lose everything I owned. Life in California is expensive, and to make it here is hard. I thought of quitting and to take the easy path, but my family supported me and motivated me to believe in myself, stay on it and put up a fight. I did, and it was worth it.

I have to take care of my family and make sure I can pay my employees, and that's a lot of responsibility that often times does my head in because there's never a guarantee I'll have customers on a daily basis. Piercings are a luxury item, not something essential.

And yet, the wish to become my own boss came true. I can come and go as I please and I can realise the ideas that come into my head. These days I give courses in my studio and make my own jewellry. I have all the freedom in the world, and it feels incredible. The most beautiful thing about it is: I learned the value of family, I experienced what it's like to have them stand behind me and support me, and that's more important than all the fame and money in the world.

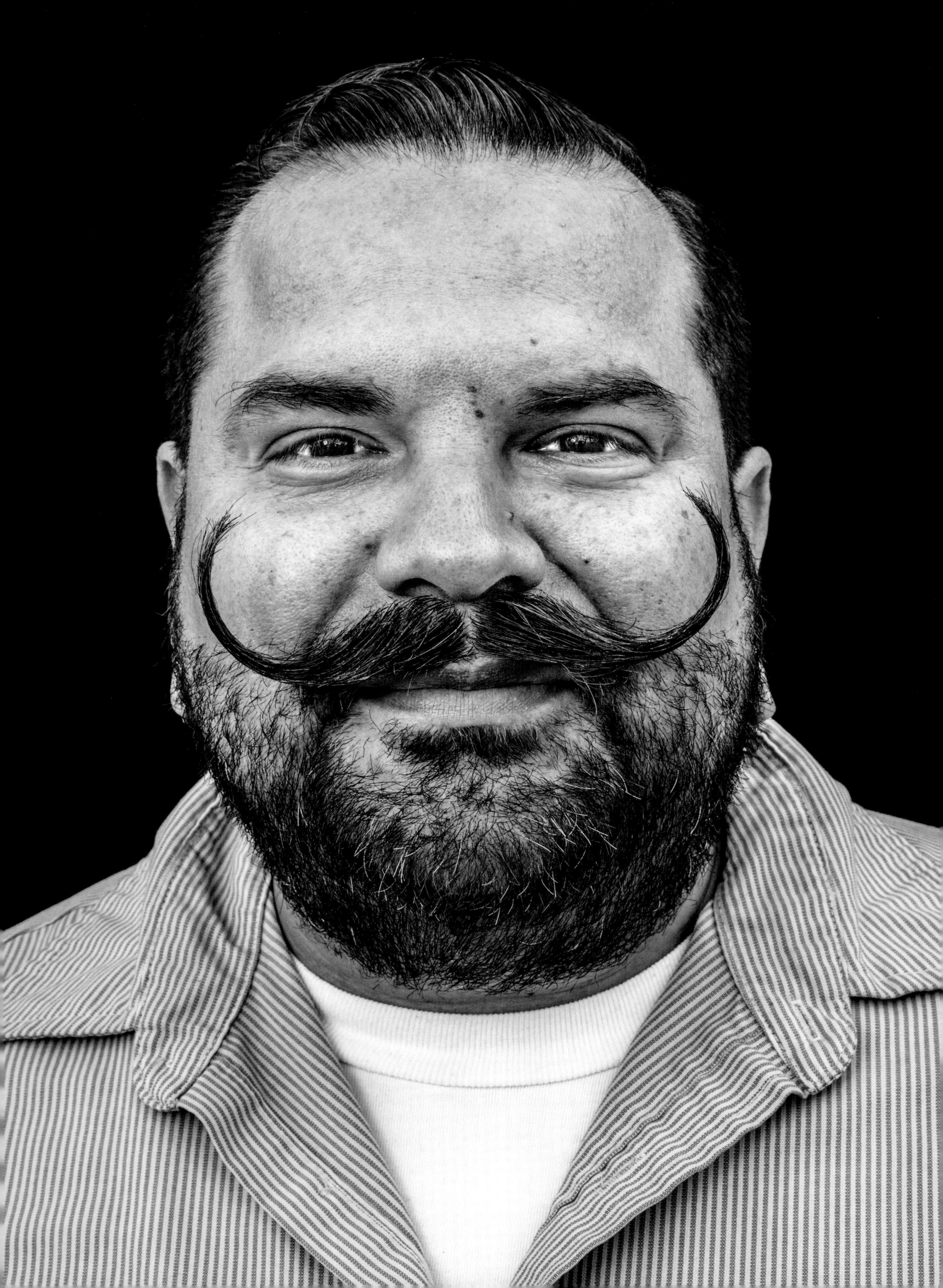

GABRIEL, 58
NOVEMBER 5ᵀᴴ, 2015, WILLOQ, PERU

Here in Willoq, we live in our own world that basically ends at the last house in our little Andes village. We speak Quechua, an indigenous language and live by following old traditions. Men wear red ponchos, wool hats, flannel pants, and sandals. Women wear traditional clothes, red knitted jackets with white buttons and headdresses with chin straps. The weather conditions are pretty rough here, and yet our houses are only covered by straw or metal sheets. Only very few of us have electricity, and there's only one telephone in our village.
This mountain landscape used to resemble a desert. The land was dry and unused. The inhabitants of Willoq mostly ate beans and potatoes. Most people here are poor, and a lot of them are unhappy, yet they weren't interested in improvements, not even when I came up with an idea to cultivate the land to plant food. I know how to plant, grow and harvest vegetables as I learned it in school.
Only very few people in Willoq get the chance to go to school as money is lacking, and the school is too far away. I was lucky enough because my parents bequeathed me with a small fortune. With what was left of it, I wanted to cultivate the fields to change life here but to convince the inhabitants of Willoq that I was trying to help them with my means and knowledge took a long time, as the people here are loners.
Two years ago I was voted to become the president of the village, and that gave me the chance to realise my project to enhance agriculture here. I bought seeds and cultivated the fields with potatoes, beans, corn, quinoa, and peas. Our landscape changed more and more and with it the people – now they are slowly waking up and are realising that life has more to offer when you seize opportunities. This is the only way we can leave something meaningful behind for our descendants.

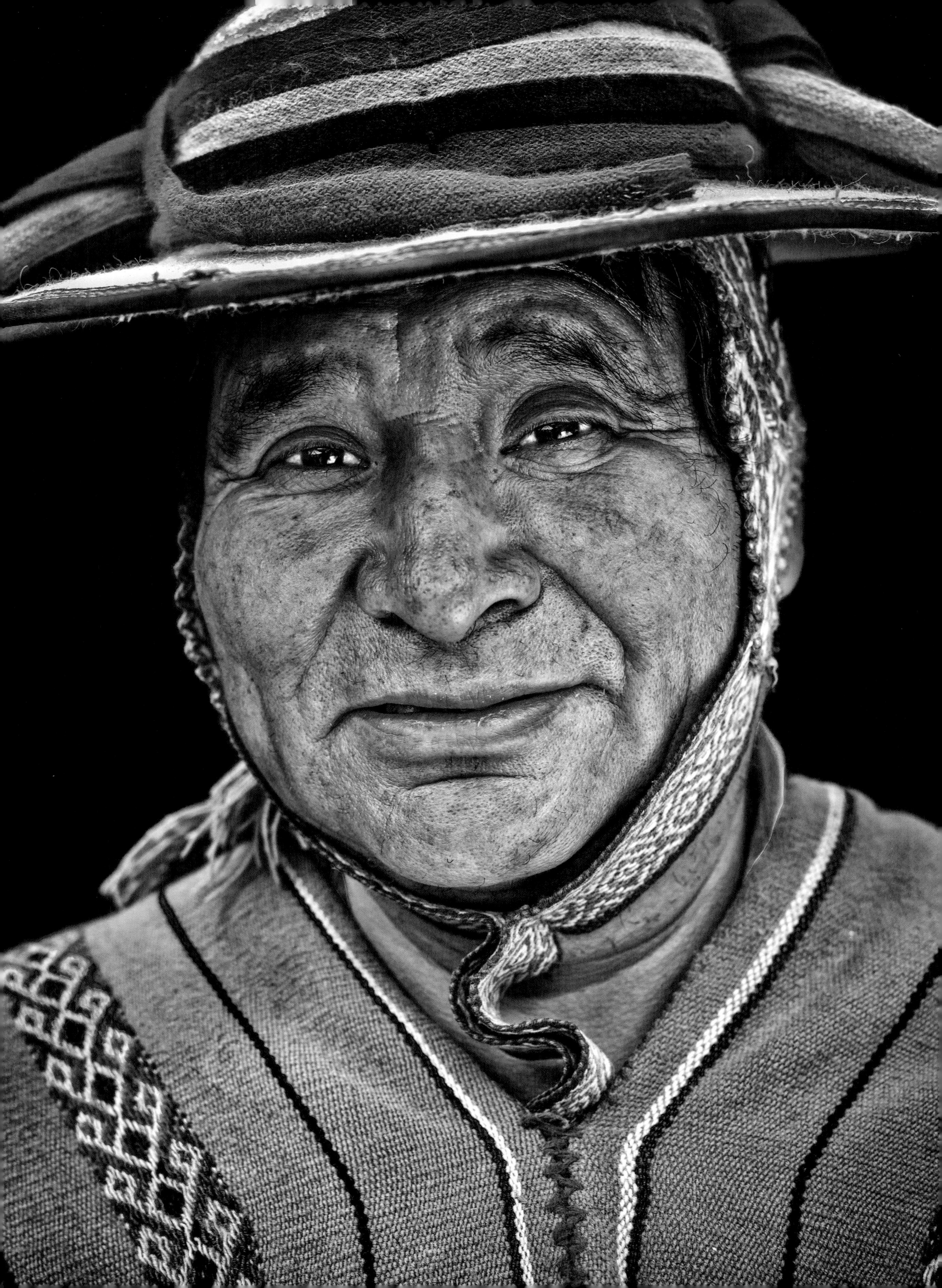

CINDY, 30
FEBRUARY 23RD, 2015, ZURICH, SWITZERLAND

I'm 5 foot 8, weigh 174 pounds and have 11% body fat. Within seven years, I transformed from a delicate woman into a bodybuilder.

I started doing gymnastics when I was four years old, then began doing rhythmic gymnastics. My father, an extremely disciplined and fanatical athlete, taught me to push past my boundaries. My mother went to my competitions and motivated me to improve. She provided me with healthy meals and made sure I had everything I need.

My ambition to be a star athlete was big, and it was my goal to participate in international competitions. But everything was over before it could start, as an injury forced me to quit sports for one year when I was sixteen years old and more injuries followed, ending my career. I was devastated.

To grow up with high-performance sport and having to suddenly do without, was hard. I couldn't live without doing some sort of sport, so I took Sundays to train with my father – bike, jog, swim or hike. I needed a new challenge at some point, and my curiosity pulled me into a gym.

I was fascinated by the world in there from the beginning – the big dumbbells, the intense smells, the people getting their bodies to sweat. At first, I trained pretty lightly. I was modelling and was keeping myself skinny. I was 20 when I won second place in the 'Miss Zurich' competition. Being skinny became a requirement, and I was never happy with that. I found satisfaction in weight training. It fascinated me to learn how

I had to train my body for it to become stronger and what I had to eat to gain strength. I was excited to learn how to create the perfect balance between physical exertion and recovery to achieve the ideal performance increase.

My training got more intense and my will stronger. With each improvement I experienced, I felt more motivated to go a step further. Each practice made me feel fantastic. I was 22 when I decided to dedicate myself to weight training without any compromises. I worked on a training schedule, changed my diet and did all this on my own.

Most people in my life didn't understand my change of lifestyle, but I no longer wanted to be controlled by others just to meet their expectations.

I like to eat at restaurants, but I also have a clear schedule that tells me when I have to eat proteins and carbs. I love music, but I don't yearn to go out clubbing as I'd rather go to bed early and go training on Sundays. My interests are extreme, but that's my way of enjoying life.

I am aware of my ability to polarise others. I hear people whispering on the streets and see degrading looks coming my way. A lot of people judge the way I lead my life, but these days my life is more structured and healthier than it ever was.

I get booked as a model from all agencies all over the world, but no-one tells me to lose weight now. I feel more beautiful and stronger than I did ten years ago, and the best thing is that I wake up every day full of joy and motivation.

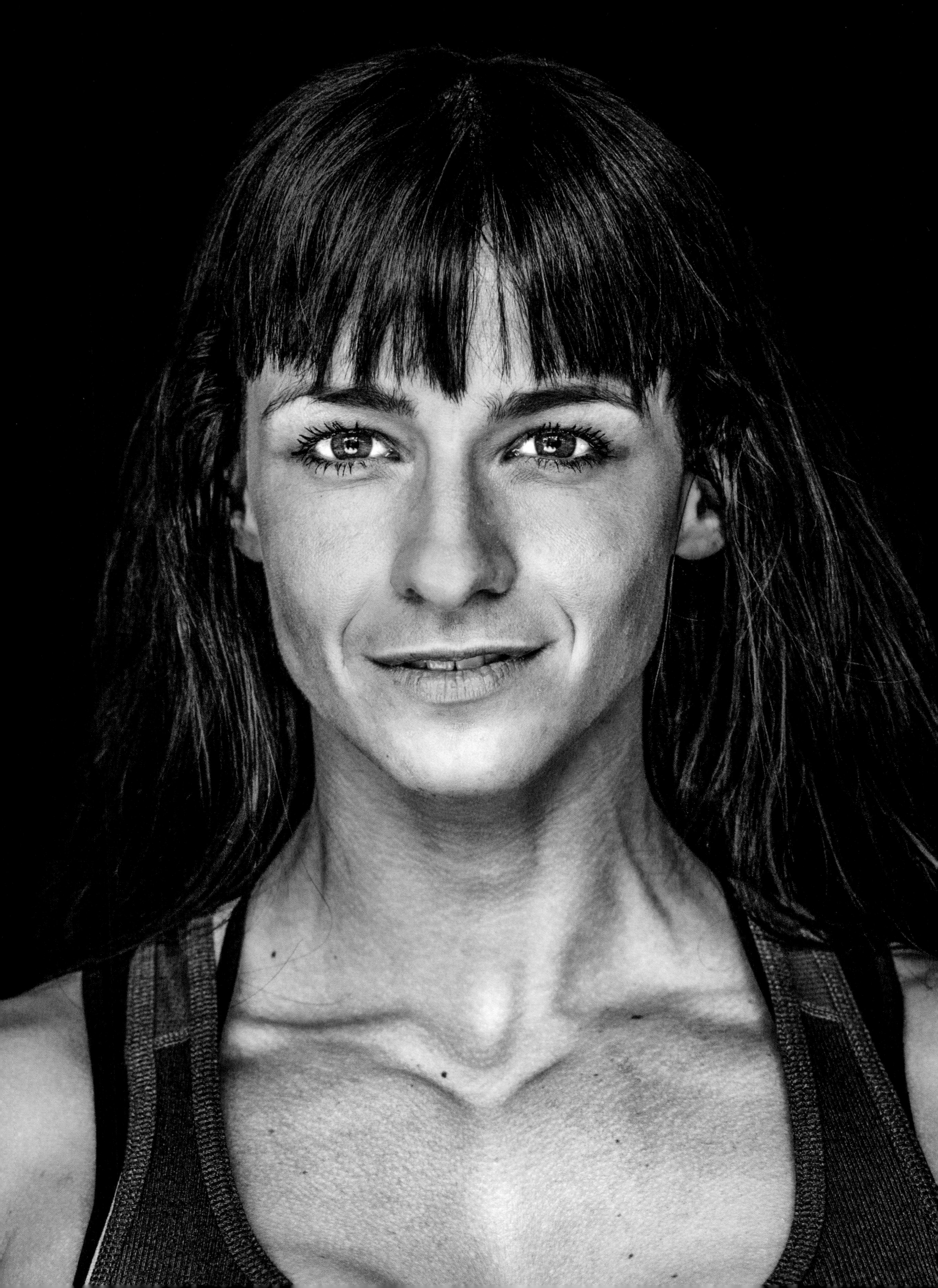

JAFET, 29
NOVEMBER 29TH, 2015, PANAMA CITY

Panama is a rich country but there's a high level of poverty, and without a job, you're forced to find other ways to survive. I wanted security and solidarity, so I joined the Ciudad de Dios when I was fourteen years old.

The name references a famous street gang in Rio de Janeiro. The group made me feel strong. Most of its members were homeless and alone, but with the gang, we felt a sense of togetherness. We fought together and for one another but daily life was hard: we stole, dealt drugs, resorted to violence to gain street credibility and killed other gang members to keep them off our territory. Bloody conflicts, rivalries, acts of revenge against traitors and even death were always right there next to us. Eighteen gang members died on the streets of Casco Viejo – they had been my brothers, my family.

Eventually, I became the most notorious drug dealer in our area and the head of the gang. I felt important as the leader, and everyone on the streets knew me. I had a lot of respect. At some point, the police began to arrest gang members even if they had no real evidence against them. I realised that my life would either end prematurely in a coffin or in a jail cell. I did end up in jail, for eleven years, and those were the most terrible years of my life. Members of all gangs met behind bars, and as the former leader, I was the centre of attention.

Most members of Ciudad de Dios were dead when I got out of jail, and I decided to lead a normal life but, as an ex-gang member, I would surely have been killed as an unaffiliated man. Gangs never forget.

I found a way out through God, as the Lord stands over everything and everyone in Panama. You don't touch the property of God here, and so I became a devout Christian and was able to move around relatively freely. The deeper I got into Christianity, the more conscious I became of the crimes I had committed. A lot of what I had done was wrong. I regret many things but when I look back on my youth I also see the hopelessness I had to deal with. I see a desperate boy who was just looking for some stability. Our government makes me sad as they don't lend a helping hand to the poor, driving kids towards criminality.

I lead a quiet and decent life these days with my wife and twin daughters. Now I'm the head of this gang, and have the responsibility to create a safe home.

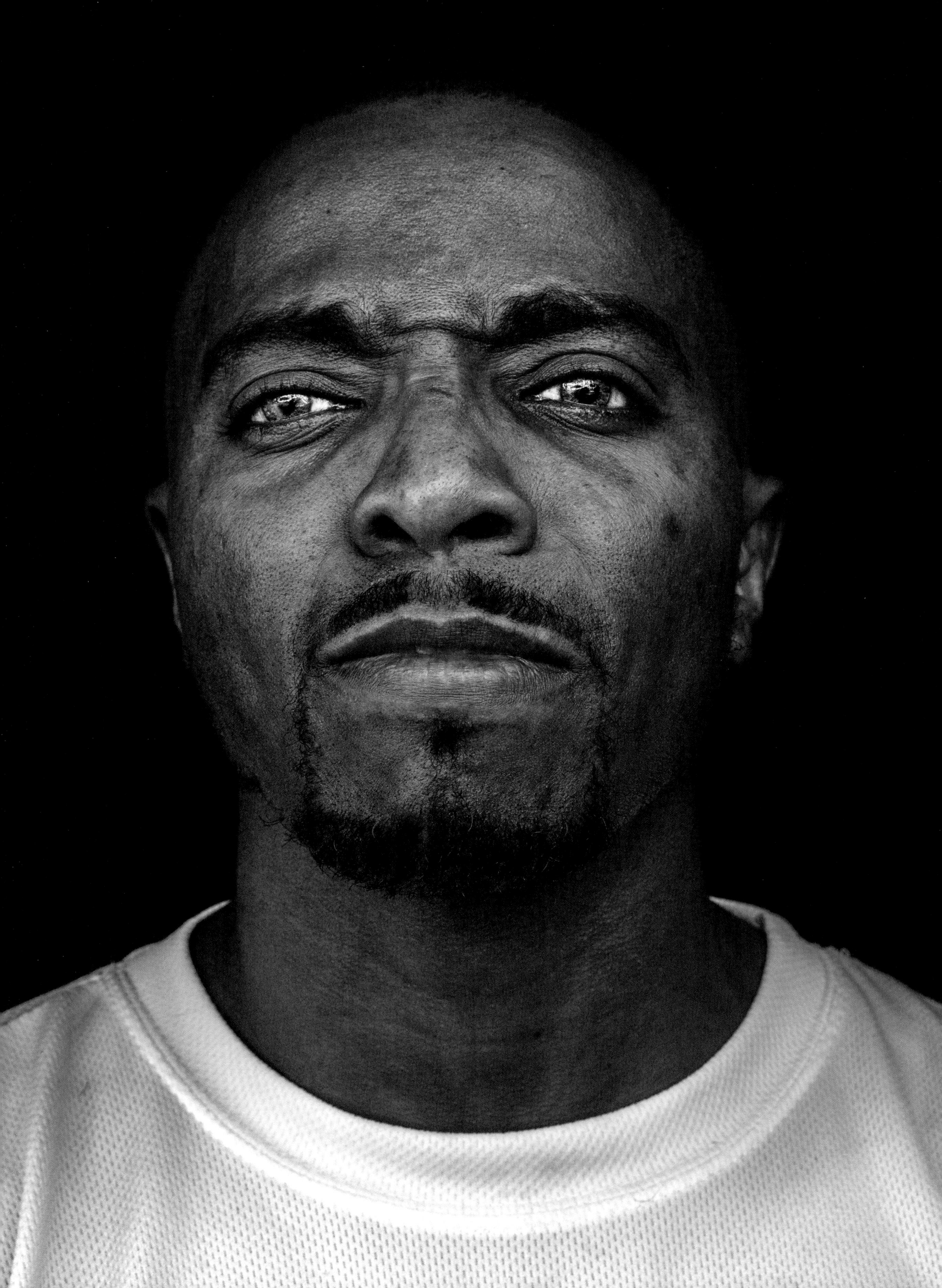

HANS, 84
FEBRUARY 4TH, 2015, DOTTIKON, SWITZERLAND

'The Russians are coming!' It was late January 1945 when the NS district manager close of Breslau gave eviction orders. The Red Army was marching across Poland to Silesia. Women and children had to leave their homes immediately, and so many fled towards the West.

Up until then, I had lived with my parents and seven siblings on a farm in Schmolz by Breslau, the capital of Silesia that was then part of Germany's empire. I was fourteen years old, one year too young for the military service. My four older brothers and my father had to join the 'Volkssturm', the German national militia of the last months of the war. They had to fight against the Russians and defend Germany's territory. I didn't know then that I would never see my older brothers again. My two younger brothers, my mother and I had no time to lose – we harnessed two horses to a wagon, filled it with food and one suitcase with the most important things, everything else we had to leave behind. Five families had to always share one wagon.

1945 was a harsh winter, and though there were snow and ice, we had to walk by foot. We walked without a goal in mind next to a convoy of 32 wagons. We would find empty barns, houses, cinemas or schools to sleep in. The heated rooms gave us a sense of security for a short amount of time, but two or three days later we were forced to hit the road again. The winter air kept our meat cold, but it started rotting when the weather became warmer. Many became sick, and when someone died, we had to leave their body at the side of the road. We had to keep going without a break.

Our route took us over a vast mountain range that is now the Czech Republic, but was Germany back then. There we came across Jews and concentration camp prisoner trains, and we walked past the 'Theresienstadt' concentration camp. We weren't allowed to comment on it, and we definitely weren't allowed to side with the prisoners, as the Nazis were still in control. We saw clothes and suitcases scattered through the Czech forests, which, as we found out later, had belonged to Jewish people. We knew they had been condemned, but we only found out to what extent when the war was over.

Once we stayed in a castle, and this was an excellent spectacle for us kids as we were able to sled down hills something that hadn't been possible at home where everything was flat. But we had to keep going as the Russian troops were getting closer. We kept hearing the sound of gunshots. Thankfully we took a wrong turn at some point because, as we found out later, many refugees who had taken the regular route had been murdered. One day we were met by American low-flying aircrafts. They were shooting at everything that moved. I was on a field with other kids when an American flew so close towards us that I had eye contact with the pilot. He let us live, maybe because he had seen we were kids.

The war ended on May 8th, 1945, but our escape went on until September; that's when we arrived Meissenheim. It was difficult to comprehend what had happened to us. As a child I was unable to grasp the severity of the situation. Our struggle to live seemed adventurous to me and only with time I realised what the war and our escape had meant. Millions of people lost their lives and families were torn apart. What happened in those years is unimaginable for today's generation.

It's been 70 years. I've written my stories down, and I've retold them many times. Images from the war still stir up feelings in me, but that's the only way I knew how to process this trauma. I went to what is now Poland, three years ago to visit the house in which I grew up. It's been renovated, and new homes have been constructed on the field next door. I stood there and thought: it's all over.

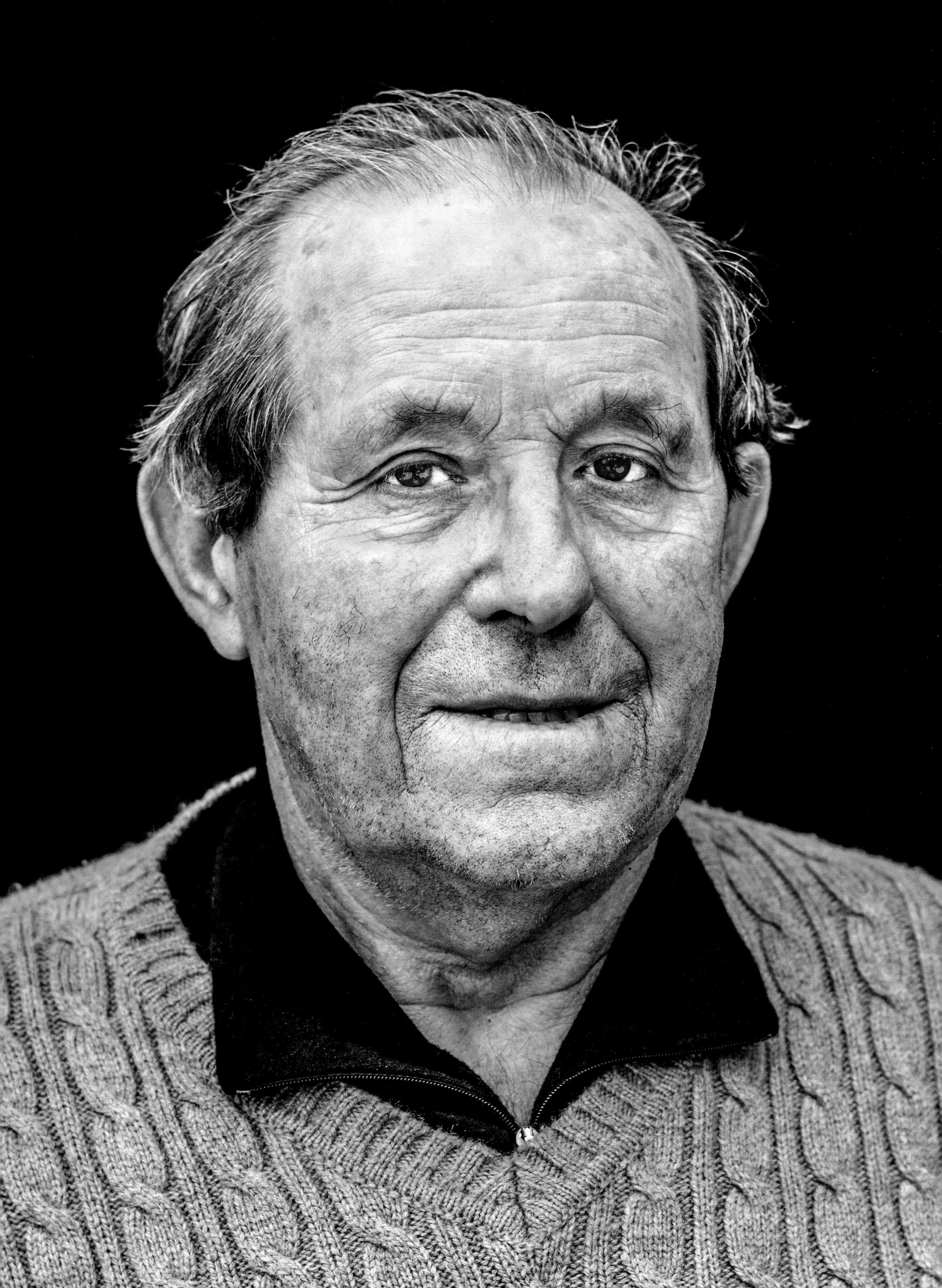

EDDIE, 50

OCTOBER 25TH, 2015, VENICE BEACH, LOS ANGELES

I was accepted to study art at two good universities after finishing high school, but my father didn't approve. He said that with my talent, I was never going to make any money with my art. He wanted me to become a doctor. Instead, I ended up managing an art supply store.

I was twenty years old when I met my wife, and we got married soon after. I now think the marriage was a means to escape my parent's house. I was too young to understand that my wife also gave me the feeling of not being enough. She had a degree in art and used every opportunity to let me know that I was merely a self-proclaimed artist, who had learned to paint from books. She turned everything into a competition and always wanted to be better than me while being jealous and possessive. By making me feel small, she was better able to control me. I was forbidden to speak to, let alone portray other women, and to exhibit my work in a gallery was unthinkable at the time.

After work, I spent a lot of my evenings in my studio, where I could paint in peace; while in the meantime my wife was meeting other men, which I accidentally found out four years later, mistaking my black diary with hers. In it, she had written where, when and how the affairs had begun. My friends had often seen her with other men, but when they told me I chose to believe that she was faithful, but she had lied to me and betrayed me. I felt useless, empty and fell into a depression. We got a divorce after twelve years of marriage.

Retrospectively it was a blessing that it all happened the way it did. After the divorce I began writing poems, I drew, sketched and painted. I finally focused on my artistic talents and gave free reign to my feelings. Slowly I realised, that I had been stuck in a dead end all these years and the more freedom I gained, the better my art became.

It's been five years now that I've been earning my living from my art. I sell my paintings on the boardwalk of Venice Beach and in several galleries. I don't make a fortune, but I feel free and careless. I live my life as an artist without having to take anyone or anything into account.

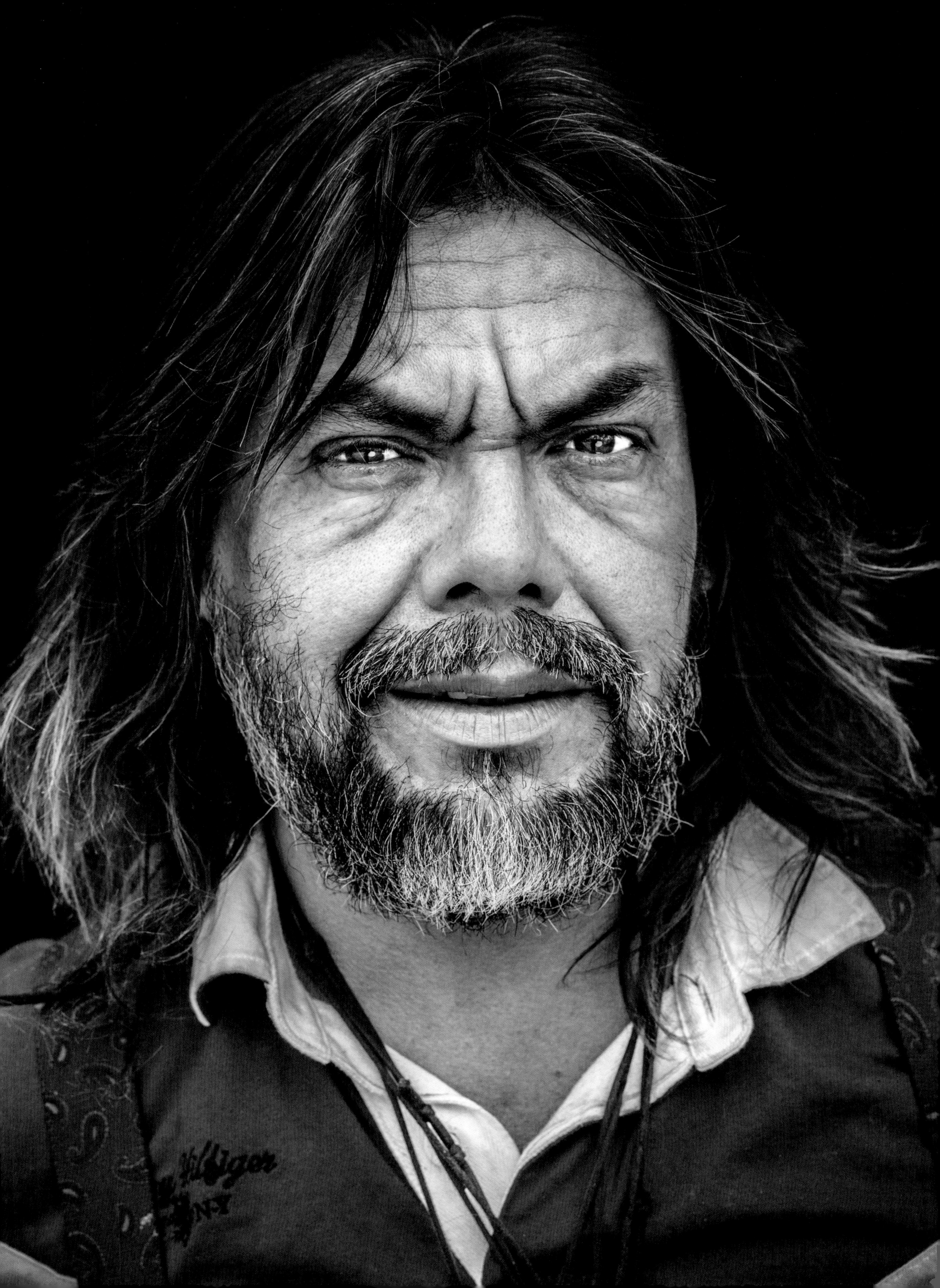

KURT, 50
FEBRUARY 20TH, 2015, ZURICH, SWITZERLAND

One should influence things that are changeable and everything else, one just has to take as is and learn to live with it.

As good as people can be, they can also go in the entirely opposite direction. If someone experienced a violent childhood, they might be more drawn to darkness. You become an imitator, or you try to do the opposite of what you experienced. I was the youngest of four children, and sometimes my mother gave me a slap in the face or she locked me away. My eldest brother was favoured and spared. I saw a massive injustice in her behaviour through the eyes of a child and to this day I react very strongly when I see unjust behaviour. I want to have an effect, bring about change.

I started to report from areas of crisis in 1984 to make a difference. I went to Afghanistan, Libya, Iraq, and Syria – I was and am wherever there is war. You need a lot of courage and trust for this kind of work. I risk going to court, to be caught by terrorists who could kidnap me, torture me or murder me. I am a single father, and still, I take the risk. If everyone just thought of their own kids, would Hitler have been defeated? I am most scared when I am still at home preparing for my next trip, and when I have to say goodbye to my children. I feel afraid of the unknown, of uncertainties and of what could happen. Days spent in crisis areas are bleak. Most of the time one is just waiting for days on end, and a lot of patience is needed. There's one day, in particular, I remember as if it happened yesterday; a Syrian airplane was circling over Aleppo. I filmed it and kept walking. Two minutes later, bombs dropped on the exact spot where I had stood two minutes prior. I had jumped into safety 150 metres from this spot. I was fortunate. Fear can be a good motor. It can make you run at record-breaking speed, but fear is a bad mentor. I try to stay optimistic and think 'Why should something happen to me at this exact moment?' Without this naivety, I would not be able to function. After my engagement in war zones, I am often traumatised and burdened by horrible nightmares. A reoccurring theme is of falling victim to terrorists who want to torture me in incredible ways, terrorists who are satisfied by using power and are driven by seeing the fear in the eyes of their victims and who abuse their religion to justify their sadism. They terrorise their victims weekly with executions, beheadings, and burnings – barbarity beyond any comprehension.

I may be unable to be myself for several weeks after coming home. I work from home and don't see anyone but my two sons, which can be quite lonely, but my kids distract me by asking me to go outside with them, by being hungry and just wanting to be close to me. They give me support and are vital to my life. It's hard for most people to get close to me, as their fear dominates. Often it helps me to digest my experiences with other war reporters and translators.

What influenced me the most was to see how people deal with war, to see how they adapt to horrible situations and use a grim sense of humour to deal with it, to see how kids use bombing breaks to play outside. I've seen kids rollerblade through rubble-covered streets. The destruction is severe, yet people keep living.

In Switzerland, I have my music, my two boys and my bed. I live in a peaceful paradise full of freedom, familiarity, and tolerance. Our country functions and we don't have to be afraid of walking on the streets, we don't have to fear to express our views, we have warm water and homes. If I'm able to have an influence on the way a few people see the world, if I can help them feel grateful and joyous for the things we have here, then I am overjoyed.

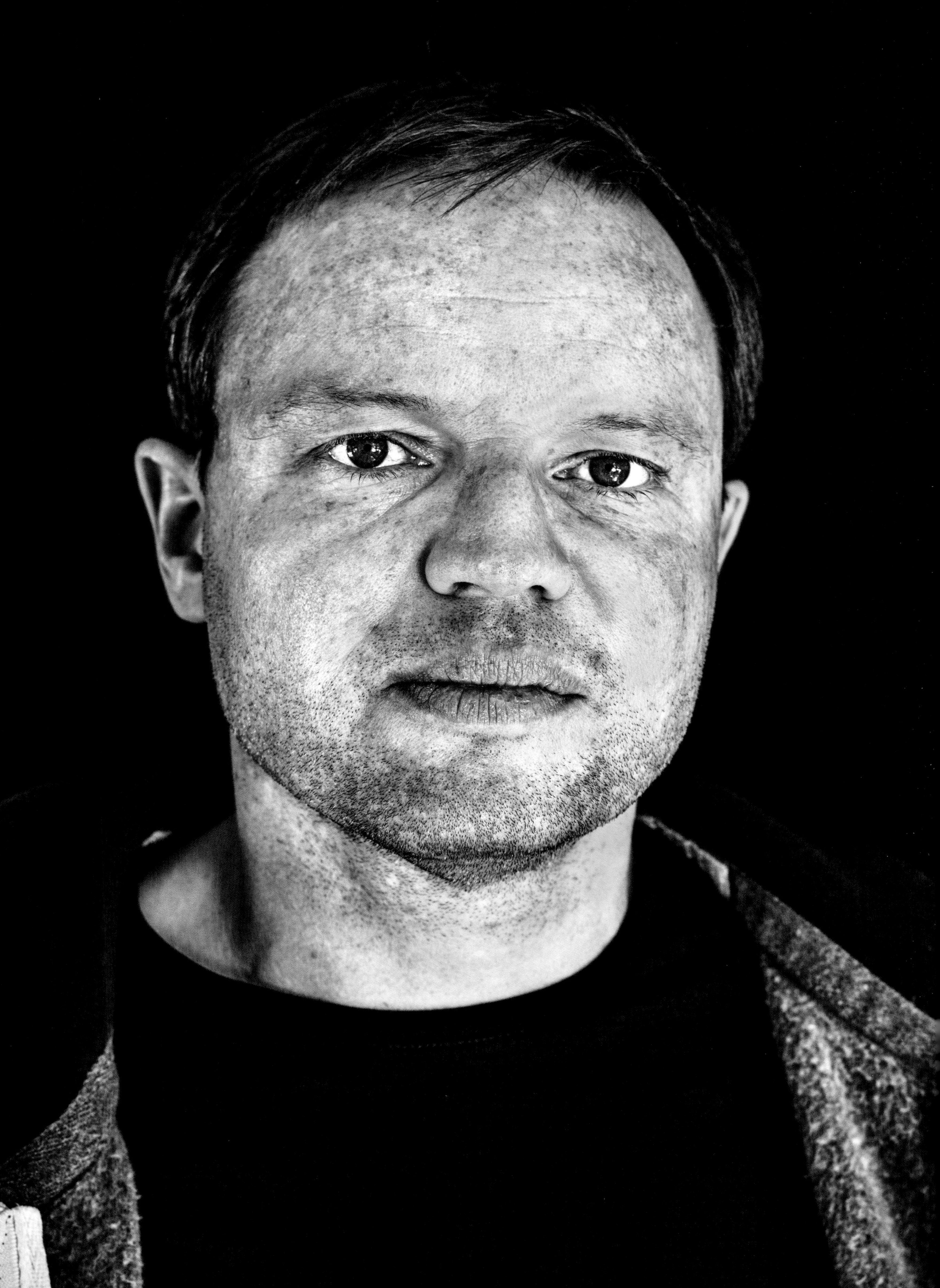

My sister died of leukaemia when I was thirty-years-old and pregnant with my fourth child. She left behind five kids and her husband. Suddenly I had to take care of two households, two husbands and nine kids while working in a hotel. I would come home in the late afternoon to cook, and two hours later I'd go back to work until the middle of the night.

My father died shortly after my sister did, and my mother became ill with diabetes and severe asthma that forced her to wear an oxygen mask every four hours. At some point, she gave up and decided to stay in bed at my house as she knew I would take care of her.

So, when I wasn't working, I had to be there for her. I washed her, cooked for her, made her tea, entertained her, and sometimes even slept next to her when she didn't want to be alone at night. I was her nurse, which in itself is a full-time job, on top of taking care of nine kids and working in the hotel – a job I needed to do to survive. Half a ton of rice lasted for about two months. My husband sometimes helped me do the laundry, but that was as far as his support went. He was an alcoholic, was frequently aggressive and eventually died from his addiction. I was tempted to give up as I felt utterly abandoned. I had grown numb and was just functioning on auto-pilot. I didn't have time to come up with a long-term solution. I would have loved to have gone dancing at the weekends, but I had to stay with my mom.

She died eight years ago, and I can remember the moment very well: I sat there thinking of all the years I took care of her and, quite honestly, her death was a relief. I had had enough. My mother took the most important time in my life away from me. I took care of her for 26 years. In this time I was unable to ever go out and enjoy myself. I missed out on having fun and on having time for myself because I was consumed by work and my responsibilities that were too big for me to really handle and this took a physical toll on me.

Today I can finally enjoy my life, but sadly I have no one to go out and dance with. My kids and my sister's kids have their own lives now and hardly visit me at all. I spent all these years taking care of others to the point where I forgot to take care of myself and yet I am satisfied. Now I'm a self-employed landlord with several vacation homes and take care of the guests, which motivates me. When I come home at night, I cook for myself and enjoy the peace and quiet.

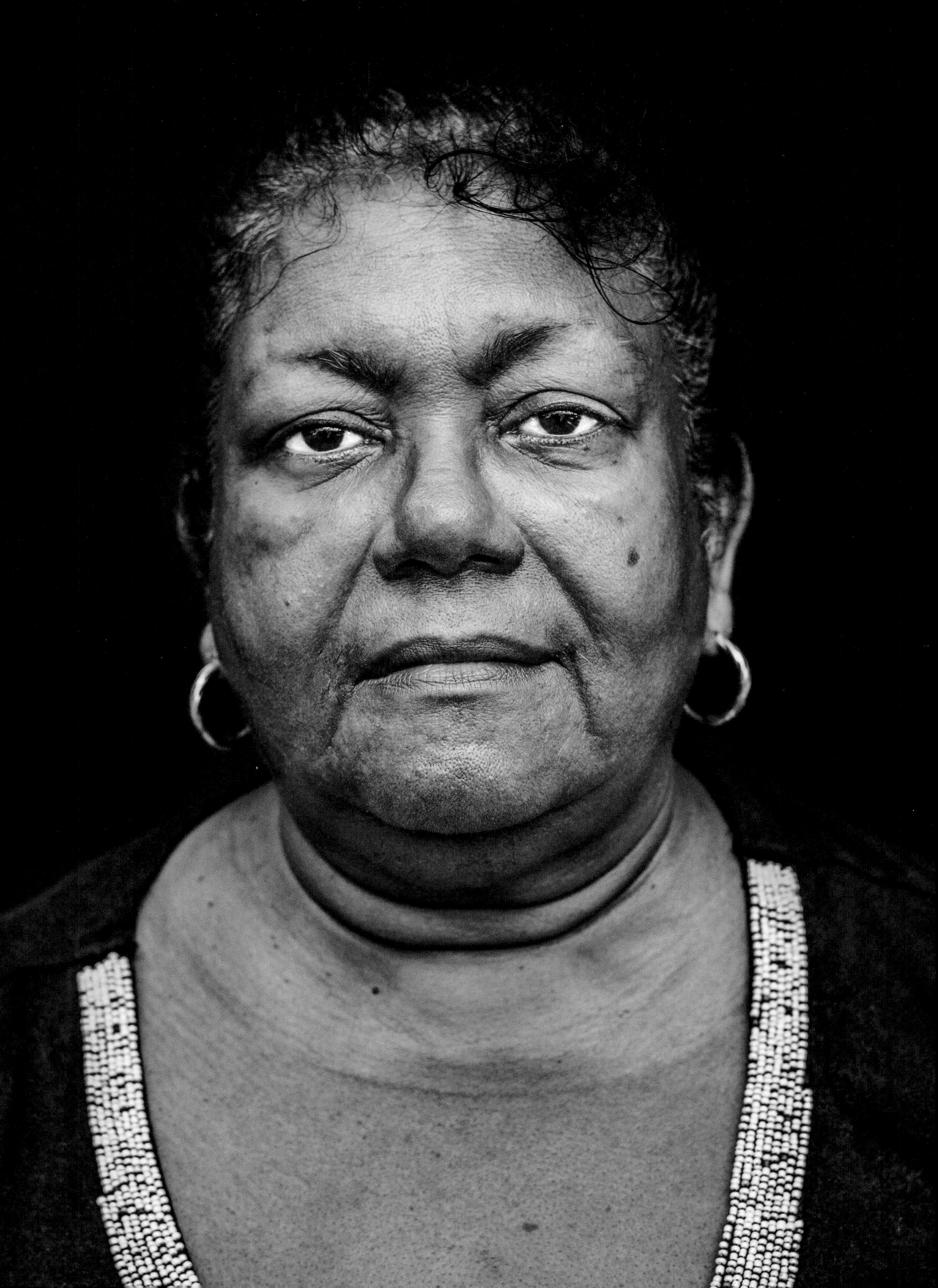

DINA, 26
FEBRUARY 5TH, 2015, ZURICH, SWITZERLAND

I needed someone who was there for me when I felt down, someone to count on. I needed a friend but found drugs instead. It felt good and was always reliable. It became both a friend and foe and changed my life drastically, taking me from down low to up high and back down again.

My mom was a single mother, and I had no contact with my father. My childhood wasn't what one wishes for. The relationship with my mother was difficult: I didn't receive any love, affection or comfort, only money to pay for bills and debts. My parents' lives had no space for me. I wasn't an easy kid to deal with, and so my mother sent me to a home when I was twelve. I had no friends there, no one to talk to and I was bullied and left to feel helpless and alone. Five wasted years.

I became addicted to drugs when I was seventeen and turned into an aggressive and violent person. I would have done almost anything to get my hands on the drug. It was a total loss of control. It was all too much for my mother, so she migrated to Spain and left me behind. All alone and sick, I broke down. I ended up in a hospital where my stomach was pumped out, and a vein was removed that was damaged entirely and black from all the shooting up; but I was alive, and that was the main thing. I lived in a rehab clinic with other junkies for one year. Yes, junkies – it's a hard word. 'None of you will manage to withdraw', the clinic's psychologist stated. He didn't believe in us, he had given us up, but I wanted to be the one to make it, the person that can prove it's possible. For a while, I managed to stay clean but then came a crash, and I was back on, and this was to repeat itself again and again.

I've been in a committed relationship for three years now. My partner has seen me suffer and despair, but her love has never wavered. She was there for me despite the daily fear of losing me to drugs.

I want to live, I want to conquer this deathly addiction but will I stay clean forever? I can't say but what I can say with pride is that I've put up a good fight and I'll continue to fight! I'm convinced that anyone who really wants to quit can make it – even the weakest person. I know that my weakness has made me strong.

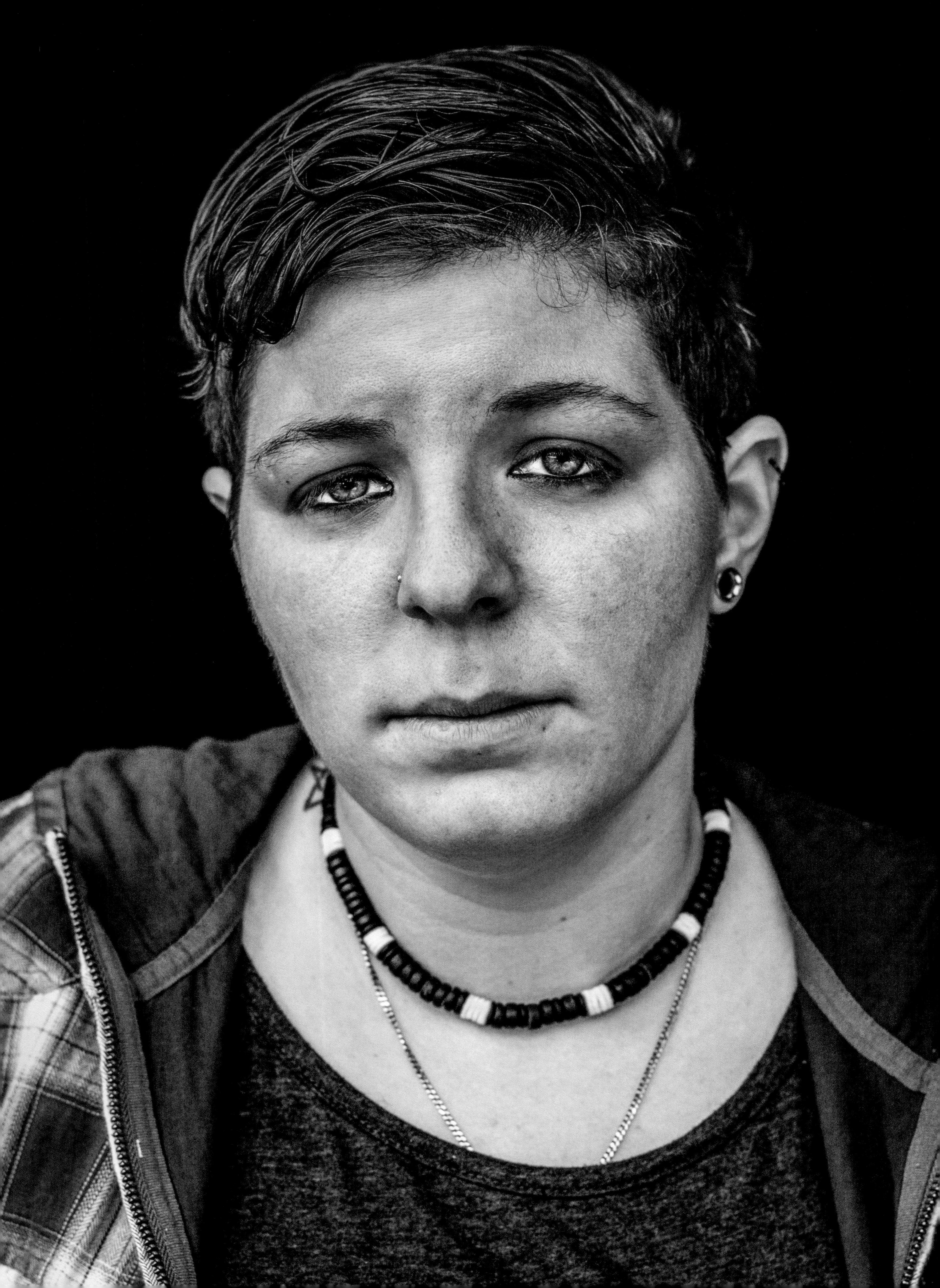

LUTZ, 67
FEBRUARY 26TH, 2014, BERLIN, GERMANY

It was the late sixties, and I was nineteen years old. The Socialist Unity Party of Germany (SED) was covering all of East Berlin with propaganda posters. As an act of resistance against the party's power and pervasive surveillance apparatus, I ripped down several posters and was immediately caught by the State Security Service. I was sentenced to 20 months of prison for 'national defamation' and that's how I ended up in the State Security prison.

But perhaps I have to first share what happened before this incident: I had done a tailor apprenticeship with 200 girls. I was the only guy, which led me to have a big mouth and being the most outspoken one when it came to political debates. I was very active in sharing my anti-SED views, as I was extremely passionate about politics. I didn't realise back then that this would lead to my downfall, as my teacher was writing a protocol for the State Security Service.

So there I was, being questioned in the prison of Hohenschönhausen for six weeks. It was psycho-terror, and I quickly realised that I wasn't there for ripping down posters but for the political statements I had made in my school. Upon arriving in prison, they let me keep on my own clothes, which seemed reassuring at first, but I later realised the degrading reason for this: only underwear and prison uniforms got washed. My personal clothes remained dirty for the whole 20 months I was there.

I was sent to an isolation cell on the third floor. The cell was dark and small with a narrow stretcher, a stool, and a toilet. There was no sink. We were given one bowl of water a day, and that had to suffice. My day started at six and ended at ten. The hours in between were endless, and it was forbidden to lie down. I was only allowed to sit or stand. Degradation, sleep deprivation and humiliation were part of my daily schedule but even worse was how quiet it was. They had placed carpets in front of all cells to absorb the sound so that prisoners were removed entirely from the outside world. The only human interaction I had was with a guard who gave me my meal without uttering a single sound. At some point, I began communicating with others by knocking on the walls of my cell. I never found out if it was another inmate or a prison guard replying my knocks.

I repressed my emotions to deal with my situation. After three months my father was allowed to send me money with which I bought sweets, fruit or cigarettes. I built towers out of my used matches and to not go crazy I started structuring my days best I could. Things got a bit easier once I was allowed to read books. I devoured five books a week and 200 in total.

Those 20 months ripped me out of my old life. I was utterly uninformed when I got out and had to reformulate my opinion about the GDR. I didn't have a high school diploma, I hadn't completed my apprenticeship – I had nothing. I had to repeat everything and start from scratch. I was banned from a lot of things due to my imprisonment; for example, I couldn't have become a teacher or a doctor.

Today I've realised that my time in jail had a more severe effect on me than I had always claimed. I suppressed a lot to protect myself. I never wanted to go back to Hohenschönhausen, fearing the pent-up emotions that might surface. Then, in 2009, I decided to face my past and anonymously participated in a tour through the prison's memorial. Now I work there and offer tours myself. I share my experiences, and this has become a sort of therapy that helps me ease the pain.

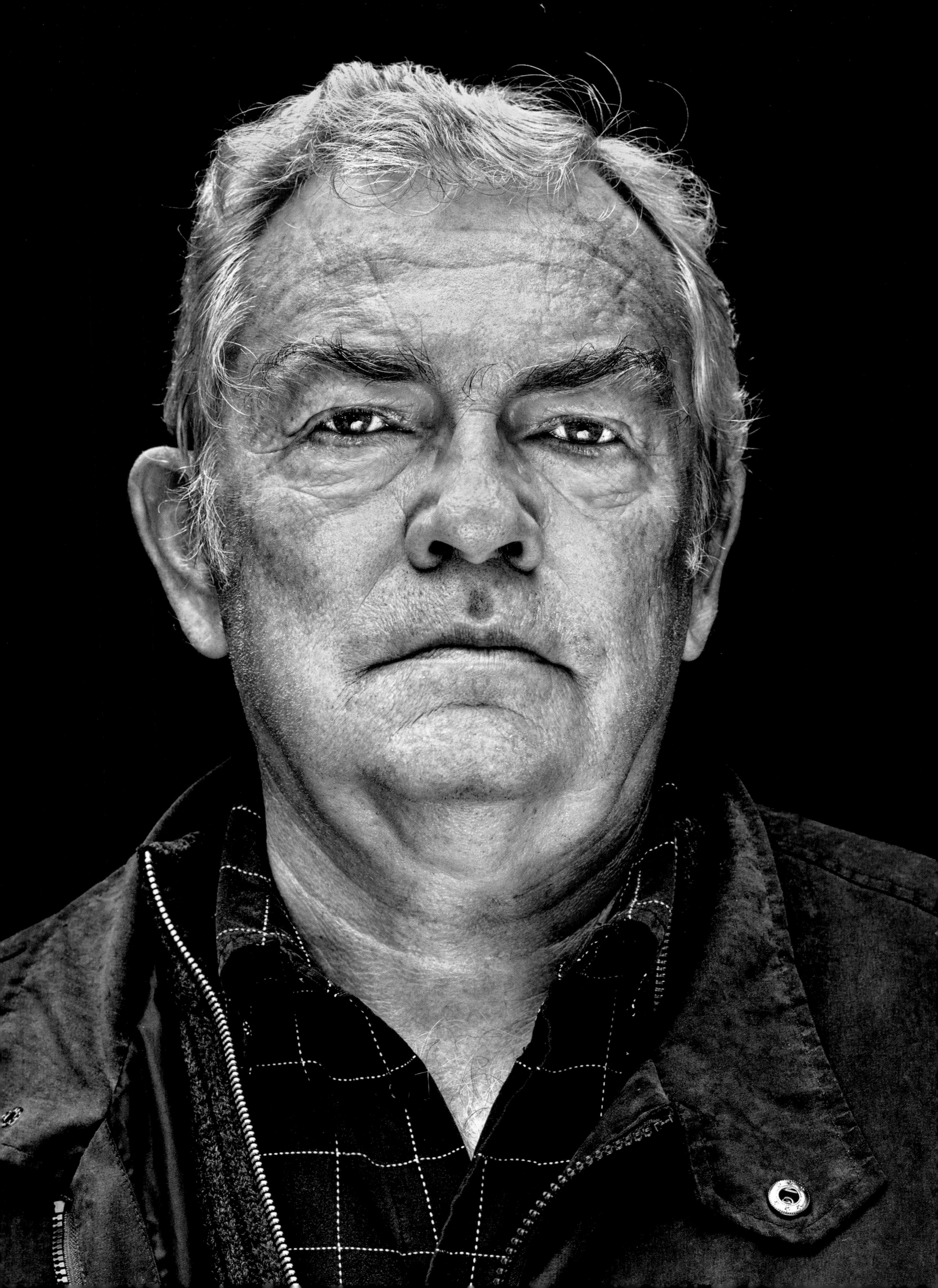

RETO, 41
MARCH 7ᵀᴴ, 2015, ZURICH, SWITZERLAND

I often get disparaging or astonishing looks on the street, presumably because my body is covered in tattoos and piercings. I might come across as harsh and intimidating but just because I don't look like the norm doesn't mean I'm a terrible person. I have a warm heart, I'm positive, kind and helpful. I'm deeply touched by the fate of others. I'm fascinated by the strength people are able to conjure in the most impossible situations and by the positive outlook and fighting spirit displayed day by day.

My life has almost just consisted of beautiful moments. The only stroke of fate occurred when my father died unexpectedly when I was seven years old. It was a shock, and I was too young to understand or accept the loss, but my family stood together. My mother's and grandparents' strength taught me to look ahead and to always see the positive in every situation. To turn back time is impossible, of course.

My mother met her present partner a few years later, and he became my father figure. The family circle closed again, and I experienced love and security. I carry this love within me, and it will protect me when something difficult happens again.

I travelled far and wide, first with my family then on my own. People from all cultures influenced my view of the world and made me feel humble. I met poverty-stricken people with a joy for life and generosity that one rarely comes across in Switzerland. People with almost nothing will give away their last shirt. That fascinates me. I live in a consumer society, in a seemingly perfect world yet people would rather save money than help others. The rich become richer while the poor become poorer. I wish for more equality and acceptance, for more people who give and not just take, people who make the time to look closely and approach one another.

Sometimes it's difficult to understand who actually needs help, like when people ask for change on the street; ultimately we have no influence over what will actually happen with the money we give, but I think the most important thing is that one attempts to help. You don't have to give much, small gestures like a smile can already have a significant effect and are worth more than any amount of money.

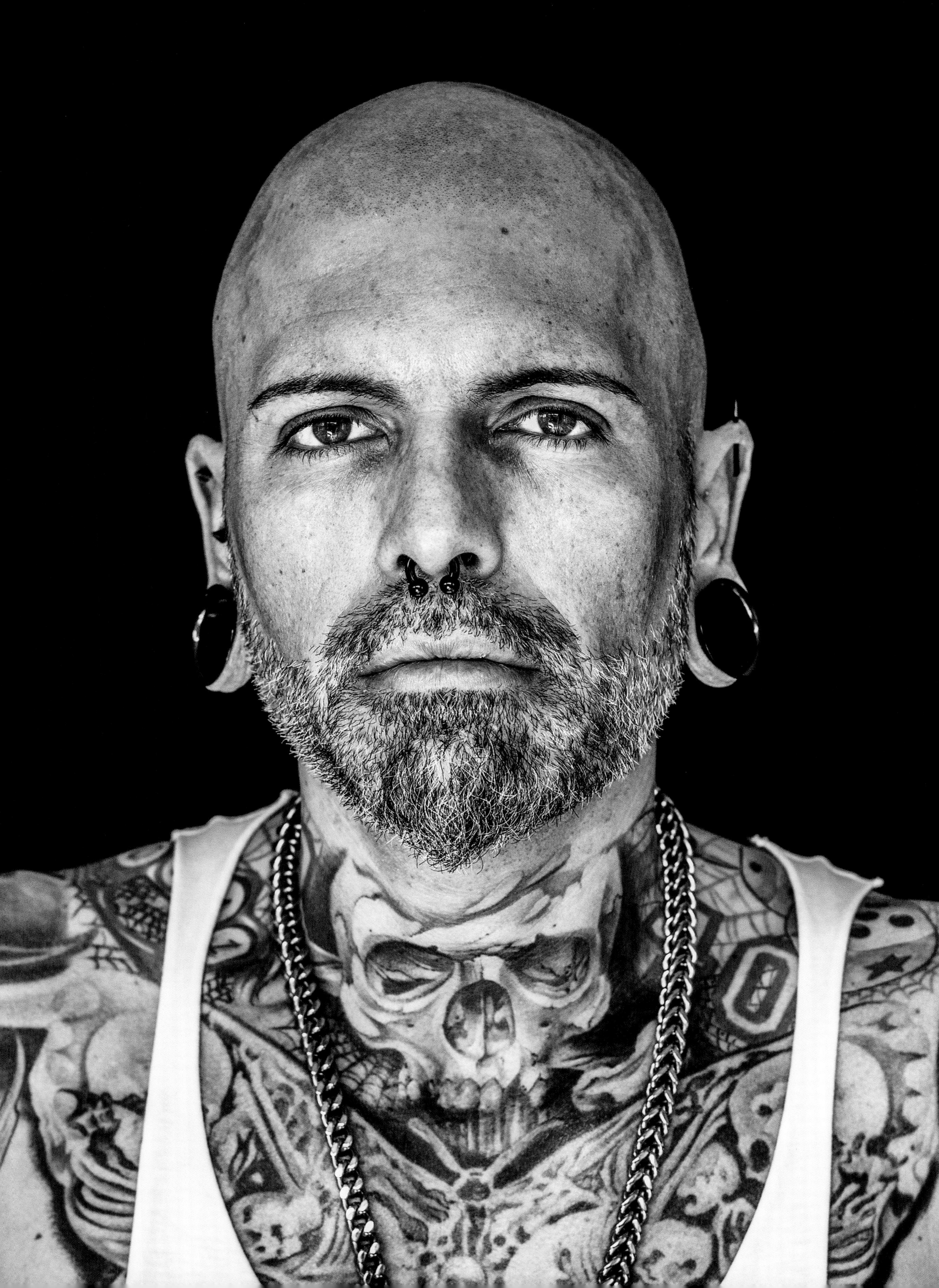

CÉCILIA, 65
OCTOBER 16TH, 2015, SKID ROW, LOS ANGELES

I had inherited a small house, a little bit outside of the city, from my parents. I don't have a husband or children. I worked at a school giving English courses, but my job was discontinued when the school had to save money. To make a living, I began renting out rooms in my house since I didn't need the whole place to myself. A lot of strangers went in and out, a lot of good people. Some stayed for some weeks, some stayed up to a year. It gave me joy to receive guests and give them a temporary home.

One day two unassuming and quiet men moved into my house. They made a good impression and wanted to pay me monthly. I hardly saw them at all for the first two months and was never sure if they were even at home. As time went on, I saw them more and more, and we also ate together in the kitchen a few times though we never talked much. Then they began to make negative comments, first sporadically then more and more. They became insulting, and at some point, I felt uncomfortable in my own house, and I wanted to end their contract. They began to yell at me, hit me and threatened to kill me if I ever dared to kick them out. From that moment on, we lived by their rules. I wasn't allowed to move around freely or go into the kitchen when they were at home, and they said that if I ever went to the cops, they would kill me. They stopped paying the rent. I felt helpless and didn't know what to do other than stay out of their way.

My room became my home, and whenever I wanted to leave it, I listened closely if I could hear them or not. Sometimes it took hours before I could muster the courage to leave my room.

One day I was inattentive and walked straight into their arms and quickly tried backing up into my room but they blocked my way and started to demand money from me. I wanted to defend myself, but one of them hit me in the face, and the other ripped me into my room by my hair and threw me onto my bed where they both raped me. My world shattered into a million pieces within a minute. I wanted to run away, but they held me down. Then they took me into a park and said that they would kill me. I was begging for my life when we were interrupted by some people strolling past, and I took this opportunity to flee. I heard them scream: 'We'll find you, wherever you go!'

I ran without knowing where to go. I had nothing with me, but I couldn't go back home. I was scared to death but didn't dare to go to the police. Those two men were dangerous and unpredictable. They would have turned the story around for their good or would have sent someone to kill me, and so I decided to keep the story to myself, and I've been living on the streets ever since. I didn't want a new apartment because they could have found me that way. They could have found me anywhere, but here they can't. Here I'm anonymous.

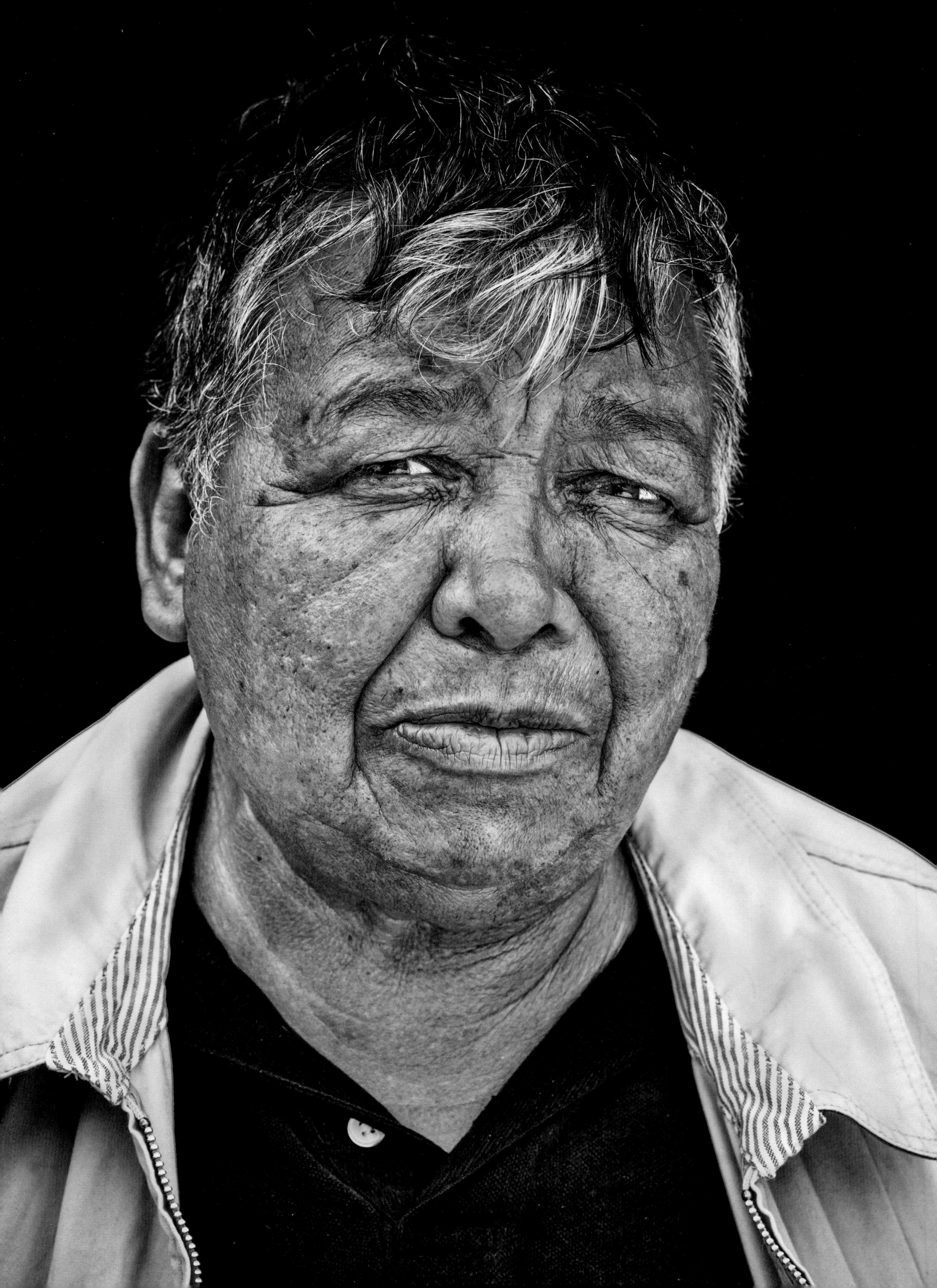

JACK, 60

JUNE 8ᵀᴴ, 2017, MANHATTAN, NEW YORK

It was a beautiful day with a bright blue sky, and like always my alarm went off at 5:45 am. I drank a coffee and then drove to work. We received an emergency call shortly before 9 am: an aircraft crashed into the North Tower of the World Trade Center. First, we thought it was an accident, but we quickly discovered that it was an act of terror.

I was the squad leader for the emergency rescue service in Manhattan, and so I had to coordinate four hundred colleagues. Upon our arrival, another airplane crashed into the World Trade Center, this time the South Tower, presenting us with unimaginable chaos. The top floors of the WTC were engulfed in flames, and emergency exits were destroyed or blocked off, leading people to jump out of the building to guarantee themselves a quick death. I saw some people holdings hands as they jumped out, others sprang in circles, and some had already caught fire. I tried to comprehend this horror scenario so that I could determine how to proceed. We fought our way to the South Tower through rubble while trying to avoid falling bodies and uncountable body parts strewn across the pavement. The South Tower began to collapse as we neared it and while debris, concrete, and metal was hurling around us we shouted: 'Run for your lives!' Everything came crashing down: a vast AC fell right in front of my feet, and a flying piece of metal decapitated a young woman next to me. I didn't look back once as I kept running. The collapse of the tower produced a pressure surge of such immensity that I was catapulted 30 metres through the air. Then I was buried beneath masses of rubble. As I laid face down, I thought of my eldest son, who's flight should have landed at JFK at 9 am that morning.

I tried to breathe, but my head laid buried in the crumbs of the concrete. When I was finally able to free myself, I vomited dust and then, with one of my men, began to search the area for our colleagues. We didn't get very far as the North Tower then also collapsed and we fled into the entrance of a bank where we stood across from each other in the door frame. The ceiling and lights came crashing down, and a big black cloud invaded the bank. I was labeled missing for seven hours until I could verify that I was alive. Then I discovered that my son had been on the last flight to land in JFK on September 11ᵗʰ, 2001.

I lost 56 friends that day. I was only able to comprehend the magnitude of the events two weeks later when I saw the images on television for the first time. Before that, I was numb and was operating in an automated mode as I was just functioning somehow. The pictures I then saw just seemed surreal.

I spent the following eight months in the ruins of WTC. I led and coordinated the operations of the local fire department, police stations, and other emergency teams. I recovered corpses and sorted through body parts, now and then I was sent to the morgue to identify colleagues and attended gala dinners where I received medals of bravery. It was a paradox, but I guess it was the way to honor our work. People declared me a hero, and I received letters and gifts from all over while flowers covered my front porch. This gratefulness hit me right in the middle of my heart yet I had to suppress my emotions to convey strength and courage to my team as that was my job. I suppressed my trauma for a long time, and it's still hard for me to talk about it today. I swallow thirteen different medications every day. I have damaged sinuses from the smoke, my shoulder is ruined, and twice a month I have to get my lungs checked as they are still full of debris. Nighttime is unbearable to me as I can only sleep a maximum of three hours and I suffer from nightmares and flashbacks. I see people jump from the towers, dismembered body parts or I see myself buried alive under tons of rubble. No matter where I go or what I do, this personal hell comes with me. I put on a smile every day, but I carry a world of pain in me, but I still try to enjoy life because I am one of the survivors.

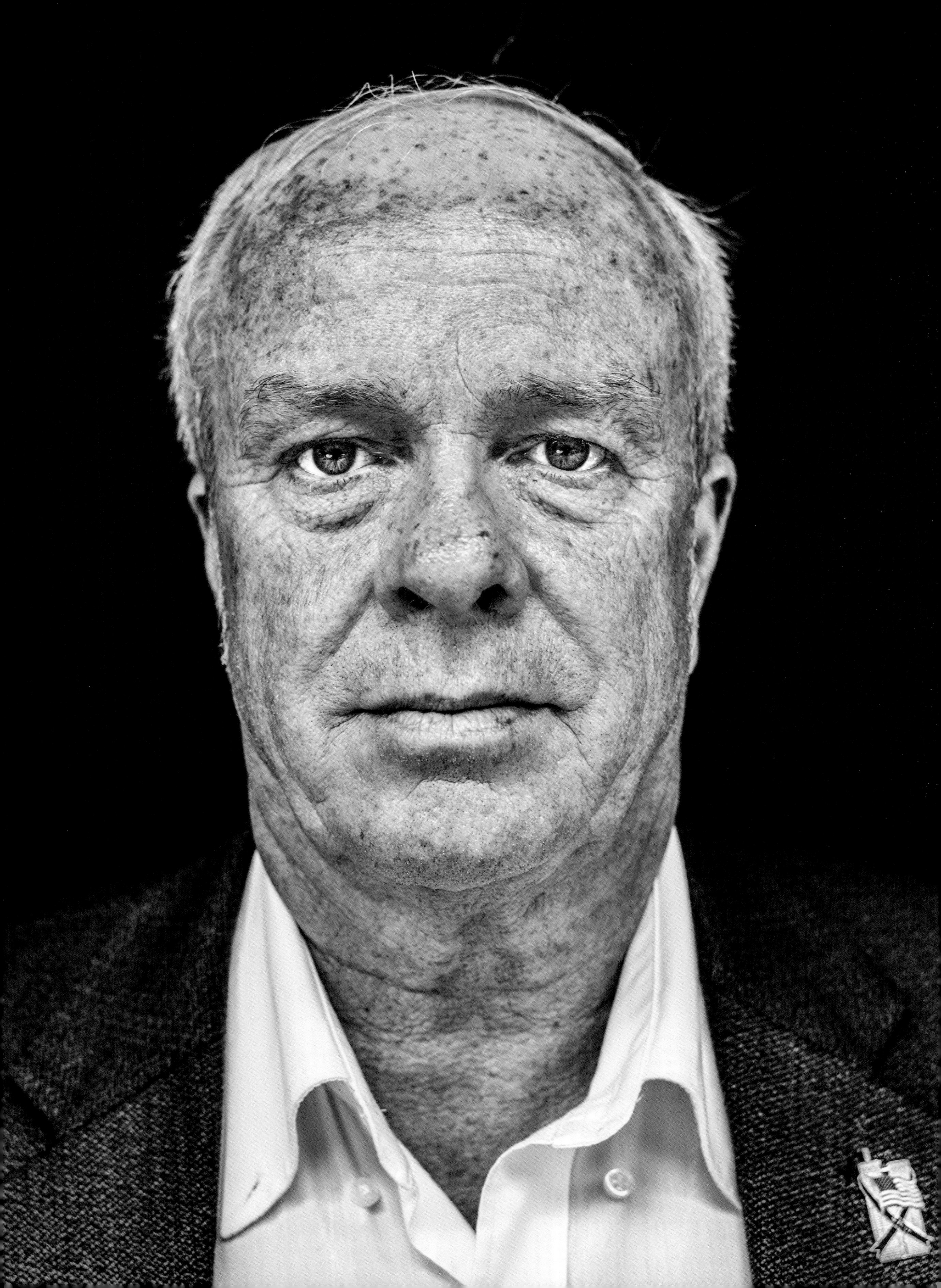

PEGGY, 27

NOVEMBER 1ST, 2016, HOUT BAY, CAPE TOWN

____

Poverty, to me, means having no money to buy food, no electricity, and no running water, but also it means not to have a safe and cosy place to call home and not to be able to live a normal life.

I grew up in poor conditions in Tzaneen, a city in the Northeast of South Africa. My parents got divorced when I was fifteen-years-old, and from that point on my mother, my two younger sisters and I were left to fend for ourselves. In the beginning, my father paid us 300 Rand (in 2016 this was worth about 15£) per month, but it didn't take long for him to be unable to pay us at all. We only had our small house left.

My mother was unemployed. She had no money for my school books or food, let alone for the shoes I needed for my long walk to school. Sometimes we had to ask our relatives to give us their leftovers. My friends shared their lunches with me at school. They were different to me: well-dressed, with enough money to go on trips. I wished to be like them. Often I asked myself why my mother didn't just put me up for adoption so that I could grow up in better conditions. I finished school when I was sixteen and couldn't wait to leave my family home. I packed my things and travelled to Cape Town hoping to start a better life with a job and a beautiful apartment, but I ended up in a township instead. They still shock me to this day: the chaos, the high rate of criminality, murders and the uncountable sick and starving people. The little shacks with metal sheets as roofs are so close to one another that they allow for no free space or privacy. Though I have a bed, light, and water, this place does not feel like a home. I will never get used to this environment, but it's through this experience that I realised my life, the way it was before, was sufficient enough. We had no money but a real home. I didn't own anything but was always healthy.

All these hurdles in my life taught me to see the bigger picture. I still don't own a lot, but it doesn't influence me as much. I wake up in the mornings and am grateful for being healthy. The townships taught me to see things in a different light. I perceive my current situation as a motivation to fight for my dreams. I have a daughter now. My boyfriend and I try to give her everything like education and enough food and I know, if I work hard, I can reach any goal. My self-confidence was at rock bottom, but I pulled myself together and grew from my experiences like a phoenix rising from the ashes.

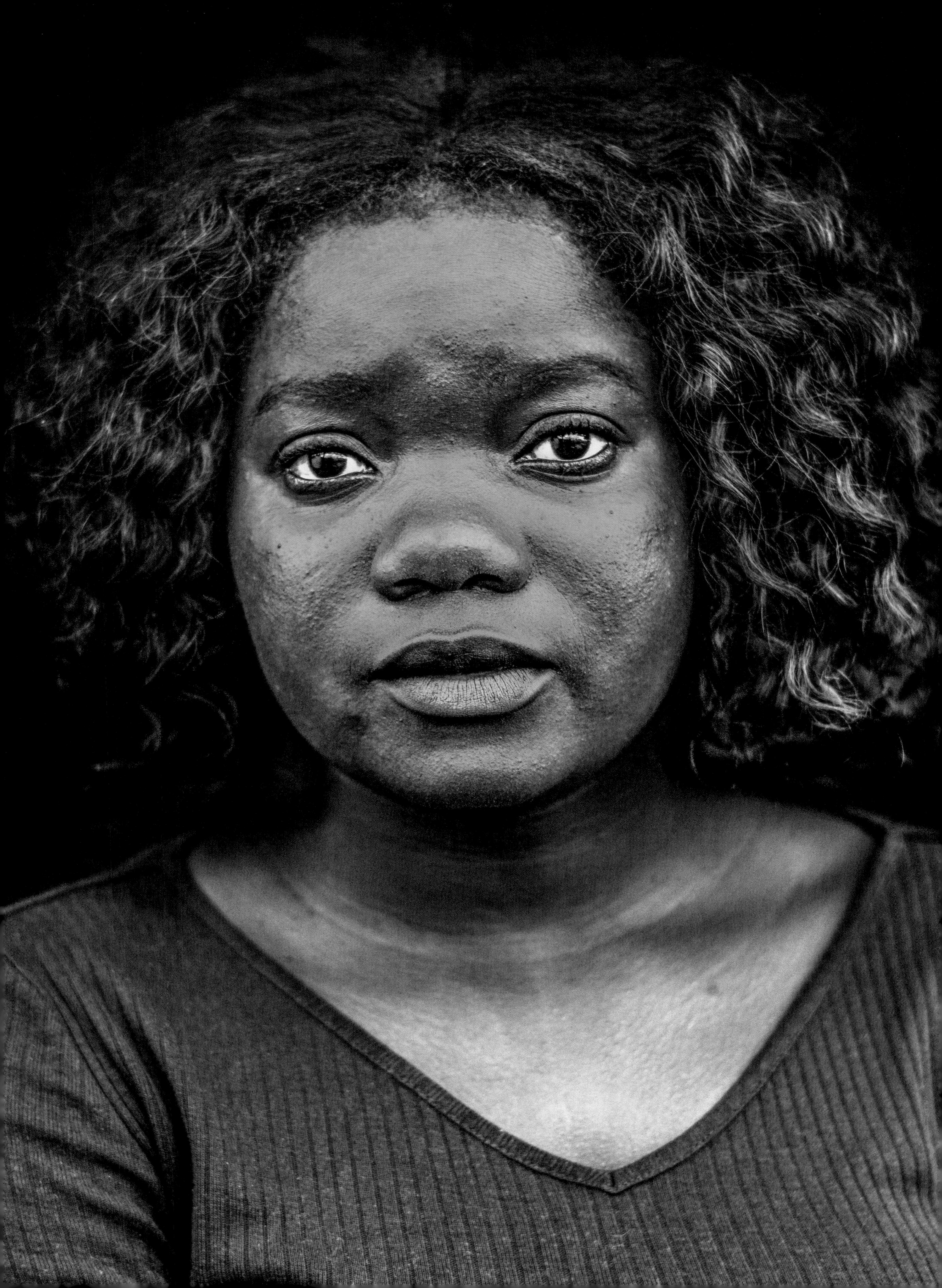

RUTH, 85
OCTOBER 8ᵀᴴ, 2017, HAEGGLINGEN, SWITZERLAND

I wanted to become a teacher, but my father thought this was a waste of money and time; he believed women should just get married and take care of the household. We also didn't have any money to spare, and that's why I had to quit school to help my parents with their farm.

I began an apprenticeship as a salesperson after working on the farm for one year. I had to bike up a steep hill every day to get to the neighbouring village. I suffered from severe joint pain, and at some point, my hip was infected.

I was seventeen years old when I was brought to the hospital where doctors attached an eleven pound stone to my left leg so to pull my bones apart. I was only allowed to lie, and the pain was so intense that I had to scream with every small movement I made. There were no painkillers at the time; I got a high fever and repeatedly asked the nurses to remove the plaster and the attached weights, but I was ignored. It took three months until I was finally freed from this weight – too long, as a hole the size of a tennis ball had appeared in the left side of my calf. The smell was horrendous, my leg was rotting away, and my bones had started disintegrating – I had tuberculosis.

Tuberculosis, at this point in time, went hand in hand with years of suffering, and sometimes death. There was no medication, no antibiotics and lying peacefully was the only therapy. I was brought to Leysin, a clinic specialised in tuberculosis – three hours by car from my home. Again, they hung an eleven pound stone from my leg, and I just had to lie there, this time on a very thin mattress that was as hard as concrete. The room was small and claustrophobic. I've thrown away all photos taken at that time to not be reminded of it. I felt as if I had been put in prison. The food was always the same, and I had to spend most of the time on the terrace in bed as bone tuberculosis was treated with sunlight and cold air back then, so I even had to spend most of the winter lying outside.

My plaster was changed every four weeks and, when it was taken off, parts of my skin were ripped off as it was on so tight. As soon as my wounds had healed, the nurses put new plasters on my leg. That's just the way it was back then, and I didn't dare protest. Back then one could only accept these things as this is what our parents had taught us.

The doctors told me that my hip would go stiff and that I would never be able to walk again, which was shocking to hear of course. I secretly began to move my leg up and down every evening. I wanted to train them to avoid them getting stiff. This slowed down the healing procedure, but I was successful. About thirty doctors came from all over the place to see me walk around. My x-rays went all the way to Paris, and I was labeled a wonder, a sensation. I never told them that I had secretly trained my leg as I had broken the rules by doing so.

I had spent over two years in bed, and when I was 20, I had to relearn how to stand on my two feet – every day for two more minutes. When I was able to stand for one hour, I dared to take the first step, then another and one more until I was eventually able to walk again. My parents were never able to visit me during this time because they couldn't afford to, but they sent me a bar of chocolate every month.

I lost an essential part of my youth but giving up was never an option. I was strict with myself and always said 'I want to and I can!' – all you need in life is a strong will.

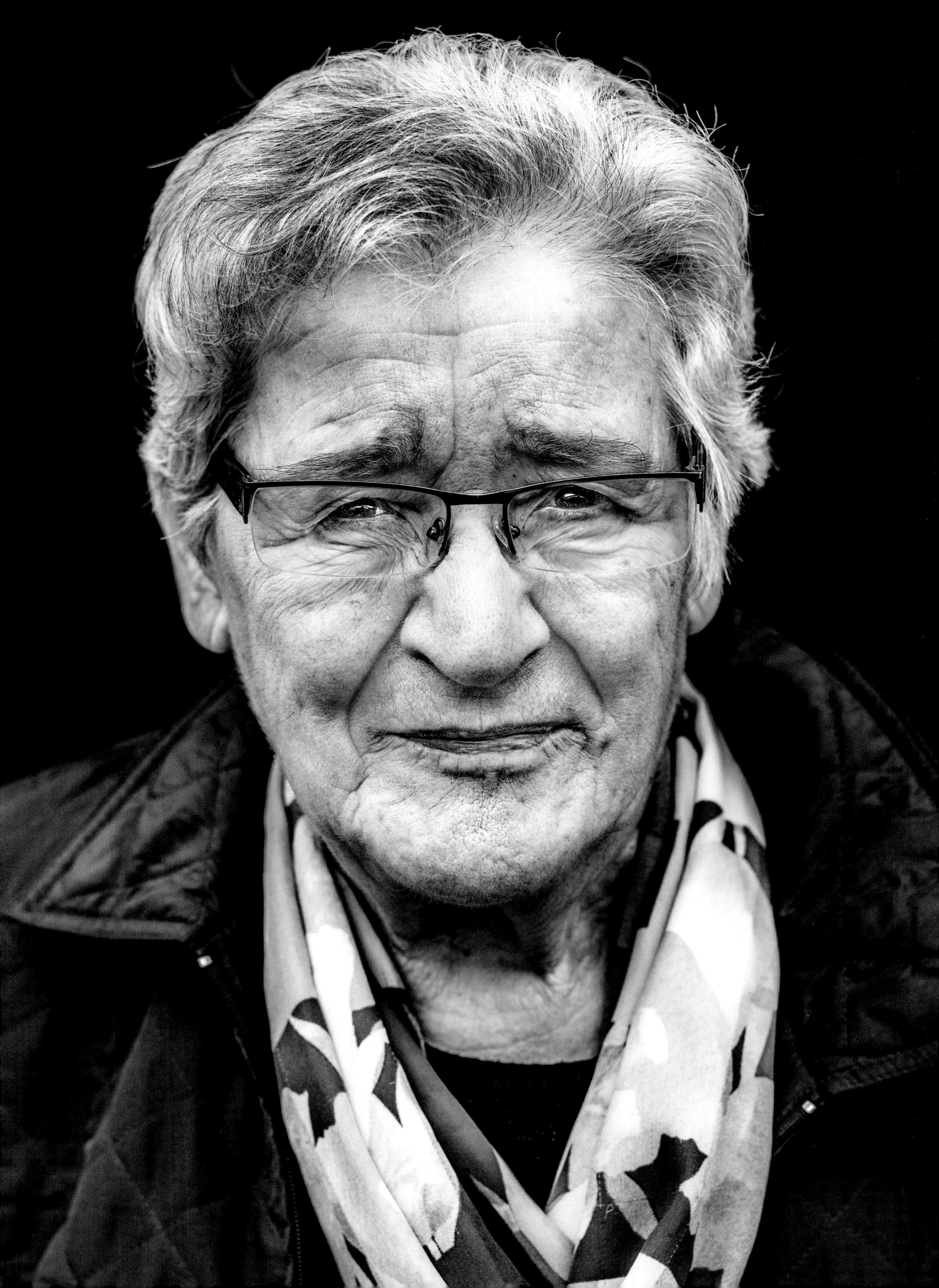

JUAN, 85
NOVEMBER 5TH, 2015, WILLOQ, PERU

I was thirteen years old when my mother fell into the river next to our house. My brother and I tried to save her, but we were powerless against the river's ripping current, and we had to watch as the river consumed our mother and carried her away.

From then on, only our father was responsible for us; but he was an alcoholic, for as long as I could remember, and aggressive – already towards our mother. There was no space to mourn after her death. When I cried, he either left our house or beat me until I didn't utter another word. I would hide from him in the fields surrounding our house.

A year had passed since my mother's death when he didn't come home after a night out drinking. My brother and I somehow survived, having the house to live in and fields to grow vegetables. I met my wife a few years later, and she moved in with me. We had three girls and four boys. The older I got, the more I resembled my father: I began to drink, became aggressive and violent. It took nothing for me to flip out and everything I had witnessed my father do, I passed on to my children.

One day I was accused of stealing from a friend and without any proof or a trial I received a nine-year jail sentence though I was innocent. The arrest took place in front of my family and just like that I was removed from my own life.

Nine years is a long time to think. It gave me the chance to work through my entire childhood and realise that my children had gone through the same as me. I had done to them what my father had done to me, and I had mistreated my wife after having promised always to protect her. I didn't know how that could have happened – perhaps this kind of behaviour is genetic, or it was the resurfacing of the uncontrollable anger and suppressed feelings my childhood had created. I don't know. The jail was a wake-up call for me, and I left utterly changed; I stopped drinking alcohol and was at peace. Even though I had been away from my family for so long, I was closer to them than ever before.

Now I'm old and time has come for me to pass away. I had many sad moments in my life, but the most important thing is that I was able to enjoy the time spent with my family consciously, I was able to give them love and eventually provide them with a peaceful home. I am grateful and joyous for this.

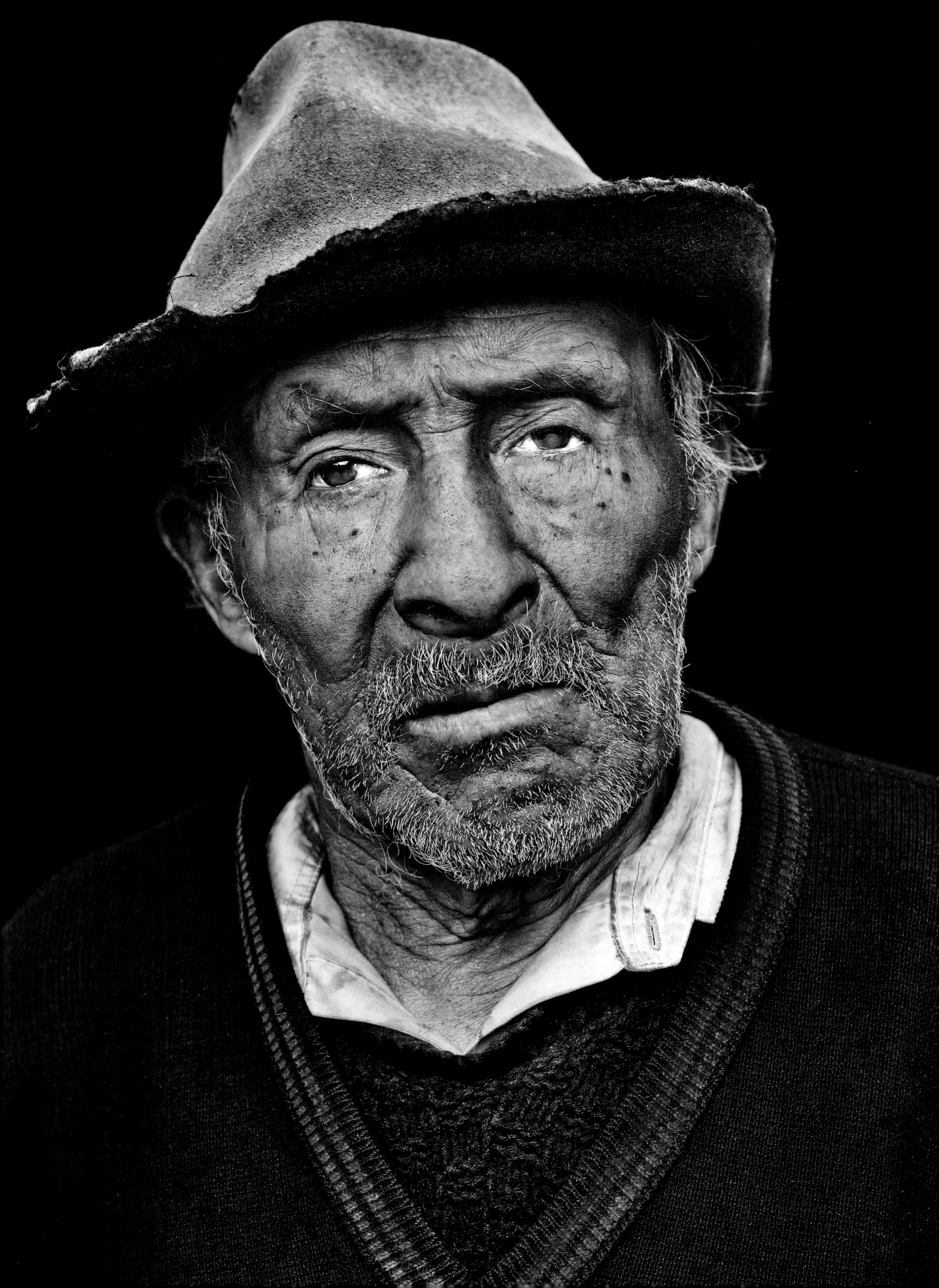

JOSE, 44
NOVEMBER 9TH, 2016, ORANJEZICHT, CAPE TOWN

It was 1988 and Angola was still in the midst of a civil war. I was fifteen years old and knew what could occur to boys my age – forceful and violent recruitment by the rebel army. It was Saturday morning at the market when a group of rebels attacked me. I tried to flee, I was screaming, and so was my mother; I can still hear her screams to this day, but they just took me with them. My childhood ended at that exact moment.

The soldiers brought many other children and me to a camp where they gave each of us a Kalashnikov AK-47 and showed us what our duties would be from then on. It was too risky to flee – they shot those who tried. Drugs stimulated me, and they manipulated me by saying that my family was dead, until I eventually believed it. They turned innocent kids into killing machines through violence and military drills. We had to plunder villages and defeat opponents. We fought to survive – either kill or be killed.

I would be awake for days with no sleep, running on the rush and numbness of all the drugs they were giving me. I had no emotions, and all thoughts were about destroying, terrorising, and torturing. The sound of bombs going off, shotguns, the smell of decay, the sight of blood everywhere – all that became normal at some point.

I spent six years living a reality made of drugs and blood until I had a dream in which I was repeatedly told: 'Why are you here? Stop it and go!' I interpreted this voice to be a message from God and planned my escape, despite the risk this entailed for my life.

One night I ran towards the river barefooted. A soldier had seen me, but I pointed to my water bottle signalling to him that I was just fetching water. Once I was out of his sight, I ran as fast as my feet would take me. I ran and ran through large bushes through the menacing night without turning back once. My feet were bloody from all the shrubs I had to pass through, and there was danger everywhere: lions, snakes, land mines and the soldiers. They noticed my escape – I could hear shots firing through the air behind me. But, as if God was guiding me, an incredible force of energy surged through me as all the images from the war turned into the beauty of freedom lying ahead of me. After four weeks I made it to the border of Namibia and was able to sneak onto a truck unnoticed. I was finally out of Angola and safe.

I still carry the war in me and think about it every day. I'll always have to live with the images in my mind. If I could, I would take back every shot I ever fired, as all I want is peace and be around people who hold together. I want to stand up for the rights of others and create good in the world. I promised myself never to use violence again or to hurt other beings. What I have kept from my life as a soldier is my endurance. I still run to this day, but I'm no longer running away – I run to keep my soul and me pure.

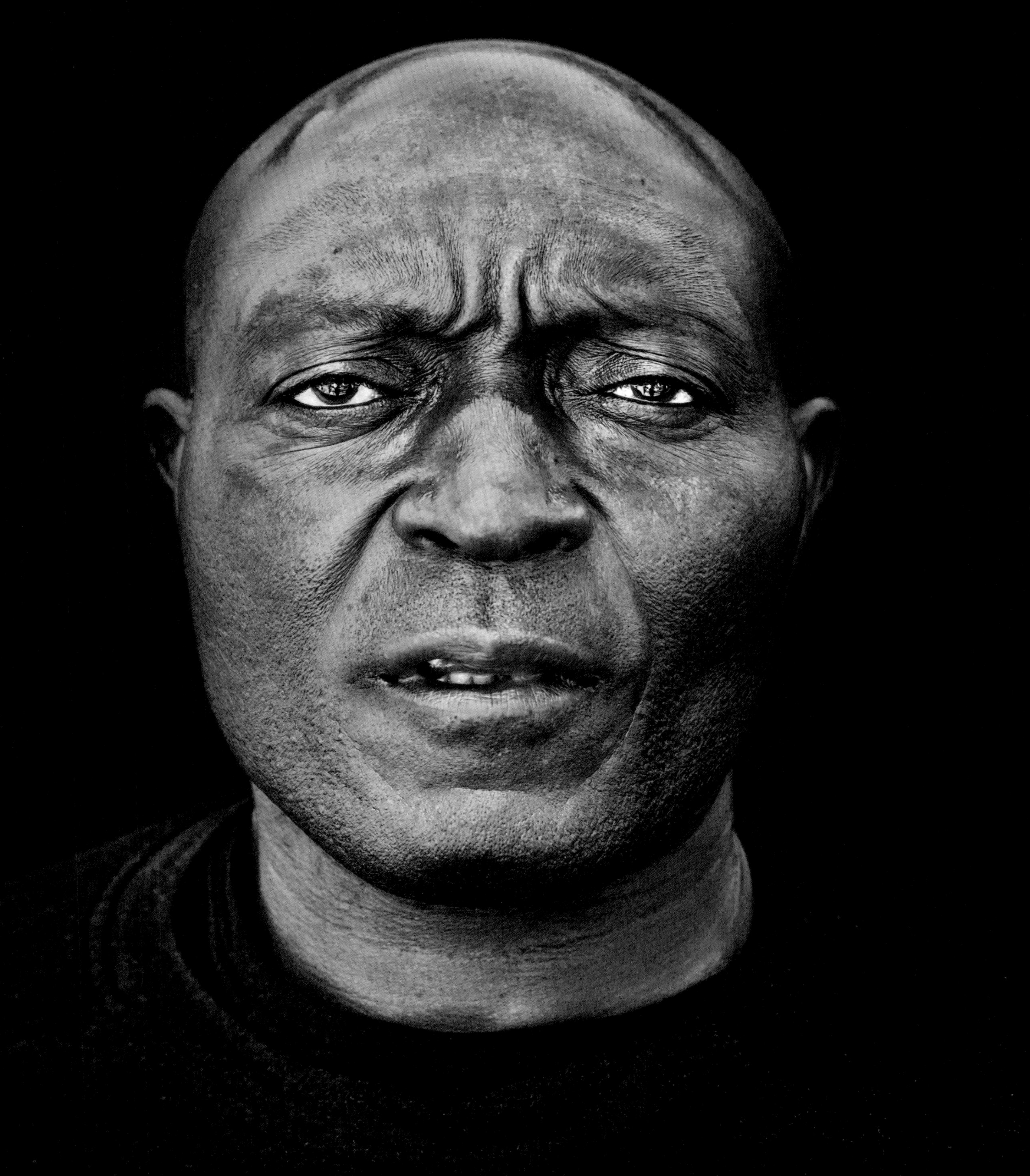

I was a hireling – meaningless, nonexistent, a nobody. The nation was scared during the war, and the government had other worries, so everyone turned away.

I was born at the end of 1933. I was the illegitimate child of a cleaning lady. My father abandoned us, and my mother's wage wasn't enough to keep me. She was called a whore – I heard it once in the hallway of the guardianship authority office.

I spent the first seven years of my life in a children's home until a childless farmer couple picked me up; not out of love, but because they wanted to use me for labour. I became their servant, and had to work until I passed out and they hit me viciously.

The guardianship picked me up two years later without any warning. These people were public officials, graduates and teachers, and they were all devious, mean and inhumane. They sent me to an educational institute called 'Sonnenberg' in Kriens. It was completely isolated from the outside world, even from the nearby village. We were free of any identity; they just called us boarding pupils, and we were punished, beaten, tortured and had to hunger. I felt as if we were all slaves. We were given sausages and bread rolls once a month, but the older kids took the food away from the younger ones. Sometimes the dog was given bread soaked in coffee, and we would fish out some pieces, and this was a banquet for us! We would sneak out of our rooms at night to steal bread, the older kids would have beaten us with leather straps if we'd refused to do it.

We were always scared and desperate. Several kids including myself were bed wetters, and the teachers would make us stand outside in the courtyard for two hours next to our urine-drenched mattresses. We were exposed before all, and even the director made fun of us. I felt powerless and helpless. I tried to escape from Lucerne to Toggenburg, but I was stopped by the police on the way. I told them every single detail yet they brought me back to the home, where I was beaten up and locked away into a small room for ten days without books or something to write with. I had nothing except white stripes on my pants, so everyone knew where I had come from.

A journalist published a report about the home in 1944 and the media scandal that followed forced the director to step down. I was eleven years old when I was again picked up by the guardianship. No-one cared how I was doing. More homes and farms followed in different states, and on top of that I had to start taking confirmation classes. One day the priest tried to pull down my pants, but I was able to run away. Later on, I found out that he had abused all the other boys. A lot of people knew about this, but it was swept under the rug.

When I came of age, I left the guardianship with the warning that prison wasn't far away, and that's where I would end up if I didn't behave as one should. I went to Engelberg and found a job. I had to manage to be a grown-up step by step. I visited my mother once without asking her. She had visitors and sent me away. After that, we kept in touch sporadically. Books gave me a sense of support during this whole time. A couple from Engelberg gave me books, and that's how reading opened new worlds for me. I was in love with it.

Eventually, I met my wife who is an incredible person. She showed me what it means to live, to be happy, to have a home and to feel sheltered – all of this had been foreign to me. Nothing has more value to me than my wife does.

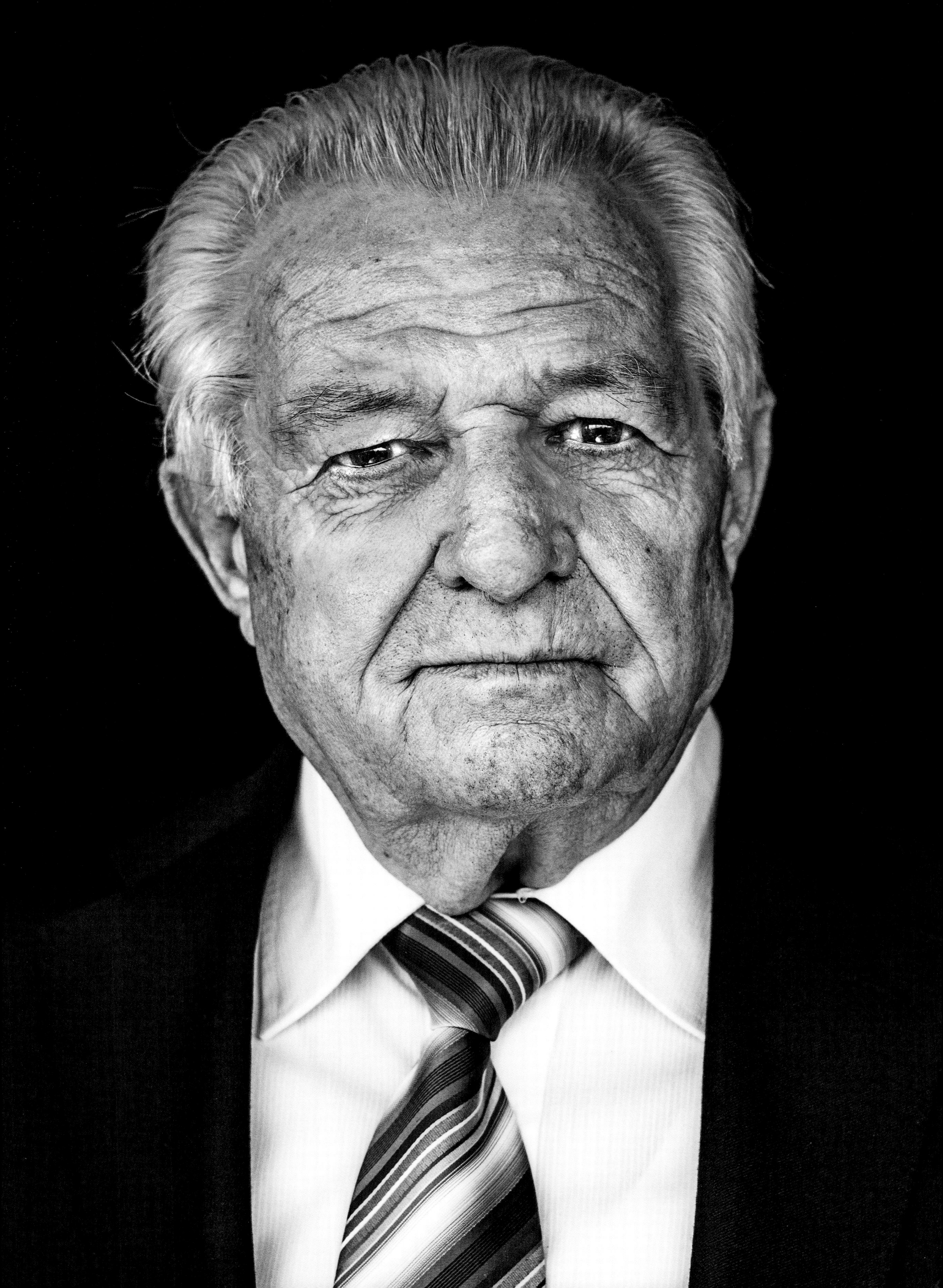

STEPHANIE, 35

OCTOBER 15TH, 2015, WEST HOLLYWOOD, LOS ANGELES

I sold my belongings, got on an airplane and pushed the reset button. I was 30 years old and had to completely restructure my life.

I had a nomadic lifestyle from day one. I moved twenty times as a child, and always had to find new friends. I had no home, and there's not one room reminding me of my childhood. My parents were unable to get used to one place or to me – I had been an accident. They gave me everything except love. They gave me access to the best education and bought me expensive designer clothes, but all I wanted was to be creative, to make music and sing. My parents didn't care about my dreams; I was meant to do what was expected of me, and so I found myself striving for the goals and dreams others had decided for me.

I used to think that I would be happily married with children by the time I was 30, but my relationship ended and my rental contract was cancelled. I worked sixteen hours a day and hadn't been on holiday in seven years. I was a stranger to myself and had reached my limit, and that's when I suffered a nervous breakdown. I had had enough and wanted to overhaul my life once again but for real this time. I saw it as a chance to do what I had always wanted to do: break out. My friends thought I had completely lost it.

Within three months, I sold, gave away or donated all of my belongings from furniture to jewellery to over 500 items of designer clothing. With every possession I gave away, I gained some freedom. I booked flights to Europe, Asia, and South America. I saw thirteen countries and 33 cities in twelve months. I discovered the world, explored cultures unknown to me and met many people. I didn't have responsibilities nor expectations, and all I did was laugh, live and make new friends.

When I felt the urge at some point to settle again, the thought of buying things was suffocating. All I needed was a roof over my head and a bed to sleep in.

Today, five years later, I still only own the bare necessities. I live in a simple apartment and don't define myself over what I own. Nothing that I had owned had ever given my life a unique sense of worth or had made me happy. Now, the things I do own have a very personal value to me.

The only thing that counts is to be happy, and that's my main focus now. I finally go after all my dreams; I work in the pharmaceutical industry, I'm writing a book, am learning the ukulele and take singing lessons. I've finally found myself, and I don't want to give that up for any amount of money.

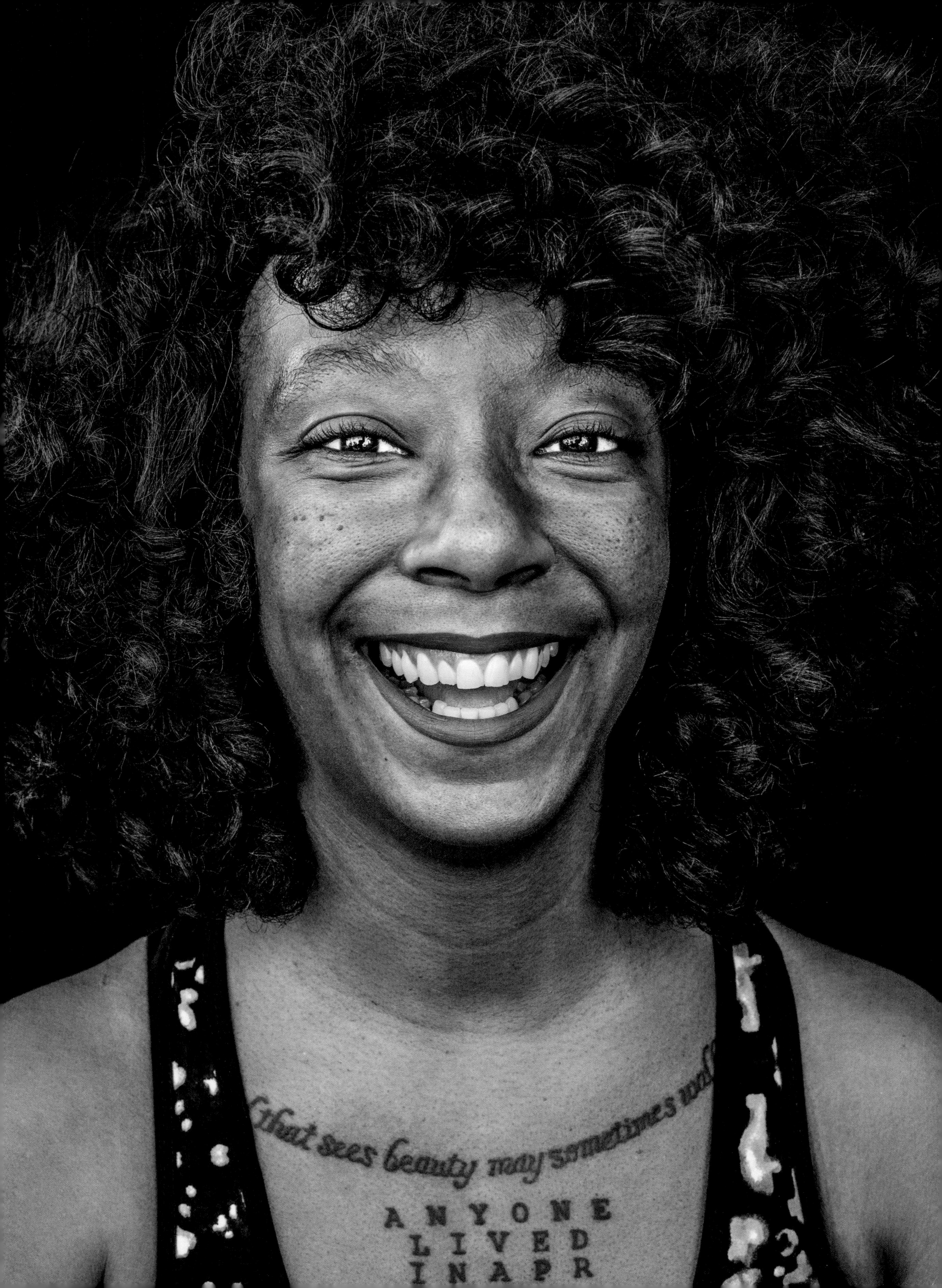
that sees beauty may sometimes
ANYONE
LIVED
IN A PR

ANDREW, 88

APRIL 16TH, 2014, CHINATOWN, NEW YORK

My wife taught me to be spontaneous, wild and unconstrained. She showed me the crazy world of Las Vegas, took me to the most beautiful casinos and revealed the adventurous sides of life to me.

Everything was wonderful. We tried to enjoy every single moment as my wife always said 'We only have this one life'. We travelled from New York to Las Vegas several times a year – it was like love at first sight.

We bought real estate all over Las Vegas and through the rents or resales we were able to live in such a luxurious way that we were able to retire at 48 in 1975. We traveled a lot after retiring and met exciting people all over the place and had a lot of fun, and though I wasn't always the easiest person to be around my wife accepted me with all my shortcomings. We were always able to work through arguments quickly by openly speaking about everything. My wife was my best friend, my love and the most loyal companion.

She passed away five years ago, though I was always so sure that she would outlive me with her energetic spirit that didn't allow anyone or anything to get in the way. From one day to the next I had to manage on my own. That was tough.

Each corner of our apartment, each bench, every shelf in the supermarket is full of memories. Suddenly I was alone in my bed, dinners at home became lonely, and the walks became boring.

Our shared life is over, but I can still hear her say 'life is there to be enjoyed until the very last second'. This I'll do, and when my last second has arrived, I know we'll be reunited.

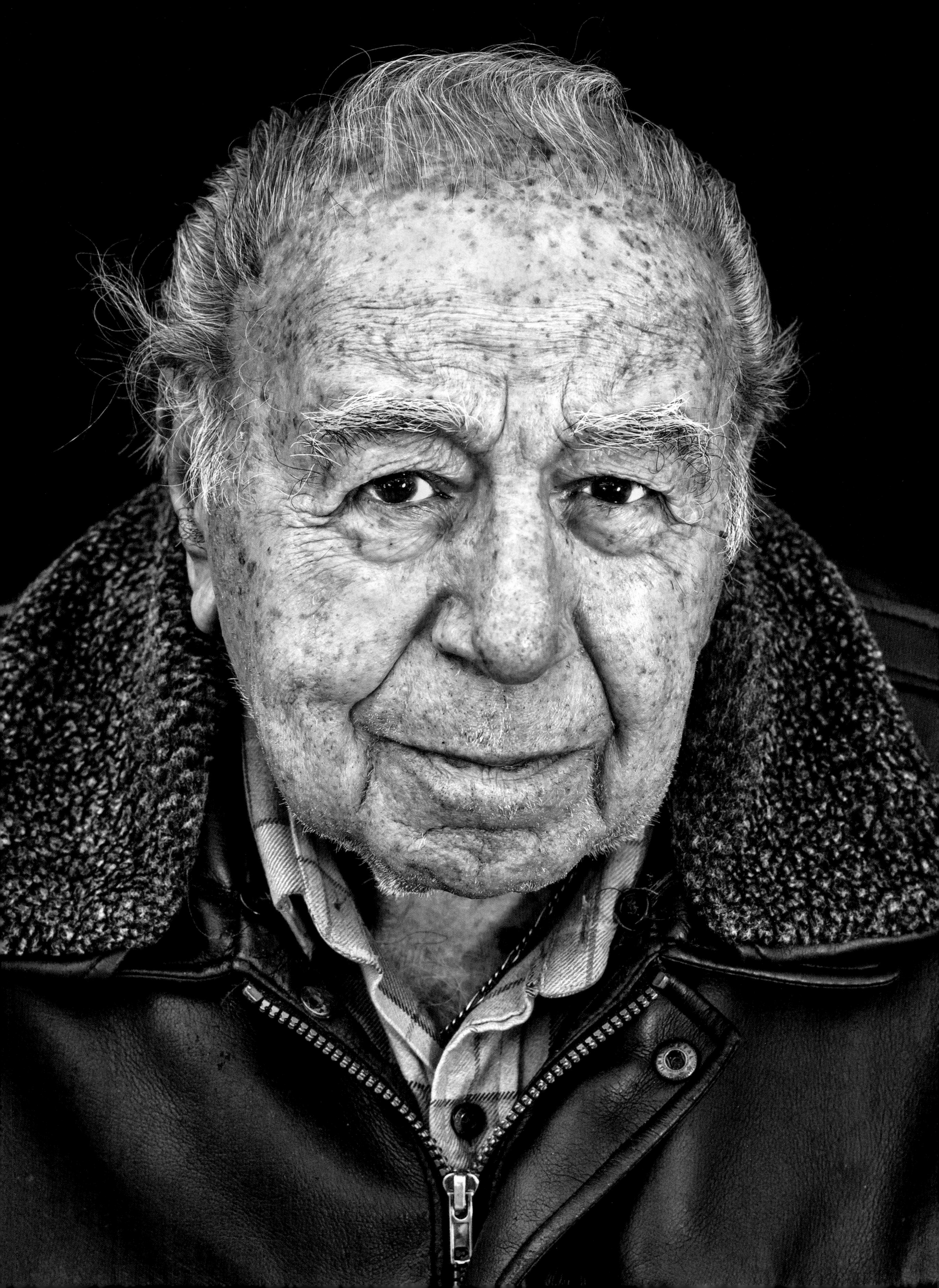

GUÉNOLA, 26
NOVEMBER 3RD, 2016, STELLENBERG, CAPE TOWN

My mother was the best person in the whole universe. She was a strong character who lived her life without relying on anyone else. My father left her when I was two years old – I was non-existent to him. The only male figure in my life was my grandfather whom I loved above all else, but he too left us five years after my father did, by taking his life. I only found out years later that he had abused my mother during her childhood. My world started to crumble.

I transformed into a party animal, became impulsive and excessive. As if alcohol weren't enough, I began taking meth too and was addicted by the time I was 20. The drug was able to suppress my pain, but it also awoke my inner demons; I became erratic, aggressive and violent – even towards my mother. Once I grabbed her by the arm and hurled her against a wall; I was abusing any morals I had remaining. Addiction's best friends are remorse and shame, and so I consumed even more drugs to forget my shame. I will never forgive myself for treating my mother in such a way. We were inseparable – it was just us two against the rest of the world. Nevertheless she was angry and worried, and so she sent me to a clinic to withdraw. I had to learn to open up and share my innermost feelings with strangers.

Eventually, this started to feel good, but I couldn't shake my reputation as 'the drug addict' once I left the clinic. I was condemned from all sides and under constant surveillance. A month after my withdrawal, my mother had to go to the hospital. The doctors found tumors in her brain, lungs, and stomach – cancer cells had attacked her entire body. I could hear in her voice that she was going to die. At this moment my emotions felt numbed. I'm not sure I felt a single thing. I needed someone to be there for me and keep me away from drugs, but I was on my own and relapsed.

My mother was a magnificent being – she was a bundle of energy and full of vitality. She gave me a sense of safety and taught me to enjoy my life to all extremes. She always said that life is too short to be surrounded by anything that's less than beautiful. She put a lot of emphasis on being surrounded by everything stunning. My mother was all that I had, and now I was to lose her forever.

She decided to die at home. She was unable to walk when she left the hospital, and her health deteriorated with each passing day. I took care of her and slept next to her at night. I was able to feel how she was slowly slipping away from me until she passed on the 17th of February 2014 at 00:01 – it was so typical of my mother, the perfectionist, to wait until the start of a new day.

I was high on meth during the last moments of my mother's life, but I was functioning normally, and no one was able to notice; but the worst part was that I was unable to feel myself. I was utterly high when I embraced my mother for the last time, and I was even high when she died. I can't believe I wasn't able to stay clean for her. She was the most important person in my life, she was the only one who got me, and now I was alone and lonelier than ever. This state of mind was fuel for my addiction – addictions live from this kind of devastation.

I asked my father to accompany me to her funeral. I just needed someone to hold my hand. He came, but shortly after the service was over, he left to take his wife out to dinner, leaving me hanging once again.

There was no-one there for me; no-one cared how I was coping. A lot of people are overwhelmed by this kind of situation, they don't know how to react and are afraid to ask the wrong questions; but is there such a thing as asking the wrong question? I was left to fend on my own at the moment I most needed someone by my side.

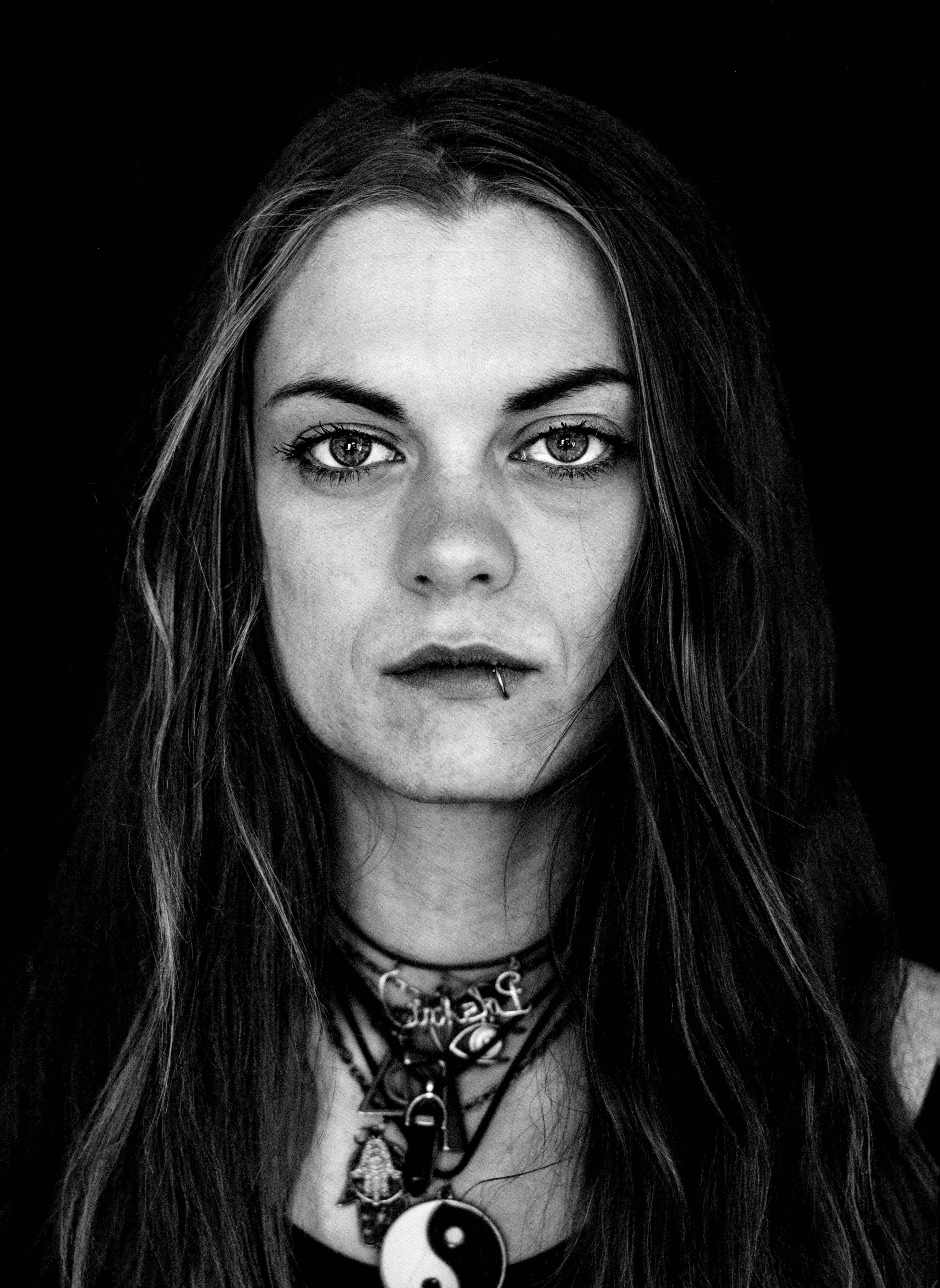

JOHN, 46

APRIL 21ST, 2014, MANHATTAN, NEW YORK

I was 21 years old when my doctor told me I had incurable leukaemia, and would die in two years. It was summer, and I was just about to fly to Ibiza to party with my friends which, of course, never happened.

The doctor said that chemotherapy might increase my life expectancy but why would I want to put such poison into my body? I felt perfectly healthy. Perhaps out of desperation and most likely to flee the unavoidable, I jumped on my motorbike and headed towards Arizona. I had no goal in mind and was internally numb. After 3000 kilometres my bike broke down, so I walked and just followed my intuition. After a few kilometres I reached a small town and stopped in front of a driveway. A woman stood there, she stared at me before asking if she can help me. I answered: 'No-one can help me now'. Unexpectedly, she asked me if I could cook, then she said I could stay with her if I wanted to. The place I had intuitively walked to was Sedona, an unbelievably mystical place. I accepted her offer, cooked an Italian meal for us and we started talking.

Lynn had grown up in New York, just like I had. She was living a hippie life and had found her purpose in this very spiritual area. I told her my story; how my father was trying to force me to follow in his footsteps as a successful agent at the DEA (Drug Enforcement Administration) and how my beloved mother had collapsed and died in the shower unexpectedly on mother's day two years prior. I told her how this had led me to party excessively and take drugs out of anger and despair. I explained that I was just about to head to Spain, but my cancer diagnosis had changed those plans. Lynn replied: 'What if I help you heal without chemotherapy or radiation?' She told me about a natural healing process consisting of fasting, detoxing and meditation. I accepted her offer and moved in – I had nothing to lose after all.

For four weeks I just consumed water and fruits followed by a few days of not eating at all. I learned how to meditate and how to focus on the positive things in life. Then I did a sweating treatment to cleanse my body and assist it in healing cancer. Then I went on a vision quest, an indigenous method to contact your guardian spirit through a hallucinogenic state of mind. Through the fasting, sweating, the solitude of nature and through sleep deprivation, I was able to enter a different state of consciousness. I was able to recognise a star constellation that showed my fight against cancer. I spoke to my guardian spirit and told him that I would defeat leukemia and that it would never return. I visualised my future and made a pact with my guardian spirit.

The things I experienced during this time of my life were purely magical. Lynn and her five-year-old daughter were by my side during these thirteen months. They supported me, gave me hope, strength, and bit by bit they gave me back my life. I felt stronger as each week went by and my outlook on my life and health radically changed through the deep belief I had in the pact I had made. I conquered cancer without any chemotherapy.

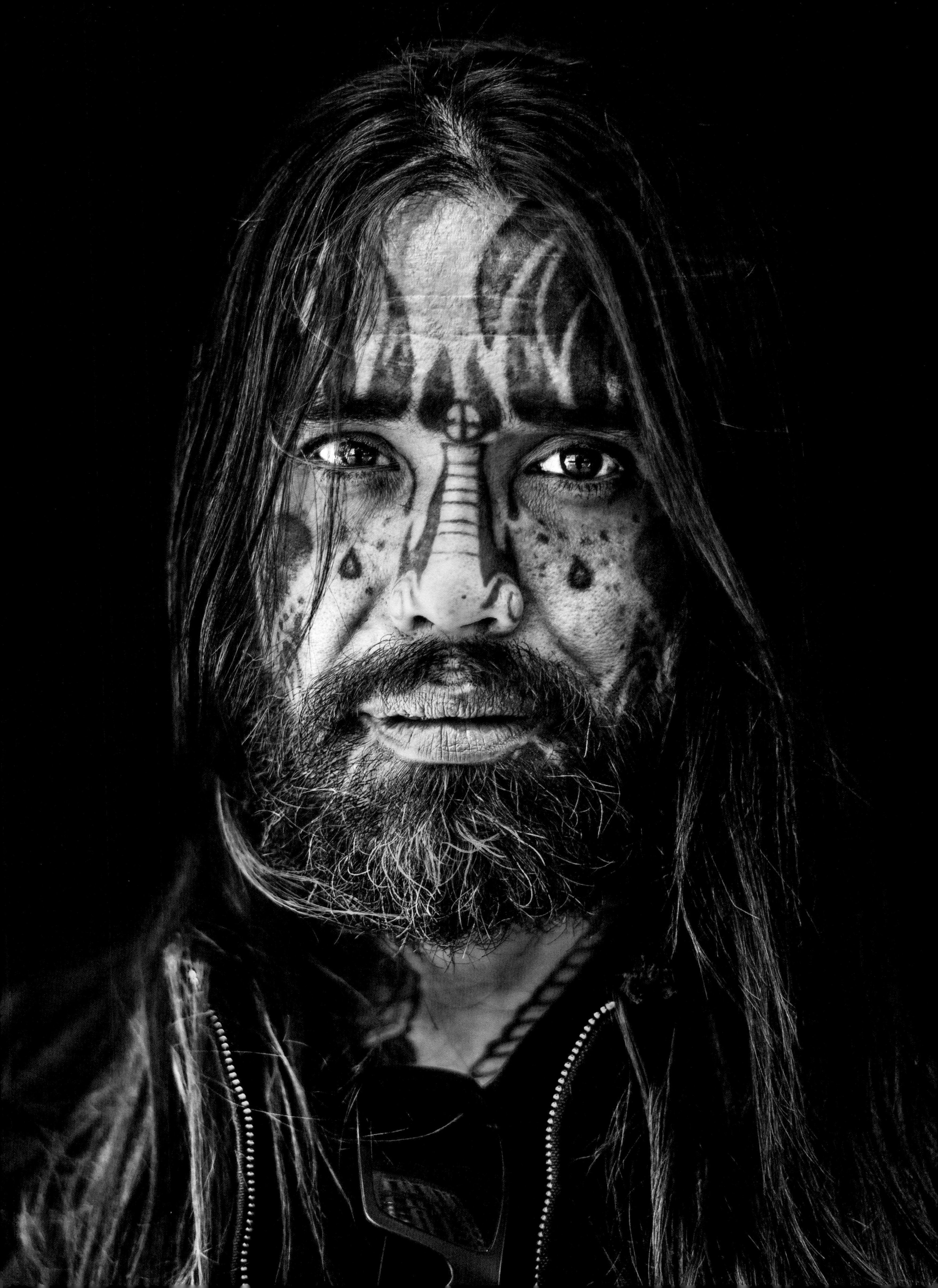

I'm 100 years old and feel like the happiest person on earth. I had what many people dream of having – the perfect life.

Upon birth, everyone gets their script, and everyone is their director. My mother taught me early on to live my own life and do so happily. My life should be fun, and I never did take it very seriously. I laughed a lot and made the most out of every moment. I blagged my way through school, which used to be a lot easier than it is now, and I quit the law degree I started.

I met many exciting characters either through my job at a music store or my travels. I remember one encounter in particular: I was in Davos to ski, and I saw a man lying on a deck chair, and I thought to myself 'He is so ugly that I could fall in love with him!'. My smile made him very happy, and when we began to talk, I found out his name: Albert Einstein.

My mother also taught me to think of others. Every evening she would light a candle and pray with me. We prayed for our family, friends and those who weren't as well off as we were. It's a ritual I do to this day. I wish happiness could be distributed equally.

I was allowed to share my joy with all the people I loved, and I fulfilled every wish I had: I got married, built a house and lived there with my husband and children. I inherited over a million when I was 75 years old. Having a lot of money is considered being prosperous where I live but what is prosperity when you are on your own? I gave all my money to my family, every cent, and sent my grandchildren off to travel the world. Having a family and knowing there are people in your life that have your back, that's real wealth.

Often I'll forget how old I am. My time is running out, but I'm not afraid to die. I knew from the get-go that I would have to go one day, but still, if I had the choice I would live forever. I like being alive, and I'm curious to know what will happen to my great-grandchildren but that's how life goes – the old has to make way for the new. I've encountered death many times. I've seen a lot of people die but being able to tell them that I love them before they passed eased the pain of saying goodbye. Death is agonising, but you have to see the meaning behind it as everything that comes, brings something positive with it even if it's not always easy to recognise the positive.

Enjoy every hour of being alive, laugh, be merry, invent something, stand your ground, believe in the impossible and find joy in it. If I were still young now, I'd climb up trees. Never stop dreaming! Because life can be a dream.

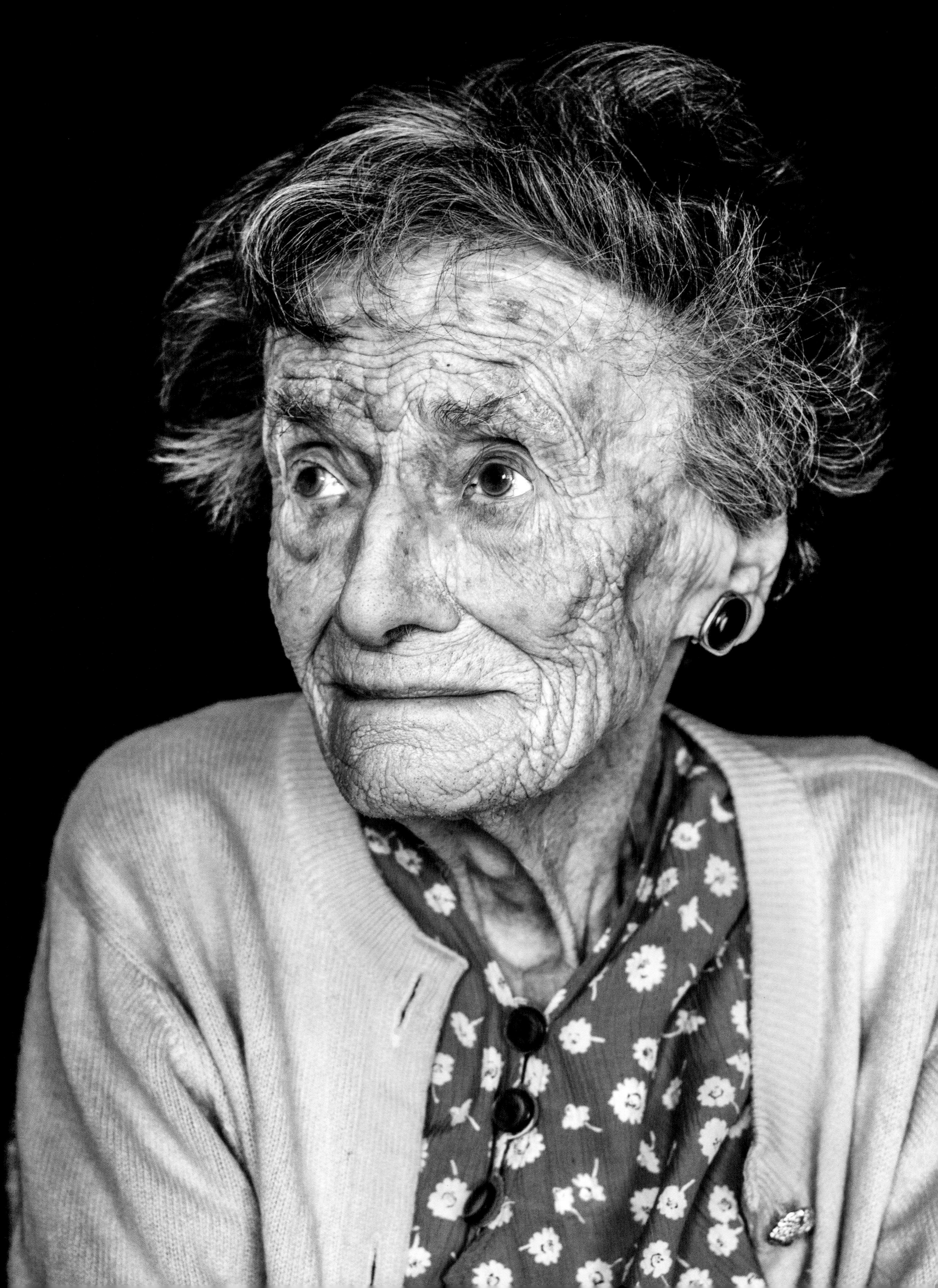

**What was the biggest
turning point in your life?**

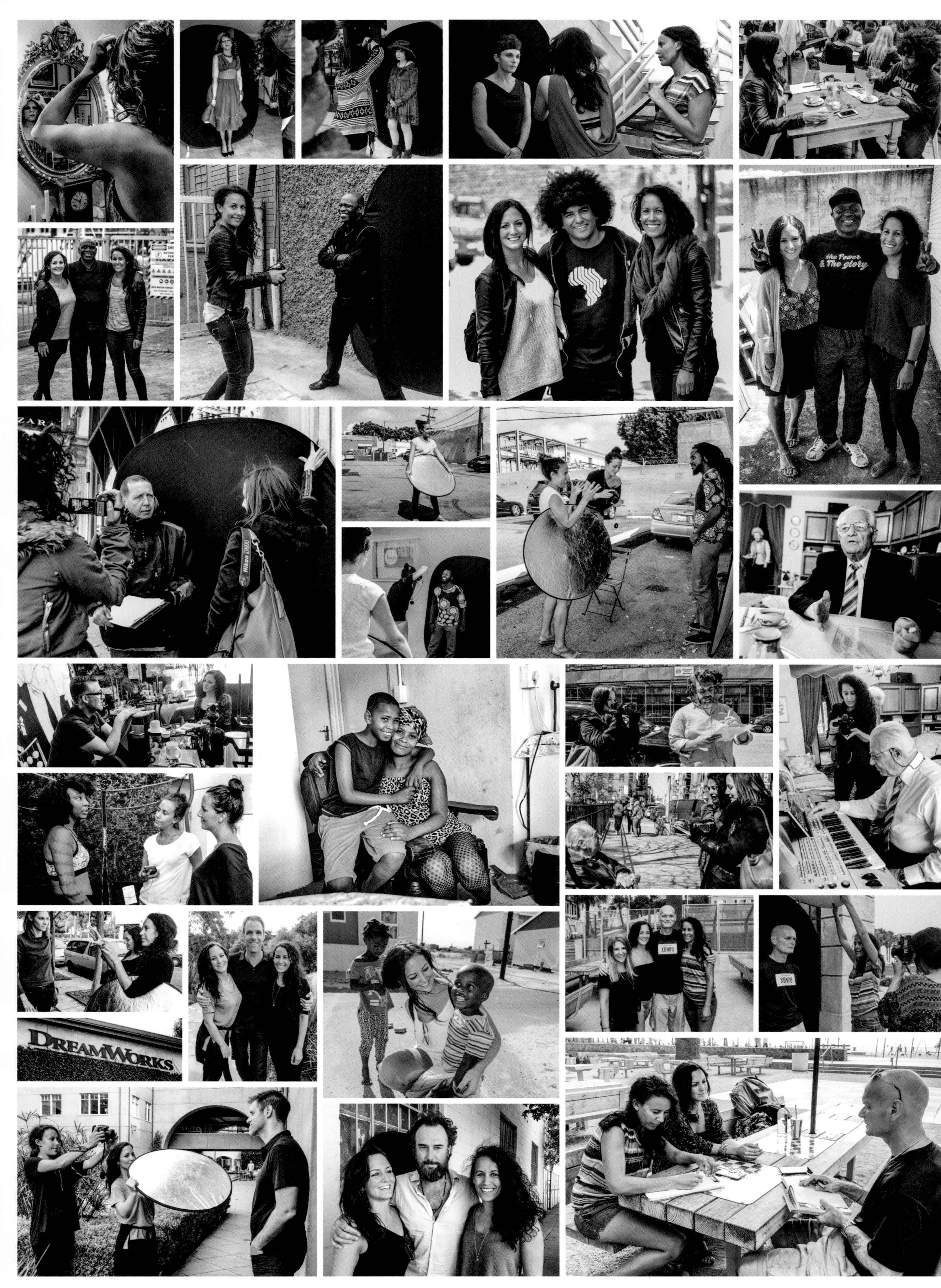

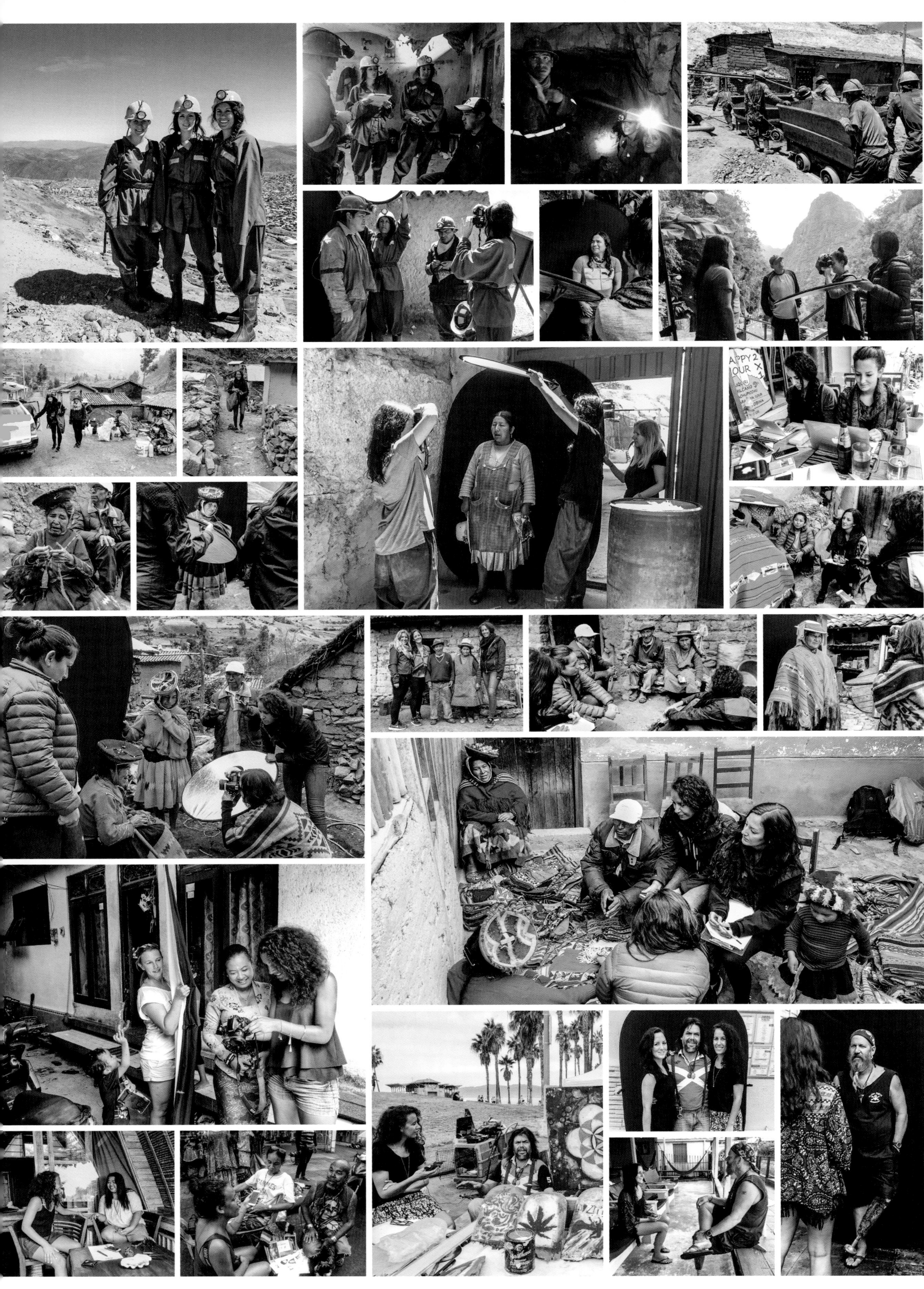

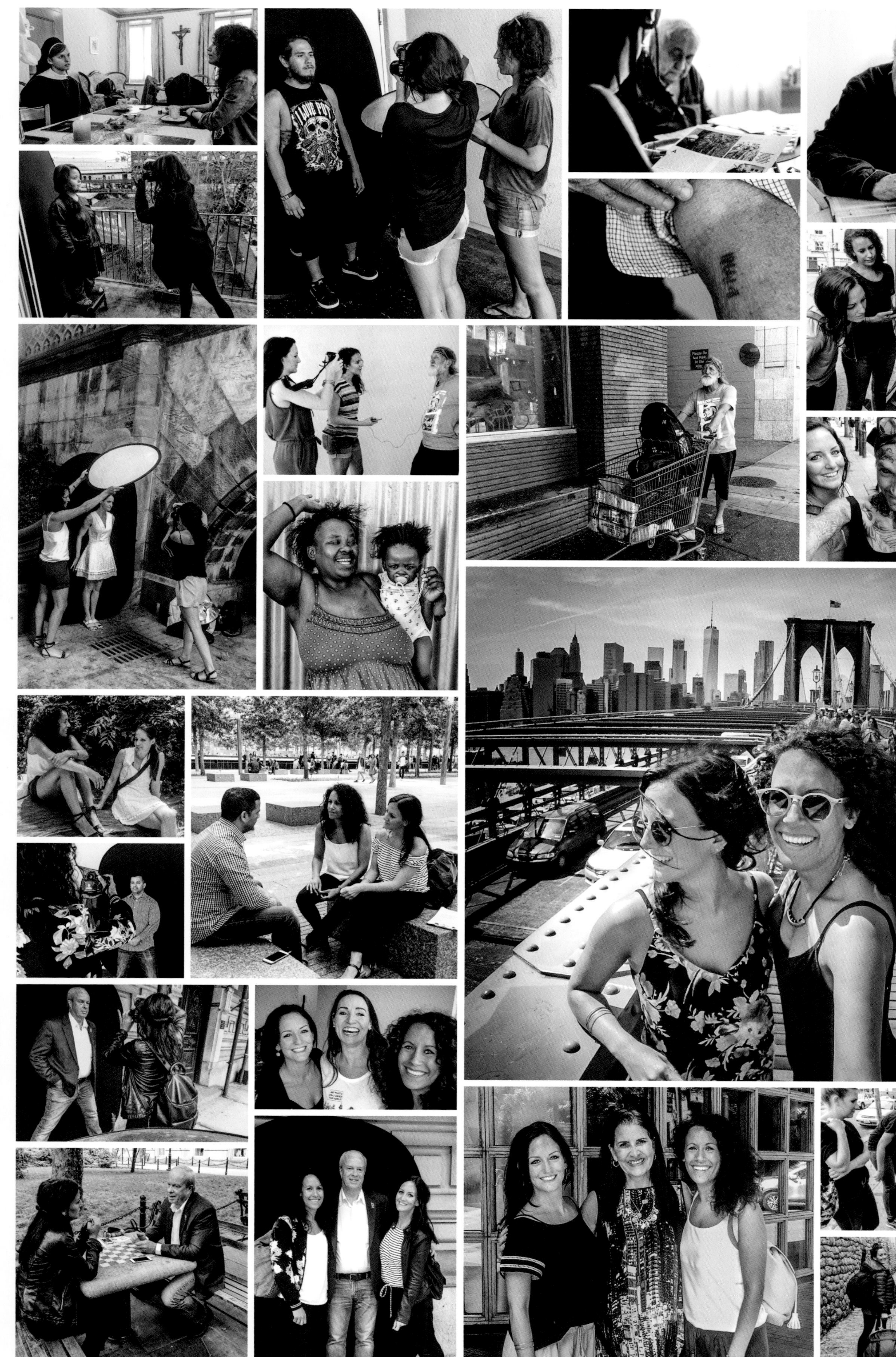

We are friends for life and have been realising many ideas together for more than ten years. Sometimes we are wild and loud, sometimes we are thoughtful and quiet, but we always feel as if anything is possible as if there are no limits. We are fascinated by life, reality, by humans. One of us will make sure the lighting is good, the other one presses the shutter. One of us writes while the other researches. Together we want to create a connection among people, we want to bring others closer together.

Sandra Schmid, loves travelling and diving into new cultures, new cuisines and into the ocean every so often. She's a perfectionist when it comes to work and is fascinated by beautiful things – art, design, photography, and film. She's got a sixth sense for small details in her work as a television video editor or as a freelance graphic designer. She has many ideas and dreams and would love to achieve everything all at once. She loves numbers and grammar as much as she loves nonsense. Unforced, adventurous, passionate, funny and spontaneous is how life should be and, of course, some sadness has to be part of it as well. Letting it all go, dancing, being free and sharing life with others are the best things life has to offer.

Sandra Buehler, half Swiss, half Seychellois. She loves exploring the diversity the world has to offer, prefers warm climates, palm trees, beaches, and the ocean. She has a deep appreciation for cuisine, but fish won't ever be allowed on her plate – she would rather observe these while diving. She likes the quiet but is addicted to music and sings at the top of her lungs under the shower and loves to hit piano keys as powerfully as she hits the ball while playing tennis or as intensely as she uses her hands to gesticulate when she tells stories of her many adventures. She's diverse, spontaneous, crazy, open for anything and a bit chaotic at times but always focused. She takes photos, produces videos and does graphic design on the side – as long as what she does is creative, she's happy.

"If you can dream it, you can do it." Walt Disney

What started off as a dream, became a reality. We started approaching strangers on the street and found witnesses of specific periods through organisations and foundations. We were allowed to experience touching, impactful, profound, despairing and hilarious moments in an array of different places. What followed is a book that is meant to create hope, courage, and inspiration. We were only able to realise this project through all the people who believed in us and the book, who understood, motivated, inspired and supported us.

A heartfelt thank you

Specifically we would like to mention

all the people, who we mostly didn't know, but who revealed their worlds to us and who became an invaluable part of our book.

Eliane Huonder, our faithful friend and a great supporter. You stood by our side from the beginning, you joined us on a lot of trips, you motivated us and gave us strength. You are an indispensable part of this project.

Madlaina Lippuner, our pearl in an ocean of words. Your constructive feedback, your corrections and clever comments shaped this book significantly. You are a true genius.

Christian Walthert, our rock, our pillar of support. Your support meant a great deal to us throughout the whole project. Your notations, your patience, and your insights were priceless. You're wonderful.

Bea Jucker and Helen Butcher, our silent heroes behind the scenes. Thank you for your valuable assistance.

Ian Strathcarron, Unicorn Publishing. Thank you for believing in our book, trusting us and supporting us in all matters.

Our friends and family. Thank you for understanding our frequent absence, the many motivating and encouraging words and tangible support. We are overjoyed at having you in our lives.

A warm thank you also goes to

all foundations and organisations
Susanne and Martin Knechtli-Kradolfer-Foundation
World Trade Center Survivors' Network
Witness to Innocence
The American Legion Post 43
Esperanza Social Venture Club
Hope Cape Town, Kerstin Behlau
Gamaraal Foundation, Anita Winter
Association of growth-restricted people Switzerland
Caritas Switzerland

IMPRINT

© Unicorn Publishing Group LLP, 2019
5 Newburgh Street, London W1F 7RG, www.unicornpublishing.org

1st edition published by Unicorn
Translated from German "Menschen wie du und ich"

Texts	Sandra Schmid
Translation	Grashina Gabelmann
Images	Sandra Buehler and Sandra Schmid
Layout	Sandra Schmid and Sandra Buehler
	crealicious.ch, Zurich
Production	Latitude Press Limited

ISBN 978-1-912690-51-0